BERKSHIRE

A COUNTY HISTORY

Daphne Phillips

COUNTRYSIDE BOOKS
NEWBURY, BERKSHIRE

COUNTRYSIDE BOOKS
3 Catherine Road
Newbury, Berkshire

ISBN 1 85306 246 4

The cover picture is by Jack Hole and was taken from
Walbury Hill looking towards Newbury.

Engraving of Windsor Castle taken from Tombleson's
Eighty Picturesque Views on the Thames, 1834.

Designed by Mon Mohan
Produced through MRM Associates Ltd., Reading
Printed in England

Contents

A view from Walbury, the highest point in Berkshire. The huge iron age Walbury Camp dominated this area 2,500 years ago.

Introduction

Berkshire today is one of the smallest English counties, locked into the centre of southern England by its larger neighbours, Oxfordshire, Buckinghamshire, Surrey, Hampshire and Wiltshire. Fifty miles of M4 motorway cross it from east to west, but, as the crow flies, the distance between its northern and southern boundaries is nowhere more than 16 miles.

The original shire, formed by the Saxons in the 9th century as an administrative division of Wessex, was larger and a different shape. Up to 1974 the river Thames formed the county boundary northwards through Oxford and westwards as far as Lechlade, taking in the whole of the Berkshire Downs, the Vale of White Horse and the towns of Wallingford, Abingdon, Wantage and Faringdon. At the eastern end, the Thames was still the boundary from Windsor to Staines. In the 1960s a major review of local authorities and the areas they served recommended that these areas 'should have some basis in socio-economic facts or in the sense of community so far as it exists today'. Statistical studies of people travelling to work and using shopping and leisure facilities indicated that the boundary between north Berkshire and Oxfordshire cut across strong commuting ties and, as a cultural boundary, was meaningless. North Berkshire people looked towards Oxford as their centre, while the influence of the Berkshire county town of Reading extended more effectively to east and west. The Local Government Act of 1972 altered the boundaries of Berkshire in accordance with these findings. The largely rural area north of the Downs and the small towns it contained were transferred to Oxfordshire, while the southernmost part of Buckinghamshire, containing Slough, Eton, Datchet and other parishes, was transferred to Berkshire.

The new county boundary lost much in the way of definition. The line of the Thames had always been visible and unmistakable; most of the new northern boundary is invisible except on maps. It is made up of sections of parish boundaries marked in former times by field endings, trees, stones, earthworks and other features, many of which disappeared long ago, although the present boundary makes use of a few miles of earthworks known as Grim's Ditch, believed to date from the late Bronze Age and to mark a boundary between political or agricultural territories belonging to Celtic tribes. The mapmaker's line runs from Weathercock Hill at the western end to take in Lambourn, East Garston, Fawley, Brightwalton, Farnborough, West and East Ilsley, Compton, Aldworth and Streatley. These parishes contain all that the county still holds of the Berkshire Downs and the turf now famous for racehorse training.

Berkshire's most celebrated horse, the enigmatic figure of the White Horse carved into the hillside above Uffington, was taken from the

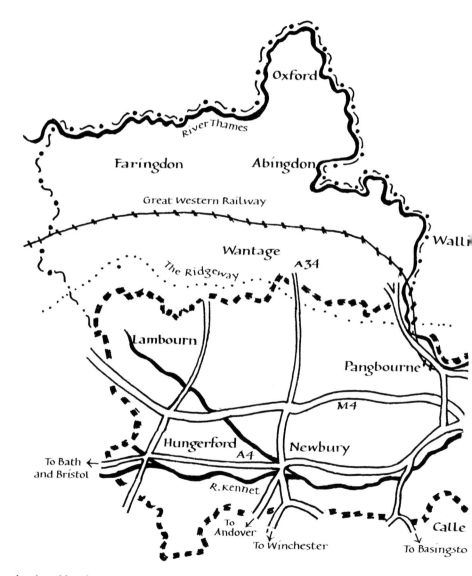

Map of Berkshire showing old and new boundaries and principal through routes.

county in 1974 and is now in Oxfordshire. Its loss aroused vigorous and emotional protests. The White Horse was Berkshire's most cherished archaeological monument and had been adopted as a symbol and as a device on the county's coat of arms. The campaign to keep it in Berkshire was fought to the bitter end, and the night before the changeover took place, on 1 April 1974, bonfires were lit around the figure of the horse and ceremoniously doused at midnight.

It has often been remarked that Berkshire is a county on the way to somewhere – from London to South Wales, or from the Midlands to Southampton – and its central, land-locked position has caused its development through the ages to follow the major lines of communica-

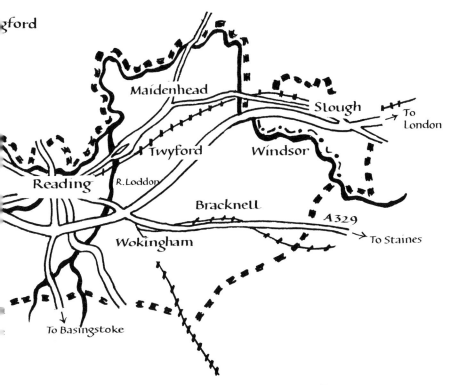

Rivers	
Modern County Boundary	
Old County Boundary	
Major Roads & Motorways	
Railways	
Ancient Trackway	

tion passing through it. The Thames and Kennet valleys provided the essential resources needed by man in prehistoric times and in the medieval period the Thames was an important highway from London into the centre of England. Most of Berkshire's early towns grew up along its banks. The development of the east-west highway which became the Bath Road, and the north-south route through Newbury, encouraged the growth of another sequence of towns and villages, some also benefiting from the Kennet & Avon canal. In the 19th century the Great Western Railway drew a new line across the map in the interests of getting from Bristol to London faster and more efficiently, and other railway lines contributed to the development of east Berkshire. In the 20th century the M4 motorway has carved its own much broader path between east and west, while the A329M and various link roads and bypasses have also taken their toll of the landscape. Berkshire, consequently, is a well-worn and heavily-used county. Its natural resources have been exploited continuously from prehistoric times, and it is now more densely populated than any of the larger counties around it except Surrey.

East and west Berkshire have always been different in character and have developed in different ways. Up to the mid 19th century the richer agricultural lands of the western and central areas were more populated and more economically productive than the forest and heathlands of the eastern part, but after 1840 new industries, the railways and the growth of commuter travel to London brought about dramatic changes, causing west Berkshire to decline while the population of east Berkshire increased. Reading, Maidenhead, Windsor and Wokingham all grew steadily, and in the present century two new towns, Slough and Bracknell, have developed. Within the last 20 years the M4 has linked east and west Berkshire more directly and closely than any previous route, promoting similar kinds of commercial and industrial development right across the county, and bringing a notable revival to the Newbury area. The motorway is also the first route to enable long-distance traffic to bypass Reading, formerly the focal point of all routes, by road, rail or water. Today, Berkshire's excellent communications with London, Heathrow and all parts of the country make it an alternative location for national and international commerce and hi-tech industry. Although reduced in size, in economic terms Berkshire is one of the fastest-growing counties in Britain, with a population approaching 725,000.

1

PREHISTORY

The great works of prehistoric man – his massive earthworks, burial mounds, the White Horse – are all plainly visible and have excited wonder and curiosity for centuries. But it is on the gravel terraces of river valleys that lesser objects have provided evidence of man's activities long before such mighty works could be conceived.

The significance of flintstones shaped into implements before the use of metals was known was not recognised until the end of the 18th century, and it was not until the 19th century that archaeologists began to divide prehistoric time into ages of stone, bronze and iron. Since then, countless finds of flint artefacts have shown that the Berkshire area was used by man at a very early period, when southern Britain was the outer limit of the inhabited world. Hunters came here in pursuit of the wild animals whose feeding and migratory habits dictated their nomadic existence. The Thames valley, with its swamps, forests, grassland and abundant water attracted a rich variety of wild life. Flints, lying in the river gravels, provided weapons and tools for men to kill and butcher their prey. Today, flints painstakingly shaped and sharpened, sometimes together with waste flakes and, occasionally, a few bones of the beasts they killed, are all that remain of the hunters and their way of life. Their own bones have rotted away, as have the animal skins they used to clothe and protect themselves against the harsh climate.

A great deal of our knowledge of the distant past has resulted from chance discoveries made when land or buildings have been disturbed for new uses. The rapid expansion of Reading in the 19th century over the gravel terraces created by the Thames, Kennet and Loddon brought about many illuminating discoveries of hand axes and other implements. In the 1870s and 1880s remarkable finds took place at Coley, Grovelands and Redlands, the two last locations also yielding the bones and teeth of animals. As the town continued to grow in the 20th century, other important finds were made at Tilehurst, near the Roebuck Hotel, and at Toots Farm in Caversham. The laying of main drainage in Caversham in the 1930s brought many more finds to light.

To the east of Reading, Paleolithic sites have been identified around

Earley, Sonning and Twyford. Near Maidenhead, at Furze Platt, the discovery of over 250 hand axes and a large number of other tools and waste pieces indicated a major flint-working site, the most important found so far in the Middle Thames valley. Other finds on the opposite side of the river, around Burnham, Farnham and Slough, show how extensively Paleolithic man made use of the Thames valley. The wide, gravelly valley of the Kennet has also yielded many working sites, while the similarity of materials found near Theale, Englefield, Sulham and Tidmarsh provides evidence that the broad valley now watered only by the Pang and a lesser stream was carved out by the original course of the Kennet. In contrast, the Downs and other parts of Berkshire have yielded only a few scattered finds of weapons, suggesting that Paleolithic man may only have gone to those areas on hunting expeditions.

The Mesolithic period, from around 10,000 BC, was marked by a warmer climate following the last ice age. People roamed more widely in search of food. Their numbers were increasing and they had learned how to make a variety of cutting and scraping tools and weapons, more finely shaped than those of their predecessors. They were skilful fishermen as well as hunters, using primitive boats and flint spears to catch fish. They were also capable of making large picks and axes which were probably used for felling trees. Many of their riverside camping and working places must have been destroyed unknowingly, but since the 1950s an important concentration of archaeological material from this period has been studied in the Kennet valley. The first discovery was made near Thatcham where, in addition to many assemblages of worked flints and waste flakes, the remains of hearths and heaps of domestic rubbish indicated that these may have been places where temporary shelters or tents made of hides were erected. Further upstream, a systematic survey of the Kennet valley near Hungerford identified dozens of Mesolithic working sites, over 50 being found in one six-mile stretch between Hungerford and Hamstead Marshall. Here the valley widens into a marshy area studded with islands of gravel firm enough to provide sites for camping. At Wawcott, near Kintbury, evidence of post holes around a pit suggested that a fairly substantial structure may have existed here for a while. In addition to flint implements, quantities of animal bones were recovered and analysed, showing that the meat of pigs, red deer and wild cattle was most commonly eaten. Fish and wild fowl, abundant in this area, and probably fruits and nuts in season, supplemented the diet. The very large number of temporary settlements in the Kennet valley suggests that they may have been used by fishermen following the migration of fish up the river. The valley would also have provided a route linking the Thames valley with south-western Britain.

The Middle Thames valley has also yielded Mesolithic evidence, notably at Braywick, where about 10,000 flint implements were discovered in 1972.

Around 4,000 BC the pattern of life was changed by new ideas and new skills introduced by immigrants from the Continent. Although still dependent on stone, bone and wood for tools and weapons, Neolithic peoples were farmers, growing cereals, herding cattle, sheep and goats, and keeping pigs. Pottery was first used in Britain in this period, and the newcomers were active traders, travelling long distances to trade pots and finely polished stone axes. The Downs were cleared of forest early in the Neolithic period, and the great overland route known as the Ridgeway came into use between south-western and eastern Britain. Daily life was more varied; there were more skills to be learnt and wits were sharpened by trading. Farming brought long-term responsibility for property, livestock and crops, so that people settled longer in one place. Although numerous small finds show that their settlements were widespread, significant discoveries of domestic sites are rare. Repeated ploughing by later generations, combined with the eroding effects of weather, are known to have lowered the surface level of chalk hills, so that systematic field exploration of the Berkshire Downs in the 1970s recovered very scanty remains from the Neolithic period. Aerial surveys of cropmarks along river valleys also identified few sites, although signs of ring ditches near Englefield and elsewhere in the Kennet valley confirmed that this area was settled by Neolithic peoples.

More evidence has been uncovered by chance as construction workers have gouged deep into the fields of eastern and central Berkshire. Trench digging for a gas pipeline from Bray to Waltham St Lawrence in 1963 discovered Neolithic flints and potsherds near Bray and Shottes-brooke. In the same year, gravel quarrying north of the A4 at Beenham led to the discovery of a large ring ditch about 180 feet in diameter, containing numerous pottery fragments and flint artefacts. The site was later destroyed by gravel digging. In 1974 the demolition of a large house and landscaped gardens at Cannon Hill, south of Maidenhead, discovered two deep shafts and pits containing worked flints, pottery pieces, charcoal and domestic rubbish indicating that Mesolithic and Neolithic peoples had lived here. In the 1980s another Neolithic site was found at Runneymede, during the process of digging deep footings for a bridge to carry the M25 across the Thames. Laying a gas pipeline from Ascot to Nuffield opened up another rich site above the Thames at Remenham. Here were quantities of late Mesolithic and Neolithic flints, together with pottery pieces of a characteristic Neolithic round-based bowl.

The Neolithic custom of raising monuments to the dead has left their most lasting impact on the landscape. Until 1974 Berkshire contained Weyland's Smithy, one of Britain's best-preserved Neolithic chambered tombs, but this is now in Oxfordshire. The most important funerary monument remaining is the Lambourn Long Barrow, on the northern boundary of Lambourn parish, and standing at the head of a shallow valley containing a group of later monuments known as Seven Barrows. The valley is dry now but may once have contained a spring worshipped in ancient times, and which, perhaps, was the reason for siting the barrows here. The Long Barrow has been badly damaged by centuries of ploughing and by a track running across one end used by farm vehicles and race horses. The barrow was excavated at least twice, but inexpertly, in the 19th century, and some human remains were removed. Rescue operations in 1964 found no great quantity of artefacts, but some of the potsherds resembled pottery found at the famous Neolithic camp on Windmill Hill, 20 miles away. A mass of sarsen stones disturbed by previous excavators may have formed a central core to the barrow.

On the slopes below the Long Barrow stands an impressive array of round barrows dating from the Bronze Age. Although known as Seven Barrows, they may at one time have numbered over 30. Many have been worn away by ploughing, leaving mounds only a few inches high, or no more than circles of chalk and rubble in the brown earth. The people who raised these monuments probably farmed on the Downs and in the Lambourn valley, and traded along the Ridgeway nearby. Their custom of cremating their dead leaders and burying the ashes under these earthen mounds, often accompanied by bronze artefacts, indicates that they belonged to a different culture from that of the Neolithic peoples. The newcomers began to arrive in Britain early in the third millenium BC and are known as Beaker people because of the distinctive type of cord-impressed pottery they brought with them. They introduced new crafts and farming methods, and traded over longer distances. They enjoyed a degree of wealth and superiority derived from their knowledge of mining and working copper and bronze; and at some time in the Bronze Age a huge technological advance was made with the introduction of the wheel. Flint and stone implements remained in general use; the Beaker people themselves developed new kinds of stone axes and barbed flint arrow heads. Metal was reserved for personal and valuable items, such as knives, ornaments and pins to fasten clothing. It was not until the late Bronze Age that the full potential of metal for weapons and armour was realised.

The most obvious remains of the Bronze Age are the numerous bell or bowl shaped burial mounds, of which Seven Barrows are the most

Two of the surviving Bronze Age burial mounds at Seven Barrows on the Berkshire Downs.

remarkable in Berkshire. But there are many others. Over 100 are scattered over the Downs and more have been located, often hidden in trees, on the sandy heaths of south-east Berkshire. In a wood to the north of Finchampstead is a large bell barrow measuring 100 feet in diameter and eight feet in height. Smaller ones survive in Swinley Park, Winkfield, at Bill Hill in the centre of Bracknell, and in the grounds of Heatherwood Hospital at Ascot, where the remaining barrow was formerly one of a group of four. Excavation of the Heatherwood barrow in 1973 dated it to c. 1800 BC. Other groups survive at Mortimer, Brimpton and Wash Common. A large Bronze Age barrow discovered in 1907 on Marshall's Hill in south Reading was destroyed by housing developments in 1932.

Until recently little was known about the lives of Bronze Age people, but within the last 20 years a good deal of new evidence has come to light in the lower Kennet and Middle Thames valleys, areas in which a number of circular cropmarks had been tentatively interpreted as ploughed-out barrows. In 1976 gravel digging north of the A4 near Aldermaston wharf produced evidence of a small late Bronze Age settlement on farmland already known to contain Neolithic, Iron Age and Roman remains. A number of post holes indicated at least two oval wooden structures, and

Remains of a Bronze Age barrow on Bill Hill, Bracknell.

there were several pits probably used for grain storage. Gravel working again uncovered a much larger late Bronze Age settlement at Knight's Farm Burghfield. This yielded evidence of occupation over a period of about 1,000 years up to c. 400 BC. Although near the Kennet, it was situated on high ground and could have been inhabited all the year round. The number of pits and post holes showed that occupation was dense, consisting of a great many of the typical round or oval wooden huts which are believed to have been occupied by families. Another Bronze Age settlement nearby at Pingewood may only have been used during seasonal cattle grazing, due to flooding in winter months. At all three of these sites, at Aldermaston, Knight's Farm and Pingewood, large number of weights, believed to be loom weights, were found, suggesting that very considerable quantities of cloth may have been made locally and perhaps traded elsewhere. Among other remains were sheep and cattle bones, supporting evidence provided by pollen analysis that the area was mainly devoted to pastoral farming.

In the late 1980s, a period of intensive development alongside the M4, several more Bronze Age settlements were found on the site of Reading Business Park, to the south of the town. Here, the pattern suggested several groups of round timber huts and granaries perched on stilts on islands of dry ground. The wet lands around them may have been used for growing flax.

The most prolific source of bronze artefacts has proved to be the bed of the river Thames, from which dredging operations over the years have retrieved numerous axes, swords, daggers, spearheads and knives. Many are of particularly fine quality, and this, together with their numbers, suggests that they were not lost but ceremoniously cast into the Thames as votive offerings. River and water gods were widely venerated. Taken altogether, the evidence points to dense and prosperous settlement in the Middle Thames valley during the late Bronze Age.

Towards the end of this period there are signs that violence and warfare became more common. Probable causes were population growth and resultant pressure on available land and resources, leading to territorial disputes. Certainly the number and types of weapons made

14

suggests a warlike society and warriors formidably armed with swords, spears, daggers and shields. Dangerous times made more securely defended sites necessary. A few hilltop enclosures had been built early in the Bronze Age, and their defences were strengthened at a later date. At Rams Hill, on the Downs about two miles north of Seven Barrows, part of the hilltop was at first enclosed by a bank and ditch; but around 1500 BC stronger defensive ramparts were put up, with stout palisades on either side of the ditch. Recent excavations suggest that Uffington Castle nearby may have superseded Rams Hill when a much larger and stronger encampment was needed. The White Horse, too, may date from the late Bronze Age, and was probably a tribal symbol.

From c. 800 BC iron began to be used for making weapons and tools. No large influx of new peoples took place; the Bronze Age merged into the Iron Age at a time when competition for land was intensifying. Warfare increased and tribes measured their status by their warriors' prowess. Native skills in fighting with war horses and chariots were to draw praise from Julius Caesar when he visited Britain in 55–54 BC. Hill forts increased in numbers. Some were no more than simple earthwork enclosures, perhaps used as temporary refuges for people, cattle and grain supplies. Others were important tribal centres, their fortifications strengthened and elaborated until they appeared impregnable. Of the hundreds of hill forts in Britain, Berkshire formerly contained at least 20, of which Uffington Castle and Walbury Camp were the most impressive, commanding the highest points of the Berkshire and Hampshire Downs. Several smaller ones remain in modern Berkshire, including Perborough, Oareborough, Grimsbury, Bussock Wood and Borough Hill camps, occupying high spurs of ground overlooking the valleys of the Pang, Kennet and Lambourn. The best preserved of these is Grimsbury Castle, now shrouded in woodlands near Hermitage. Unlike the other univallate (single ditch) camps it had a second line of earthworks protecting its western entrance, but partial excavation resulted in few finds. The other hill forts in this group have been largely destroyed. In east Berkshire the only hill fort was Caesar's Camp, situated on a high plateau to the south of Bracknell. Its bank and ditch fortifications follow the irregular contours of the ground in a characteristically Iron Age fashion, although its name appears to have been derived at a later date from the nearby Roman road and the many finds of Roman coins in this area.

Hill forts represent the most obvious remains of the Iron Age. People of that time lived and farmed everywhere; their homesteads and settlements were scattered over the Downs, the valleys and the heaths. The need for more land to produce food, combined with the demand for timber to build huts and for fuel, led to the clearance of more woodland. Increasing knowledge of farming enabled them to make better use of land, and improved skill in draining allowed them to settle in areas formerly too wet for permanent habitation. In recent decades evidence has been found of many hitherto unsuspected Iron Age settlements, particularly in river valleys. Aerial photography has recorded cropmarks of complex patterns of circles, parallel lines and sub-rectangles, indicating ditched enclosures containing huts, granaries and storage pits, trackways and animal compounds. The extent and density of the marks show that communities were not only larger but more closely knit than formerly. Evidence of this kind has been found in the Kennet valley near Aldermaston wharf, on a site occupied since the Neolithic period, and in other continuously exploited areas around Englefield, Ufton Nervet and Pingewood. Other settlements identified so far were in the Thames valley near Remenham and Datchet, in the Loddon valley south of Swallowfield, and the Enborne valley near Brimpton. A site discovered at Binfield shows that Iron Age farmers were moving into an area where heavy clay soils had previously been too difficult to cultivate.

Towards the end of the Iron Age more than enough food was being produced and there was a surplus for trade. Corn and wool were exported to the Continent; wine, spices, oil and luxury goods were imported for the enjoyment of the leaders and wealthy men of the tribes, who controlled trading activities. Through trade Britain was brought into closer contact with the Roman world, and the influence of Roman culture began to be seen in southern Britain. Around 50 BC Commius, a refugee from Gaul and a leader of the Atrebates tribe, fled to Britain with his followers, and carved out a territory south of the Thames. His tribal capital was Calleva, founded between 50 and 20 BC. It is now known by the name of the nearby village of Saxon origin, Silchester.

2

THE ROMAN COUNTY

The Iron Age territory of the Atrebates extended over a large area which, some 900 years in the future, would contain Berkshire and parts of Hampshire, Surrey, Sussex and Wiltshire. After the Roman conquest this territory was much reduced to the south, leaving Calleva nearer the centre and still in control of the Berkshire area.

The site of Calleva, whose name means 'a place in the woods', may have been chosen because it was hidden and protected by its environment. It stood on a gravel spur overlooking the Loddon valley. Timber and water were abundant, and although there was only one small stream within the enclosure, water was easily obtained by sinking wells only a few feet deep. Iron Age earthworks protected the eastern end of the spur and were doubled in strength on the western side, where more level ground offered easier access. Parts of these earthworks survive today outside the walls of the Roman town. Originally the Iron Age settlement consisted of round huts and grain stores casually grouped in the Celtic manner, but by the beginning of the 1st century AD these had been replaced by a formally planned settlement with streets approximately at right angles to each other, and running between regularly spaced buildings and enclosures. The plan closely resembled that of Roman towns on the Continent and showed clearly the influence of Roman culture.

Trade throughout the territory would have been well organised, for the Celtic rulers of Calleva drew a valuable tribute in corn, cattle, hides and slaves, for all of which there was a ready market in the Roman world. In return, they bought wine, olive oil, exotic foods, fine pottery and ornaments. Coins were used by the Atrebates in the 1st century BC, crudely shaped to begin with, but redesigned later in Roman style, bearing inscriptions in Latin, and sometimes their place of origin: 'CALLE' or 'CALLEV'. Coins show that Epillus and Verica, the sons of Commius, styled themselves Kings of the Atrebates. About AD 42 Verica fled from Britain, probably driven out by the Catuvellauni, an aggressive tribe whose territory lay across the Thames. His plea to Rome for help in regaining his kingdom is said to have provided the excuse for the Roman invasion of Britain in AD 43, although the Emperor

Claudius had other motives of more benefit to himself and to the empire. The Roman legions landed on the south-east coast, defeated the Catuvellauni and captured their capital at Colchester. In the west country they overcame the Durotriges and took the mighty hillforts of the Dorset region. Between these campaign areas the Atrebatic kingdom seems to have offered no resistance, but soon after the invasion a Roman garrison was established at Calleva. One of the earliest Roman buildings discovered in recent excavations resembled a military headquarters. It was situated in the centre and clearly in control of the whole town. On the south coast a military supply base was established at Chichester.

Towards the end of the 1st century AD the civil administration of Calleva was restored to the native leaders and the town underwent a radical change. Another street plan was laid out and a major building programme included a new administrative and market centre, a bath house, temples, shops, private houses and, a short distance outside the town, an amphitheatre for public entertainments. Buildings of this period were still of timber, and were not replaced in masonry until the 2nd or 3rd centuries AD. Calleva functioned not only as the principal market town of the region but as the centre for the administration of justice and for the collection of taxes.

All major roads across Berkshire led to Calleva, and formed part of the Roman network built across Britain to provide a rapid means of communication between all military and civil centres. At least six great Roman roads converged upon Calleva, making it an important staging point for civil and military travellers. An inn near the south gate grew into the second largest building in the town. Its three wings set around a large courtyard provided a working arrangement adopted by inns in medieval and later centuries, except that the Roman inn had a bath house – not an amenity commonly provided in medieval hostelries.

Because Calleva was abandoned soon after the Roman occupation, the roads leading to it fell into decay and have only survived here and there as rough trackways. The road from London crossed the Thames at Staines and continued over wooded heathlands to a high point now known as Dukes Hill, where the Roman surveyors

Iron Age earthworks still survive to the south-west of Silchester, the Roman town of Calleva.

This aerial photograph of Silchester shows the Roman street grid of Calleva, and the line of the road to London leading away from the east gate.

realigned it so that the next 17 mile section ran directly to Calleva. Remains of the agger (earthen embankment) of this road are still traceable along the track running through Sunninghill, Crowthorne and Finchampstead, known locally as the Devil's Highway. A ford still exists where the Romans crossed the river Blackwater, and west of this the Berks-Hants boundary follows the road for most of the way to the east gate of Calleva. Out of the west gate a south-westerly road ran to Old Sarum and Dorchester; and a north-westerly road to Cirencester and Gloucester. The latter has been traced through Aldermaston Park and across the Kennet valley to Thatcham, where there was a small Roman settlement. From Thatcham to Speen its course is uncertain, but it must have crossed the river Lambourn near Donnington Grove. Speen is identified as the Roman posting station of Spinae, listed in the Antonine Itinerary of routes along which the imperial post travelled. From Speen the road continued through Wickham, where there was another small settlement, to the next posting station at Wanborough, where aerial photography has discovered the outlines of a large Roman inn. Between Speen and Wickham another road branched off to cross the Kennet near Chilton Foliat, and the site of the fine Roman villa at Littlecote, to continue westwards to Bath. A northbound road from Calleva ran to Dorchester-on-Thames, but beyond the first 1½ miles most of its course to Streatley has been obliterated. In recent years an important clue to its direction has been found by aerial photography, showing a short length of Roman road crossing the modern A4 between Ufton and Bradfield, and heading more directly for Streatley than the previously suggested route via Pangbourne. From Streatley the continuation of the road is traceable via Moulsford and Cholsey to Dorchester.

Southbound roads from Calleva linked it with Winchester and Chichester. A north-easterly road is believed to have crossed east Berkshire to a ford at Hedsor, on the way to St Albans, but few traces of this have been found. This road would have passed to the south-east of the site of Reading, an area where numerous finds of coins and other objects indicate Roman occupation up to c. AD 400. As well as the main Roman roads, numerous tracks connecting the settlements of native peoples must have remained in use, and the Roman villas and farms whose remains have been located in north-east Berkshire must have had adequate means of transport and communication with Calleva and with each other. Of the several villas in the Maidenhead area, the first to be discovered, in 1886, was on Castle Hill, and contained a suite of baths with furnaces and underfloor heating. In 1959 one of the largest villas in the county was discovered at Cox Green, by means of aerial photography, in a field about to be covered by a housing estate. The area had long been under cultivation and cartloads of rubble were known to have been removed from the site. Excavations showed that the original farmhouse was enlarged in the 2nd century AD into a winged corridor villa with a heating system and a suite of hot, cold and tepid baths. Further enlargements and elaborations were carried out in the

Remains of a late 3rd century Roman wall at the south gate of Calleva. Southbound roads linked the town with Winchester and Chichester.

3rd century, and the villa was occupied for at least another 100 years after that. In addition to numerous pottery pieces, iron slag was found, showing that the villa had its own forge, producing nails, ring staples, knives, door handles and other useful items.

The owners of Cox Green villa did not lack neighbours. A flourishing Romano-British society in north-east Berkshire is indicated by the discovery of other buildings of the period near Maidenhead, Knowl Hill, White Waltham and Waltham St Lawrence. A site on Weycock Hill in Waltham St Lawrence had been attracting the attention of antiquaries since the 16th century, owing to the large numbers of Roman coins found in the area. Camden, Ashmole and Hearne all commented on the phenomena; Camden stating that 'the foundations of an old fort' were to be seen there. By the 18th century nothing remained to be seen except a scattering of broken masonry and, later, the exact site of the 'fort' was lost. Then, in 1837, during excavations for the cutting for the Great Western Railway below Weycock Hill, a Roman cemetery was unearthed, containing more than 30 skeletons. In 1890, when the railway cutting was being widened, several old wells and rubbish pits were found, containing domestic animal bones, broken bricks and tiles. Altogether, the finds pointed to a place of importance somewhere nearby, but it was not discovered until aerial photographs showed the outlines of a building on top of Weycock Hill, and subsequent exploration found that it was not a fort but a temple. Like many Roman temples it was octagonal in shape and probably consisted of a central room with a domed roof, surrounded by an ambulatory. The large quantities of coins, mostly from the late Roman period, found in the area may be explained as votive offerings to the god to whom the temple was devoted.

The villa farms of north-east Berkshire were engaged in the production of corn to help feed the Roman army. In contrast, south-east Berkshire appears to have been thinly populated, and may have been reserved as a source of timber. Finds in the area, such as those at Wickham Bushes and Finchampstead, have been minor, and all of them close to the Roman road. West Berkshire was a huge grain producing area, and several villa farms have been identified along the river valleys. In a field near the Thames at Lower Basildon two fine mosaic floors were discovered during construction of the Great Western Railway approaching Gatehampton bridge in 1839. The floors were subsequently destroyed by the workmen but numerous fragments of red tiles and pottery have been found in the fields round about, and aerial photographs have recorded marks of rectangular enclosures and pits beside the railway line. Another enclosure and part of a trackway have been found a short distance downstream from Basildon church.

In the Pang valley, remains of two Roman villas were discovered by ploughing in the parish of Hampstead Norreys, and roughly excavated in the 19th century. One site, at Well House Farm, was reported to have consisted of a large enclosure containing several buildings. Among the broken bricks, tiles and tessellated floors were lumps of molten glass and metal, and two skeletons lying face downwards, suggesting that the villa may have been sacked and burnt. The second site, at Eling, uncovered in 1863, was described as a villa of the corridor type, with a hypocaust and part of a mosaic floor, badly damaged by ploughing. In 1970, a mechanical digger preparing the ground for the advancing M4 motorway struck the foundations of another villa at Maidenhatch, on the north side of the Pang near Tidmarsh. Hurried excavations before the bulldozers destroyed the remains established that the villa measured 100 feet by 50 feet, and had consisted of a number of small rooms opening onto a long corridor, and possibly a patio facing south. The outer walls were of flint and stone, the roof of baked red tiles.

There was a well-preserved underfloor heating system at the eastern end. The villa had provided living accommodation for a small farming community, while another building nearby was probably the working farmhouse. There was evidence of facilities for storing grain, and of iron smelting and pottery making, showing that the community was self-sufficient. The villa dated from the 4th century but there were signs of a small earlier building underneath it. The probable course of the Roman road from Calleva to Dorchester-on-Thames would have been about a mile to the west.

The Kennet valley continued to be extensively farmed in the Romano-British period. To the south-west of Reading, coarse pottery and associated finds suggesting humble farmsteads were found during the extension of a housing estate at Southcote in 1952 and at Pingewood, south of the motorway, in 1970. In fields alongside the A4 at Ufton Nervet, cropmarks showed three farm enclosures dating from the late Iron Age into the Roman period. About a quarter of a mile away, a previously unknown length of the Roman road from Calleva to Dorchester was found, crossing the Kennet by a ford also used by a trackway from the farm. Pottery found on the site showed this was a small, not very prosperous farm, and, as at Pingewood, many of the pots were of coarse Silchester ware. A wealthier late Roman settlement existed near Aldermaston wharf, in an area being used for gravel extraction. The remains of a Roman bath house only were identified, the rest of the building having already been destroyed. A similar bath house has also been excavated further west along the Kennet valley at Kintbury. Numerous Roman finds at Newbury, and the discovery of a Roman cemetery near the railway goods station in 1856, indicate that there was a considerable settlement here, although no buildings have been located.

On the Downs, Roman potsherds and the survival of field systems bear witness to the intensive cultivation of the region for the production of cereals. Few substantial buildings have been located, and the scanty remains suggest an area of small farmsteads. At Upper Lambourn, three Roman burials were revealed by the uprooting of a tree, perhaps marking the site of a small cemetery. In recent years interest has centred on Maddle Farm, near Lambourn, where archaeological studies have identified a villa constructed, in its initial stages, of chalk blocks. Associated farm buildings show signs of corn drying and milling processes in the 3rd and 4th centuries.

On Lowbury Hill is the site of a Roman temple, dedicated, like the one on Weycock Hill, to pagan gods. If Christianity ever reached these remote places in Roman times, it has left no signs. Pagan temples continued to be built after the Christian religion was officially recognised by the Emperor Constantine in AD 313. The small apsidal building, with its distinguishing transept, discovered during the excavations at Calleva in 1892, is therefore all the more remarkable. It may be a unique instance of a Romano-British Christian church dating from the 4th century. Compared with other buildings in the town, however, the church was small and unpretentious, suggesting only a small Christian community. Few Christian objects were found there, and none from that period had been found elsewhere in Berkshire, until the discovery, in the 1980s, of a lead font in a gravel pit at Caversham. It has been suggested that the font may have been buried by a Christian community to save it from barbarians during a raid, and never recovered.

In the 4th century the great Roman empire began to break up under pressure from increasingly powerful barbarian attacks, and Britain, too, suffered repeated raids and incursions. The Roman legions withdrew, and an appeal to Rome by the British civitates proved useless. After the sack of Rome in AD 410, the Emperor could only advise the British to look to their own defences.

3

SAXON BERKSHIRE

Saxons had begun to settle in small numbers in the upper Thames Valley before the end of the Roman occupation. Graves of men and women of Germanic origin, some with Roman weapons, have been discovered in the Oxford-Abingdon area. These people may have been some of the foreign mercenaries invited by the British authorities in the late 4th century to help defend the country against increasing barbarian attacks. Finds of pottery and metalwork dating from the 5th century in cemeteries at Dorchester, Wallingford, Reading and Aston near Remenham indicate a gradual spread of Saxon settlements along the Thames. It is possible that groups of soldiers and their families were placed there to help protect the boundary of the territory centred on Calleva, and, so far as is known, there was no early Saxon settlement near Calleva itself. Nor is there any evidence of a barbarian attack on the town. The Romano-British way of life seems to have continued there for a generation or more after the departure of the legions, although living standards declined as the town's control over its territory weakened. Some indication of shrinking horizons and fear of attack can, perhaps, be seen in the earthworks two miles away at Padworth. These could have been thrown up during this period to guard the north-western approach and the road from Dorchester-on-Thames. By c AD 450 Calleva was deserted and falling into ruins. It had long ago ceased to be a place of any importance.

The Anglo-Saxon invasion of Britain was quite different from that of the Romans before them or the Normans after, which were planned military operations designed to seize control of the country as quickly as possible. The Angles and Saxons arrived in boatloads on different parts of the coast, taking over the country gradually as they searched for living space in a land already well populated. The early peaceful settlers were probably followed by more numerous and warlike hordes, and it is likely that some fighting took place as the British tried to protect their properties. But, after four centuries of Roman rule, the British were unaccustomed to warfare, and it may be significant that the only evidence we have of a period of alarm and danger is the number of coin hoards hidden away and never recovered by their owners. The Christian font found buried at Caversham also suggests flight from a barbarian invader.

The *Anglo-Saxon Chronicles*, relating the deeds of the early kings of Wessex, claimed that Cerdic and his son Cynric landed on the south coast in AD 495 and after several battles founded the kingdom of Wessex in 519. It must then have been small in area, for their descendants fought for another 50 years to extend their territory as far as the Thames Valley. Cerdic's grandsons won a battle in 571 which gave them Eynsham, Benson and Aylesbury. The chronicles contain no references throughout this time to any place in Berkshire, so the story of local resistance, if any, like the story of King Arthur's heroic defence of the west country, remains one of the mysteries of the Dark Ages.

In the end, by whatever means, the Saxons became the masters and imposed their way of life on the countryside and their language on the people. Essentially they were farmers and their primary concern was food production. The changes they made stemmed largely from their involvement with the land and natural resources. Margaret Gelling, in her *Place-names of Berkshire*, has shown how basic resources influenced the names by which Saxons identified settlements and localities. Those believed to have been earliest, because associated with the earliest archaeological findings, were often given names concerned with water supplies, fording places or sites sufficiently drained for habitation. Place-names ending in -well, which could mean a spring, -ford or -ey, meaning an island of dry ground surrounded by streams, are very common in the upper Thames and Ock valleys. When the Saxons penetrated the river valleys of west Berkshire, the need to establish themselves at crossing places on the Lambourn, Pang and Kennet gave rise to the names of Shefford, Welford, Boxford, Stanford (to which Dingley was added later), Denford and Hungerford. Shefford, 'the sheep ford', is known to have been settled by the middle of the 5th century from the evidence of a large Saxon cemetery discovered during the construction of the Lambourn Valley Railway in 1890. Here, many men, women and children were buried in pagan style together with their weapons, ornaments and other prized possessions. At the head of the Lambourn Valley, Saxons also made use of the Bronze Age Seven Barrows for the interment of their own dead. Some riverbank settlements were given names ending in Old English -hamm, meaning a meadow. Greenham, Midgham, Benham and Thatcham are examples.

A second essential resource was wood for building and firing. Woodlands and clearings, made by tree felling and the extension of land available for growing crops, were the origin of names ending in -ley.

Chieveley, Ilsley, Langley, Fawley, Lilley and Woolley identify woodland clearings in west Berkshire. Streatley, Purley and Hurley were clearings made for settlements along the Thames, and the wooded nature of the country around Reading is indicated by Coley, Whitley, Woodley and Earley. To the south and east, Farley, Riseley, Hartley and Whistley show how the forest area was being reduced. The name Kentwood suggests that a wood once extended here between the Kennet and the Thames. The -hurst of Tilehurst was applied to a wooded hill where tilemaking, carried on in Roman times, was later revived. Timber in use is suggested at Theale, from Old English thelu, meaning 'planks'. In this area, even today threaded by many streams, the number of plank bridges may have given rise to the place-name.

A remarkable feature of central Berkshire is the sequence of places with names ending in -field, from Old English -feld. Bradfield, Englefield, Burghfield, Wokefield, Stratfield, Swallowfield, Shinfield and Arborfield cover between them a huge area of fertile land along river valleys which may have been heavily wooded when the Saxons arrived and was systematically cleared for cultivation. In east Berkshire there are three more such places: Binfield, Warfield and Winkfield, again in an area where woodland clearance was needed to extend lands which had been cultivated since Roman times and perhaps earlier.

In south-east Berkshire heavy clays and sandy soils were too poor for cultivation and were left to support forest and heath. Woodlands near settlements were used for feeding swine, and place-names such as Bearwood, Billingbear, Bear Grove, Bearhill, with Bere Leys and Bere Court near Pangbourne, are all indicative of woodland swine pastures. Swinley, near Winkfield, had a similar origin. The survival of wolves in the forest is, perhaps, indicated by Woolley, 'the wolves' wood', near Maidenhead. The common Saxon personal name of Aethelwulf, 'noble wolf', suggests a particular admiration for this animal.

Another group of place-names which may have been introduced when the settlers were established contains the endings -ham or -hamstead, meaning a farm or homestead, and later a village. These endings could be associated with a crop, a topographical feature or a personal name. At Beenham, beans were grown; at Leckhampstead, leeks or garlic. Sulham and Sulhamstead were farms in steep-sided valleys; Frilsham belonged to a man named Frithel. Another group signifying ownership of a farm or enclosure included Aldworth, Chaddleworth and Padworth, the enclosures belonging to Ealda, Ceadela and Peada. Names ending in -ton are believed to date from late Saxon times, as they indicate a large farm or estate granted to an important official or king's thegn. Aldermaston, Brightwalton, Donnington, East Garston,

Pangbourne village sign commemorates the Saxon history of the village, which was first recorded in a 9th century charter.

Eddington, Leverton and Ufton were all estates of this kind.

In central Berkshire there are several names derived from –ingas, a group or tribe of followers. Reading and Sonning began as settlements, perhaps controlling large territories, inhabited by Reada's and Sunna's people. Such groups were formerly thought to have been among the first Saxon arrivals, but this theory is now in doubt. The territory of the Sunningas, on the evidence of a 7th century charter of Chertsey Abbey, extended over much of east Berkshire, and certainly these people gave their name to Sunninghill. Wokingham, too, had links with Surrey, and may have been started by a breakaway group from the Woccingas' main territory around Woking. Pangbourne originated from a territory and stream held by Paega's people.

Among the former Buckinghamshire places now in Berkshire, there was a recurrence of the -ey names found along the upper Thames. Here, too, was a low-lying area laced by many streams forming islands. Eton was an island farm, and adjoining it are Chalvey, Boveney and Dorney. Another group of farming communities lived at Cippenham, Burnham, Farnham and Wexham; while Upton, Ditton and Horton were later estates bordering the great mire which gave Slough its name. Langley was a long clearing at the foot of the Chilterns.

Very few Celtic names survived, showing how completely the Saxons gained control and adopted only the names of major topographical features such as the rivers Thames, Kennet, Loddon and Ock. The place-name of Datchet is unusual in that it contains a Celtic word for wood, suggesting that a British enclave may have remained here. In the forest, the legend of Herne the Hunter lived on. His name is derived from Cernunnos, the Celtic god of the underworld. Pagans worshipped many gods and easily absorbed other people's.

The re-establishment of Christianity in England in the 7th century was

28

accomplished slowly and with many setbacks. By repute in Rome, the English were a barbarous, fierce and pagan people, and even after the eastern and northern parts of the country had been converted, the west remained heathen. Christianity made no progress there until Birinus was sent, in AD 635, on a special mission from the Pope. His success in converting Cynegils, King of Wessex, was followed by the endowment of a church and bishopric at Dorchester-on-Thames, which remained the centre of religious life in Wessex until 676, when the bishop's see was moved to Winchester. From Dorchester, Birinus and his monks went out to preach to the people and set up Christian altars in place of pagan idols. Most early churches were built by landowners on their estates, often close to their own houses but sometimes in the largest settlement on an estate which might include several hamlets and farmsteads. As Christianity spread, more churches and more priests were needed. In areas where some of the new Christian communities were small, their needs could be supplied from a minster church, which supported a group of priests who went out to serve the dependent communities. Minster churches were usually quite large and well-endowed with lands and revenues. Thatcham church, founded in the 7th century, was a minster, and there were others at Reading, Lambourn, Kintbury and Cookham. In later centuries the tendency was for each village to have its own church and priest. There are very few remains of Saxon churches, because most were built in wood, and even stone ones largely disappeared in later rebuildings. The most substantial survival in Berkshire is the tower of Wickham church, of which the lower two stages are Saxon work, although the top dates from the Victorian restoration of the building.

The Christian Church, with its need for administrative and financial organisation, gradually imposed a new order and uniformity on the countryside and its settlements. At a higher level, it brought kings a new kind of counsellor in abbots and bishops, whose authority increased as the Church grew richer and more powerful. Contacts with Rome and the rest of Christian Europe were maintained, encouraging scholarship and the spread of literacy and learning, at least among clerics and in monastic institutions. Berkshire's first abbey was founded at Abingdon in AD 675.

The Church, together with a more settled way of life, helped to raise living standards, which were fairly primitive in the early Saxon period. Unfortunately, remains of Saxon homes are even more elusive than those of churches, so that the remains of a Saxon hut near Ufton Nervet represented a rare find indeed. A sunken floor surrounded by post holes, and fragments of coarse, undecorated pottery, suggested a poor standard of living, and the hut probably dated back to the 6th century. A piece of loomweight showed that weaving was carried on in the home, and the sunken floor, characteristic of Saxon huts found on the Continent, is believed to have created the kind of cool, damp atmosphere best suited to making cloth.

In the 7th and 8th centuries, living standards rose. Ornaments and other metalwork show that dress became more sophisticated. Food production increased as more land was cultivated to supply the growing population. Traps and weirs were constructed in rivers to catch fish, especially eels, in larger quantities. A major technological advance was achieved by the introduction of water mills to replace hand milling with querns. By the beginning of the 9th century millwrights were capable of building, on a royal estate at Old Windsor, a large and elaborate mill with three vertical wheels working in parallel and driven by water drawn from the Thames along a channel 20 feet wide and three-quarters of a mile long.

Important developments in local administration began to take place in the 8th century, when the first shires were formed as divisions of Wessex. Hampshire was recorded as early as AD 757; Wiltshire in 801. In the first half of the 9th century Wessex emerged as the most powerful of the English kingdoms, largely owing to the campaigns of King Egbert, who reigned from 802–839. During the reign of his son, Aethelwulf, the ancient dispute between Wessex and Mercia, concerning territory south of the Thames, was finally settled. The river was established as the boundary between the two kingdoms, and sometime in the 840s Berkshire was formed, containing all the territory lying between the Thames and Hampshire.

The creation of the shires reflected the increasing responsibilities of kingship and government. In each shire, the king appointed a deputy to deal with routine matters and oversee the administration of justice. In time of war he was responsible for summoning the shire levies and leading them into battle. This officer was called an ealdorman, and like the king, he had official estates within the shire. In Berkshire, Aldermaston was the ealdorman's estate. It was well situated in the centre of southern Berkshire, and on roads leading in one direction to the Wessex capital of Winchester, and in the other to Wallingford, the chief town of Saxon Berkshire. In the 11th century the Domesday survey recorded that the Aldermaston estate owned two houses in Wallingford, perhaps formerly used by the ealdorman for himself and official guests.

Accord between the English kingdoms was achieved at a time when the whole country faced a growing menace from Viking raiders. Attacks on coastal towns had begun in the last years of the 8th century and had increased in frequency and ferocity as the raiders penetrated further

St Swithin's church, Wickham. The lower two-thirds of the tower is late Saxon work and the tower may originally have been built for defence. The only entrance was the now blocked up doorway in the south wall, about eight feet above ground level.

and further inland. It was in the context of one of these raids that Berkshire was first recorded in the *Anglo-Saxon Chronicles*. About the year 860, 'a great pirate host landed and stormed Winchester; and against the host fought ealdorman Osric with the men of Hampshire and ealdorman Aethelwulf with the men of Berkshire, and they put the host to flight and had possession of the place of slaughter'. By AD 865 Danes had established bases in Kent and East Anglia, and by 867, in Mercia. Towards the end of 870 they reached Wessex and set up a fortified camp at Reading. From there they rode westwards, perhaps with the intention of sacking Aldermaston, but at Englefield they were confronted by a Saxon force commanded by the ealdorman Aethelwulf, and after a fierce encounter the Danes were forced to withdraw. Four days later, King Aethelred of Wessex and his brother Alfred arrived with a large army and attempted to recapture Reading; but although 'a great slaughter was made there on either side, and ealdorman Aethelwulf was slain', the Danes remained in possession of the town.

The English army withdrew to Ashdown (the name by which the Berkshire Downs were then known), and took up a position astride the Ridgeway near Compton. The Danish army drew up its lines on slightly higher ground, giving them an advantage in attack. According to Asser's account of the battle in his *Life of King Alfred*, King Aethelred was still in his tent at prayer, 'and declaring firmly that he would not leave that place alive before the priest had finished Mass', when Alfred realised that he must attack immediately in order to prevent disaster; 'and acting courageously, like a wild boar . . . and strengthened by divine help, when he had closed up the shield-wall in proper order, he moved his army without delay against the enemy'. The battle was long and fierce, ending in the deaths of 'many thousands', who lay 'over the whole broad expanse of Ashdown, scattered everywhere, far and wide'. The Danes were put to flight and chased back to their camp at Reading.

Far from being a decisive victory, Ashdown was only the beginning of seven years of intermittent warfare in Wessex, and it was not until 878 that Alfred was able to dictate peace terms and rid his kingdom of the Danes. In the 880s he set in motion plans for its future defence. Determined that the enemy should not again succeed in a surprise attack while all his own men were scattered at their homes, he reorganised the army in two parts, so that at any time half his thegns and fighting men were ready in arms, while the other half remained at home, attending to their estates and farming the land. Next he planned a network of fortified sites, called burhs, throughout Wessex, each of which could protect an area from attack and provide a refuge when danger threatened. Oxford and Wallingford were fortified along the

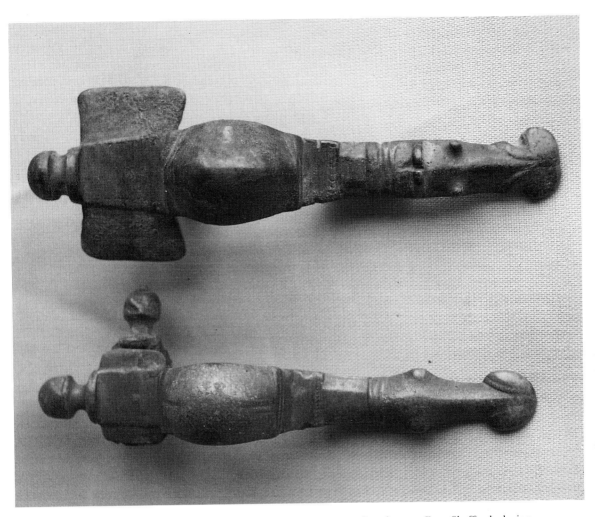

An early Saxon cemetery containing pagan burials was found near East Shefford during construction of the Lambourn Valley Railway in 1890. Among numerous finds on this site were two brooches made of bronze, the lower sections in the form of horses' heads.

upper Thames, Reading and Sashes Island, near Cookham, along the middle Thames, all guarding routes into Wessex. After Alfred's death in 899, his policies were continued by his son, Edward, whose conquests made him the first king to rule all England. The wars of the 10th century were fought in other parts of the country and it was not until 1006 that another Danish army burst into Wessex and rampaged through Berkshire and Hampshire. They spent Christmas at Reading, feasting on plundered food supplies, and burned Wallingford to the ground before going on their way to Winchester and the sea, laden with booty.

4

BERKSHIRE UNDER NORMAN RULE

Among the buildings sacked and burned by marauding Danes may have been a royal house or hunting lodge on the banks of the Thames at the village now known as Old Windsor. Although there is no written record of such an event, archaeological research has uncovered evidence of a particularly fine building, with stone walls, a tiled roof and glazed windows. The high quality of the materials, together with that of pottery and metal pieces found on the site, point to an owner of great wealth and status. The house, a large and elaborate mill and associated buildings, were in use in the 9th century but apparently destroyed by fire around the year 900. In the 10th century the complex was restored, the house rebuilt in timber and the mill, which originally had three vertical wheels, replaced by one of different design with two horizontal wheels. By the 11th century a major Saxon settlement had grown up here and was recorded in 1061, when King Edward the Confessor was in residence at his house in Windsor. Edward, like other Saxon kings, and the Normans after them, was addicted to the violent sport of hunting, but he was also a deeply religious man and his later years were devoted to rebuilding Westminster Abbey. In January 1066, shortly before his death, he gave his Windsor estate as part of his endowment of the Abbey, but when, in the autumn of that year, William of Normandy seized the throne, he lost no time in reversing Edward's grant by exchanging it for estates elsewhere. In the new charter the Abbot agreed that Windsor should be 'for the king's use, the place appearing proper and convenient for a royal retirement on account of the river and its nearness to the forest for hunting'. The wording makes plain the role of the Thames as a major highway between Windsor and the capital.

William's most pressing concern after his victory at Hastings was to secure his hold of the country and its largely hostile population. He did this by giving the lands and possessions of English thegns who had fought against him, or refused to accept him as king, to his Norman supporters, and by building strong castles at strategic positions throughout the land, from which Norman barons could subdue the local people and prevent uprisings. His decision to build a castle at Wallingford was inevitable, in order to control the former Saxon burh and the important river crossing, and work began there in 1067. His choice of a second Berkshire site fell on a chalk cliff dominating the middle Thames Valley a few miles to the north-west of his Windsor residence, and around 1070 work commenced there on the motte and bailey castle which would bring the town of New Windsor into being.

All land was deemed to belong to the king, and estates, or manors as the Normans called them, were held in fief from him in return for allegiance, military service and taxes. Soon after the Conquest, changes in land ownership affected almost every part of the county. The 22 manors formerly held by King Edward or his Queen and which had passed to Harold, William took for his own maintenance. Henry de Ferrers, one of the most powerful Norman barons, was granted most of those belonging to the English sheriff, Godric, as well as those of a dozen other thegns. Geoffrey de Mandeville, William, son of Ansculf, Ralf de Mortimer and the Count of Evreux were also generously rewarded, Geoffrey's estates including those at East Garston, Streatley and Hurley which had formerly been held by Esgar, staller of King Edward's horses. Lesser knights and officers of the royal household were given smaller estates. To Walter FitzOther, Keeper of the Forest and Constable of Windsor Castle, went Orton (later absorbed into Windsor), together with other manors across the river at Eton, Burnham and Horton. To Bernard, the King's Falconer, went the manor and mill of Wasing; to Hugolin the Steersman, a small estate and mill at Hamstead Marshall. Hundreds of Englishmen were dispossessed but among the few who remained in favour was Theodoric the Goldsmith, in recognition of his craftsmanship and willingness to serve the new monarch. Theodoric was given lands at Aldworth, Hampstead Norreys, Sulham, Purley and Whitley. Another goldsmith, Alfward, was allowed to keep the Shottesbrooke estate which had belonged to his father, and in due course descended to Alfward's son, tactfully christened William.

The estates of great abbeys remained, for the most part, unchanged, for William I was a pious son of the Church and had received the Pope's blessing on his invasion of England. Next to the king, Abingdon Abbey was the largest landholder in Berkshire, with many estates in what was then North Berkshire as well as the manors of Farnborough, Chieveley, Welford, Beedon, Winkfield and Whistley (Hurst), which remain in modern Berkshire. Chertsey Abbey retained its estate at White Waltham; Westminster Abbey, its estate at Easthampstead; and Amesbury Abbey its estates at Kintbury and Fawley. Battle Abbey, Sussex, founded by William after his victory at Hastings, was endowed with a manor at Brightwalton and another, which became known as Battle Manor, adjoining a royal estate at Reading. The Bishopric of Salisbury held a huge estate around Sonning, comprising much of the former territory of the Sunningas, and including Ruscombe, Arborfield, Wokingham and Sandhurst.

Within 20 years of the Conquest, land ownership had so changed that an orderly and up-to-date record of holdings was needed, setting out exactly who owned what, together with the extent of the resources and value of each estate. The great Domesday survey was planned by William and his counsellors at Christmas 1085, and carried out in the following year. The means for gathering, with such speed and efficiency, the mass of information required already existed in the shire and hundred courts and local juries which had survived from Saxon times. These ensured that men with local knowledge were available to answer, under oath, all the questions of the king's commissioners concerning each estate, as it then was and as it had been in the reign of King Edward. The manors were assessed as agricultural units, in which the extent of arable, pasture and woodland, and the value of mills and fisheries were of first importance. The workforce of peasants, graded as villeins, bordars, cottars or serfs, had few entitlements and many obligations towards their lord.

West Berkshire was the most widely inhabited and cultivated area, and contained the majority of villages and farmsteads. Extensive tracts of arable land produced wheat, barley, oats and beans; and there was also ample pasture for cattle and woodland providing food for pigs. Most manors contained some of each kind of land, and wherever possible part of a stream to drive a mill and provide fish. Manors without a mill often owned a share in one belonging to a manor blessed with sufficient water power to drive several mills. Downland manors, such as Aldworth, Compton and Beedon had no mills, whereas Bradfield had three and Welford five. Altogether, the area of modern Berkshire had about 80 mills at the time of the survey. One of the largest corn-producing estates was the king's at Lambourn, where there was enough land to provide work each year for 42 plough teams. Lambourn also had two mills, but very little woodland and no meadow. Aldermaston, another large but more balanced estate held by the king, contained ploughland for 30 teams, 124 acres of meadow, a mill, fisheries and some woodland. At the lower end of the scale were estates such as that enjoyed by Humphrey the Chamberlain at Bagnor. Here, Bagnor mill was already working, and Humphrey had a modest acreage of arable land for three teams, plus

Padworth church, showing the rounded Norman apse and later bell turret, the latter typical of the churches built in the wooded parts of south Berkshire.

22 acres of meadow and a small wood. Many small manors listed in the Domesday survey represented only parts of modern parishes of the same name. Enborne, for instance, contained three small estates, two with land for only two ploughs and 13 acres of meadow. One of these contained no woodland, although the other had woodland producing material for fencing. The third, and more valuable estate, contained a mill, land for three ploughs, 20 acres of meadow and a small wood for feeding pigs.

Bread, cheese, pork and beans were the staple diet of medieval man, but only in old North Berkshire were dairy farming and cheese making recorded. Nowhere in the county was sheep farming specified, although ewes' milk was commonly used for drinking and cheese making, and small flocks were probably pastured as well as cattle. Certainly there were none of the great wool-producing flocks enumerated in other counties. Cattle were kept mainly to breed oxen, which were used everywhere for draughtwork. Each plough team could consist of up to eight oxen. Horses were bred for riding, although there is only a retrospective reference to this on the king's manor at Kintbury, where, in King Edward's time, Godric the Sheriff made 43 acres of land into pasture for his own horses, by what right the shire court giving testimony did not know. (There are indications elsewhere that Godric used crown property for his own benefit.)

East Berkshire remained more sparsely inhabited, with most of its villages occupying gravel terraces beside the Thames or the clay belt between Reading and Maidenhead. Elsewhere, heath and forest prevailed. On his manors of Cookham and Windsor, William had extended the area of forest; and at Winkfield, which belonged to Abingdon Abbey, the monks had reluctantly surrendered four hides of land for enclosure in the forest. William's successors were to continue to enlarge the forest until it covered most of Berkshire south of the Kennet. Punitive laws protected the deer and other game from poachers, and the forest itself from wood cutting or the enclosure of plots around cottages or the houses of other forest tenants. Woodland constituted the major part of many East Berkshire manors at the time of the Domesday survey, and pig production formed the most valuable part of their economy. A proportion of those bred was rendered to the lord of the manor in return for the right of pannage in his woods. Among manors held by the king, Finchampstead supplied 200 pigs a year, Waltham St Lawrence 150, Warfield, Wargrave and Cookham 100 each. The bishopric of Salisbury received 300 pigs a year from its Sonning estates.

Fish, particularly eels, were an essential part of the food supply. They were trapped in weirs and mill pools, and dues were paid either in quantities of eels or in money. The royal manors contained many rich fisheries. Those on the Thames at Wargrave yielded 3,000 eels a year; at Remenham 1,000; but at Cookham 13 shillings and fourpence was paid in lieu, the fish evidently being sold profitably elsewhere. From the Loddon at Shinfield 550 eels were due, plus a further 150 from the mill pool as part of the miller's rent.

Norman enterprise had started an experiment in viticulture at Bisham, where Henry de Ferrers had planted a vineyard of about twelve acres.

The Domesday survey depicts a rural and agrarian economy with very few indications of towns. The Saxons were not, by nature, townsmen, and had done little to develop them. It was left to the Normans, with their European and more cosmopolitan background, to promote towns and increase their numbers. Town planning began when landholders granted leases of plots of land along either side of a main street, where the lessees could build houses or set up workshops. These plots usually had a narrow, uniform frontage but extended some way back, so that there was room for extensions or outhouses. If trade or business affairs increased, the leasing of such plots could be very profitable. Most towns had started with a market held regularly at the intersection of trade routes or at a river crossing, and soon craftsmen found it advantageous to settle there, where they could compete with each other and profit by a wider market and cheaper supplies of raw materials. In large towns local affairs could be conducted by the king's or the county officers.

In 1086 Wallingford was the chief, and by far the largest, town in Berkshire, with a built-up area containing several hundred properties. These were leased to a variety of individuals, officials or manors in Berkshire and Oxfordshire. There were several churches; a market was held every Saturday; a mint was in operation; and a strong Norman castle had been built within the walls of the former Saxon burh. The population included 22 Frenchmen. No such sophisticated urban community is indicated elsewhere in the Domesday survey of Berkshire. The next largest complex of buildings was at Old Windsor, where many of the 95 recorded may only have been occupied while the king and court were in residence. A few properties were held by royal servants: Eudo the steward was mentioned, as well as Albert the clerk, a priest and two sergeants of the court. A little farming, fishing and pig-keeping were carried on, but some of the woodland had been enclosed within the forest. Across the river, the manor of Wraysbury supplied hay for the cattle of the court. Windsor was obviously not a trading place at this time, but on the king's more productive manor at Cookham the survey referred specifically to 'the new market' which yielded 20 shillings in tolls. The king's long-term plans for his own and future royal accommodation were centred on the castle under construction at Clewer. There, defensive ditches had been dug around the hill and a fortified tower established on the inner mound. During the next 30 years the original timber buildings were replaced in stone and the castle enlarged, so that, by 1110, it was sufficiently well advanced and habitable for Henry I to hold court there for the first time. After that date, the royal residence and its associated buildings at Old Windsor were allowed to decay, and the town of New Windsor grew up around the castle.

Reading, in 1086, appears to have been less than a quarter the size of Wallingford, and was divided between the king's manor, containing the burh, and Battle Abbey's manor containing the church. Both manors included rich farmlands, woodlands and fisheries; the king's, of course, larger than those of the abbey, and having four mills against the abbey's two. Both manors were increasing in value; the king's Reading manor was valued at a higher figure than any other in the county, reflecting the growing importance and potential success of the town. Reading had taken over the role fulfilled in earlier times by the Romano-British town of Calleva as a focal point of major roads through the region. It was better situated than Calleva and more accessible, standing at a

Avington church, one of the best preserved of Berkshire's Norman churches.

busy Kennet crossing and near enough to the Thames to benefit from waterborne trade with the capital. A road from Oxford to Winchester and Southampton passed through it, and in course of time it drew the main London to Bath and Bristol highway away from the abandoned Roman town. The Danes found Reading worth taking and holding onto when they chose it for their base camp in the 870s; and again, in the raids of the early 11th century, they had been able to rely on an abundance of food supplies here. A church had been built there, very likely on the site of St Mary's, by the 10th century; and the name of Minster Street (which ran directly to the church before the extension of the graveyard) confirms its one-time status. Early markets were held in the open area in front of the church and near the junction of the principal roads. Reading was a royal possession in the reign of Edward the Confessor, who founded a mint there; and up to the time of the Conquest, Godric the Sheriff maintained property in the town for the entertainment of official guests. Reading's future as a trading and communications centre would have been assured even without the foundation by Henry I of the great Benedictine abbey in 1121. Henry gave his Reading estate as part of his initial endowment of the abbey, and soon afterwards added the

Battle Abbey estate, which he had regained in exchange for property in Sussex.

In West Berkshire, Lambourn and Thatcham had been places of some importance in Saxon times, but neither proved well situated for the trade and traffic of the Middle Ages. Lambourn, the centre of a large corn-producing estate, had long been a royal possession and was recorded c 888 among the bequests of King Alfred to his Queen. By 1032 it had a church, which was replaced in the 12th century by a larger building in stone. By that time a small town had developed along the main road leading to a market place in front of the church and the place became known as Chipping Lambourn, chipping or cheping meaning a place for buying and selling. But Lambourn achieved only a moderate degree of prosperity, based almost entirely on local trade. No major road passed through or near it, and the area it served was thinly populated.

Thatcham, too, was well endowed with natural resources, having 147 acres of meadowland (the second largest to Reading's 150 acres), two mills and woodland rendering 60 pigs to the king, who was lord of the manor at Domesday. The Saxon church had served as a minster over a wide area since the 7th century, and by 1086 the settlement was one of the very few in which building plots were mentioned, although the twelve recorded here must already have seemed insignificant in comparison with the 51 at nearby Ulvritone. There had been a Roman staging post at Thatcham on the western road from Calleva, and when that road was abandoned in favour of the Kennet Valley route, Thatcham was still well-placed. But it lacked a good crossing over the Kennet for north-south traffic, and the existence of such a crossing a few miles further west had created an important junction at Ulvritone, where roads from Oxford to Southampton, Basingstoke and south-eastern England, Andover and the south-west, converged and met the London-Bristol road a short distance to the north.

Although Newbury was not mentioned in the Domesday survey, it must then have been represented by the large settlement still known by its Saxon name of Ulvritone. The new Norman lord was Arnulf of Hesdin, described by a medieval chronicler as a man of commanding stature, abounding in energy and wealth. No doubt it was due to his enterprise that the 51 regular building plots had been laid out, ready for leasing, and certainly the value of his manor had increased nearly threefold since the reign of King Edward. The first plots were to the south of the Kennet, along the present Bartholomew and Cheap Streets, leading to the Market Place, where a weekly market was held by the end of the 11th century. Northbrook Street was developed as the town prospered and more houses and workshops were needed.

41

Hungerford was a later Norman development. It was not named in the Domesday survey and any small settlement here may have been included in the lands belonging to the manor of Kintbury. But the ford provided a better crossing place and lined up with an easier route to the south-west than that at Kintbury, hemmed in by a steep ridge of the Downs. The Oxford to Salisbury road and the London to Bristol road met here, and lesser roads from Lambourn and Cirencester used the same crossings. Hungerford became a separate manor by the 12th century, with its own parish church, and the first town plots were laid out along the Salisbury road to the south of the river Dun. The crossing had been bridged by 1275, and by the end of the 13th century a weekly market was being held in the main street.

In East Berkshire, two new market towns were promoted in the 13th century to serve the area between Reading and Windsor. Wokingham was first recorded in 1146 as part of the manor of Sonning, and early in the 13th century the Bishop of Salisbury chose it for the site of a new market. In 1219 Wokingham received its first market charter, which was confirmed by Henry III in 1227, and the nucleus of the town was laid out along the main roads (now Broad Street, Rose Street, Peach Street and Denmark Street) leading to the market place. A rival market was started about the same time by the Bishop of Winchester, who held Wargrave manor from the end of the 12th century. A market charter was granted in 1218, and by 1225 Wargrave had acquired borough status; but in spite of its initial success, Wargrave market did not prosper, and both market and borough status had lapsed before the end of the 13th century. The final decades of this century saw the beginnings of Maidenhead, a place brought into being by the requirements of traffic and trade, rather than by the designs or ambitions of a landholder.

5

THE CHURCH IN THE MIDDLE AGES

The rebuilding and enlargement of existing churches and the foundation of new ones was one of the outstanding achievements of the Normans, and their energies were allowed full scope at a time when more churches were needed due to rising populations and the spread of the parochial system. This process had begun before the Conquest as the need arose for new churches and these became separated from the minster which had formerly served their congregations. By the 13th century most parishes had been formed and each had its own church, but some small rural communities were still served by chapels subject to a mother church. Records of a visitation of Sonning in 1220 show that the parish church of St Andrew had dependent chapels at Earley, Ruscombe, Hurst, Sindlesham, Arborfield, Wokingham and Sandhurst, a situation indicative of the remoteness and slow growth of villages in the Forest area. In 1256 Sir John le Despencer obtained permission to build another chapel and keep a chaplain on his manor of Swallowfield, pleading that the journey through the forest to hear Mass at Sonning church was beset with dangers to himself and his family, from robbers in summer and floods in winter.

Some Norman building work survives today in the majority of Berkshire parish churches, although nearly all have been greatly altered over the centuries in response to changes in population, economic prosperity, architectural fashions and forms of worship. Generally, the fewer changes in a village and its way of life, the more Norman work is likely to survive, albeit restored. Avington and Padworth churches retain their basic early plan of nave and chancel without substantial later additions, while the unusual length of Aldermaston church is due to the enlargement of an early Norman church by the addition of a new chancel in the 13th century. Tidmarsh retains a 12th century nave and a rare apsidal chancel dating from the 13th century. Towards the end of the 12th century the distinctive round arches, plain columns and small windows of the Norman style began to give way to the pointed arches, more elaborate columns and larger windows of Early English Gothic. One of the least altered churches from this period is at Beedon, built c 1220. The 13th century also saw the decoration of church interiors with coloured wall paintings, presenting in vivid detail, scenes from the Bible or the lives of the saints. The Annunciation, the Nativity and the Last Judgement were popular subjects, while among individual saints, the large and reassuring figure of St Christopher, patron of travellers, very often occupied a wall facing the main entrance. Few of these paintings, whitewashed or plastered over during the Reformation, have survived in good condition, but those in St Clement's church at Ashampstead are particularly fine.

Beedon and Ashampstead are among the many small country churches which have never had a tower. Such churches are common in the wooded parts of south and east Berkshire, where timber bell turrets and small shingled spires made the best use of local materials. Flint and sometimes rubble were used for walling. In towns and large villages, bell towers soon became essential enhancements and were added usually to the west end but sometimes at the crossing of nave and transepts. Early towers were massively constructed and rather squat, and most were heightened at a later date. Lambourn's fine crossing tower, begun in the 12th century, has a top stage added in the 15th century. Aldworth's sturdy tower dates from the 13th century, as does the lower part of Chieveley's tower.

The round Norman tower of Great Shefford church is topped by a 15th century third stage. Round towers were dictated by the lack of a local building stone in Berkshire.

Some early flint towers were round, their shape being due to the lack of stone for strengthening the angles of buildings. The tower of Great Shefford's church has round lower stages and an octagonal top added in the 15th century. At Welford, the medieval church was carefully rebuilt in 1852, copying the original 12th century round tower with its 13th century spire.

The power and magnificence of the Church in the Middle Ages was amply demonstrated by the great Benedictine abbey founded at Reading by Henry I in 1121. The abbey was not only a monastery, providing a life of prayer and seclusion for monks, but an institution playing an important role in

Reading Abbey waterfront, at the confluence of the Kennet and Holy Brook, was enlarged in the 14th century. This artist's impression conveys the busy life of the abbey in the 15th century. (Copyright Trust for Wessex Archaeology Ltd)

the affairs of the town, the county and, to some extent, of the nation. Situated immediately to the east of the town, it shared with it all the advantages of well-developed access by river and road. Its monastic buildings and massive church, which rivalled those of Gloucester or Tewkesbury, could not have been built without the importation by water of huge loads of stone from Caen in Normandy, which was cut into smooth blocks and used for facing the rough core of flint and rubble which remains today. From the beginning the abbey was richly endowed. Henry's gifts included the manors and churches of Reading, Cholsey and Pangbourne, the manors of Thatcham and Bucklebury, and the church of Wargrave. In addition there were gifts of gold and silver plate and rich vestments for the church, and numerous holy relics which made Reading Abbey a great centre of pilgrimage. By the 14th century these and subsequent gifts of lands and revenues had made it one of the wealthiest abbeys in England.

The Benedictines had a reputation for hospitality and were called upon to provide accommodation and entertainment for kings and noblemen on their journeys. Grand weddings and other splendid ceremonies were held there, as well as royal and ecclesiastical councils and meetings of Parliament. The Abbot was invested with temporal as well as spiritual responsibilities. In addition to administering the affairs of the abbey and its many estates, he was lord of the manor of Reading and therefore closely involved in the government of the town. In the king's name he administered justice, punished offenders, and through his bailiffs collected taxes, controlled markets and fairs and ordered the repair of roads and bridges around the town. His powers included the right to choose the warden of the Reading Guild of Merchants (later the mayor), a right deeply resented by the guild and a cause of much ill-feeling between town and abbey. On the other hand, the abbey stimulated trade by bringing large numbers of travellers and pilgrims to the town, and gave employment to local people. An abbey the size of Reading's would have employed up to 100 paid servants in domestic chores, building repairs and maintenance, or in the abbey stables, the mill, or on the wharf beside the Kennet.

Reading Abbey promoted the reputation and growth of the town, and although its ruins today appear insignificant, the outline of its precincts around the Forbury can still be seen in the road system. The important west gate opened onto the Market Place, to which the market had been moved from its previous site outside St Mary's church, and where it was held under the supervision of the abbot's bailiffs. A second town church, St Lawrence's, was built beside the west gate before the end of the 12th century, and a third soon afterwards on the outskirts of the town, a traditional site for churches dedicated to St Giles, patron of beggars and lepers. The need for three parish churches reflects the growth of the town and its area of development. London Street and Friar Street were laid out as principal approach roads to the abbey, and High Bridge was built over the Kennet.

Berkshire contained several smaller monasteries. Although the Normans were arrogant and ruthless in their dealings with the common people, they were devout and held the Church in deep respect. It was customary for rich lords and landholders to give part of their wealth for the support of churches or religious houses, and in this way a priory of monks subordinate to Westminster Abbey was founded at Hurley in 1086 or 1087. The founder, Geoffrey de Mandeville, held estates in several counties but most notably in Essex, of which his grandson became the first earl. In the preamble to his charter, de Mandeville said that he founded the priory for the salvation of his soul and of the souls of his first and second wives, his heirs and successors. His endowment included the church, village and woodland of Hurley, together with gifts and tithes from other estates in his possession which would, in effect, supply the monks with corn, pigs, cheese, fowls, horses, calves, orchard fruits and wine. To these he added a fishery in the isle of Ely which supplied 1,500 dried eels and 40 fat eels a year, while the Essex village of Mose supplied 3,000 dried herrings. Hurley Priory was supported by many gifts from other sources, of which the most important in this county were the church and manor of Easthampstead, granted by Westminster Abbey.

The monks of Hurley were better provided for than the nuns of Broomhall Priory in the forest near Sunninghill. Broomhall was founded c 1150, some years after the foundation of Sunninghill church, which was bestowed upon it by King John in the year 1200. Otherwise it was ill-endowed and the nuns lived very simply, enduring considerable hardships. Later royal gifts, granted to relieve their poverty, included free pannage for 36 pigs and three lengths of timber from the forest for the repair of the priory roof. In 1228 the king's forester was ordered to allow the nuns free access to 100 acres of waste in the forest, and in 1283 the Prioress and nuns obtained a royal licence to enclose this land, which they had laboriously brought into cultivation, with a small ditch and hedge, provided that the latter was low enough to allow the king's deer to get in and out.

Another cause close to the hearts of Norman barons was that of the crusader knights, whose orders were formed to protect pilgrims to the Holy Land and to fight the Infidel. The most famous in England were the Knights of the Temple and the Knights of the Hospital of St John of Jerusalem. Members of these orders had taken vows similar to those of monks, but they chose to serve God by fighting as well as praying. Lands and money were given to these orders for their support, and preceptories were founded where, in peace time, the knights could live in monastic communities and devote themselves to charitable work among the poor.

The Order of the Knights of the Temple was founded in France c 1118, and c 1140 Robert de Ferrers, recently created Earl of Derby by King Stephen, gave them his manor of Bisham, with its lands, woods, mills and fisheries. A preceptory was founded there, parts of which, rebuilt in the 13th century, survive in the building later known as Bisham Abbey. The Templars were suppressed in 1307, after the crusades had ended and their order had fallen into disgrace, but Temple Mills at Bisham have preserved the name of their medieval owners.

The Knights Hospitaller were granted the manor of Greenham for

Bisham Abbey, showing the 13th century doorway surviving from the preceptory founded by the Knights Templar.

the purpose of founding a preceptory at some time in the reign of Henry II, and the grant was confirmed by King John in 1199. Other endowments included Brimpton church and a house and lands nearby at Shalford. The Hospitallers survived until their order was suppressed during the Reformation. They received continuous support from various west Berkshire parishes as well as the proceeds of occasional collections at churches throughout the county.

Another popular order in the 12th century was that of the Austin Canons, who followed the rule of St Augustine, leading a disciplined monastic life whilst carrying out parochial duties. Ralph de Chaddle-worth founded Poughley Priory for them c 1160 on the site of an ancient hermitage, and endowed it with Chaddleworth church and woodland, a chapel at Woolley and other lands in west Berkshire. Papal support came from Rome in the form of exemptions from tithes and the enjoyment of other privileges. In 1313 the Bishop of Salisbury granted 40 days' indulgence to everyone who gave assistance to the priory after a serious fire destroyed its granaries, mills and storage barns.

A smaller priory of Austin Canons was founded c 1193 at Sandleford. The founder, Geoffrey, Count of Perch, endowed it with the church and lands of Sandleford, together with the right to build a mill on the river Enborne and an income of 13 marks to be paid yearly from the mill at Newbury. The last named gift was not always paid willingly, although it was confirmed by King John in 1204 and again by Henry III in 1231, when the sheriff of Berkshire was ordered to ensure that the prior and canons received the money regularly after Newbury mill had come into the possession of the crown on the death of its previous owner. At Sandleford, as at other monasteries, it was not unusual for aged royal servants to be cared for and maintained for the remainder of their lives.

Greyfriars of the Franciscan order arrived in Reading in 1233. Although under royal patronage they were not welcomed by the abbot, who would only allow them a piece of waste land outside the town on which to build a friary, and that on condition that they were content to hold no other property and did not infringe on the rights of the abbey. The land was marshy, lying beside the road to Caversham bridge, and frequently flooded, but the friars, true to their vows of poverty and humility, endured appalling discomforts for nearly 50 years before they were given permission to move to higher ground within the town. Even there they were subject to severe restrictions, and their new friary and church might never have been completed if King Edward I had not taken pity on them and sent a generous gift of 56 oaks from Windsor Forest towards the buildings under construction.

The Greyfriars worked humbly among the poor and sick people of the town, work which the monks of the abbey were no doubt willing to share with them as the numbers of such people increased. From the 12th century the care of the sick had been a recognised duty of monasteries, where some of the earliest hospitals were founded. With the state of medical knowledge at that time these were not so much places where diseases could be treated and cured as refuges where the sick, aged and destitute could be cared for and, if need be, isolated. At Reading Abbey, Abbot Anscher founded a leper hospital in the 1130s, and c 1190 Abbot Hugh II founded another hospital to house 13 poor persons and provide daily assistance for 13 others, as well as for needy wayfarers. This hospital, later dedicated to St John the Baptist, was on the north side of St Lawrence's church, whose vicar acted as chaplain and visited the hospital every day. Leper hospitals were found to be necessary in most towns: one was founded at Windsor by Henry II in 1168, and there were others at Newbury and Hungerford in the 13th century. Leper hospitals closed in the 14th century, when the disease was almost extinct. At Newbury, St Bartholomew's Hospital was founded perhaps in the early years of the 13th century, and certainly before 1215, when King John granted it the benefit of a two-day annual fair. Although not attached to a monastery, St Bartholomew's was a religious foundation;

its warden was a priest and the brethren and sisters who ministered to the poor and needy lived under religious vows. The hospital was allowed to collect alms and was supported by small gifts of money and land from local townspeople. It was never wealthy.

In the 14th century the power and influence of the Church began to decline. Some of its teachings were questioned, as was its right to own so much land and wield such authority. Monks and nuns, as Chaucer made plain, were no longer so deeply respected, and people were less willing to give money or lands to monastic houses. As the numbers of travellers and pilgrims, and of the poor and needy, increased, monasteries found their resources draining away and many fell into debt. At Bisham, where Austin Canons had founded a priory in 1337 (30 years after the departure of the Knights Templar), the canons had sunk deeply into debt by the 1390s. In pleading for help from the Pope they complained that their rents had diminished as a result of the plague, their church was still unfinished, and the situation of the priory, beside a busy highway leading to various markets, brought multitudes of travellers demanding hospitality. To make matters worse, the Thames in flood had damaged the priory buildings and ruined the crops in the fields, while the murrain had killed their cattle, sheep and horses. Their resources were no longer sufficient to support the canons, the 30 servants they employed and the hospitality demanded of them.

Other monasteries were suffering for similar reasons. In 1392 the Prior of Hurley petitioned the king to approve the appropriation of Warfield church to the priory, to alleviate poverty caused by Thames floods and 'modest endowments'. Even at Reading Abbey the entertainment of guests and pilgrims, to which the monks were bound by their foundation charter, became a crippling burden, particularly when the king and some of his household stayed for several days at a time. Gifts received on these occasions hardly compensated for the cost involved. The king's patronal rights also allowed him to use the abbey as a home for retired royal servants, in return for their years of faithful service.

6

MEDIEVAL TRADE AND TOWNS

In the Middle Ages navigable rivers were prized above roads as a means of transport. Along the four great rivers, Thames, Severn, Trent and Yorkshire Ouse, the nation's trade moved most easily, and all the important towns of the Middle Ages grew up beside one of these, or a lesser navigable river. Jurisdiction over the four great rivers was a crown prerogative, and various royal edicts were issued concerning waterborne trade before 1350, when Parliament passed the first of many acts for the removal of obstructions and the improvement of the navigation.

From prehistoric to Saxon times the Thames Valley was one of the first regions to be exploited by each new wave of inhabitants, and by the 11th century thriving towns and villages were established throughout its course. Apart from Newbury, all the principal towns of medieval Berkshire – Abingdon, Wallingford, Reading and Windsor – developed through trade along the Thames. It was to riverside places that the necessary loads of stone and timber were most easily delivered for the Normans' most ambitious building works. Windsor and Wallingford castles, Reading Abbey, Hurley and Bisham priories, and many other buildings owed their stone to the Thames, supplies being brought at first from Normandy but, by the 13th century, very largely from quarries in Oxfordshire.

Although lacking stone, Berkshire was well stocked with timber, still the most abundantly used building material, and for hundreds of years timber formed a valuable part of the local economy. Huge quantities were sent by water to help build London and Westminster, and a grant of oaks from Windsor Forest for the repair of a bridge or ecclesiastical building was one of the most welcome of royal gifts. There were wharves along the Thames from an early period: the remains of one dating perhaps from the Bronze Age has been found near Runneymede, while the name of Windsor is believed to contain the word 'windlass', indicating a Saxon, or earlier, wharf at Old Windsor. In the Middle Ages, every riverside town looked towards its wharves, and there were others at lesser places, such as Hedsor opposite Cookham and Water Oakley near Bray. The establishment of the new wharf called Maidenhythe in the 13th century points to the need for increased facilities in this area, to cope particularly with the traffic in timber out of Windsor Forest. Other goods carried along the Thames in the medieval period included corn, malt, wool, cloth, bricks, floor tiles and hay; while boats on the return journey brought hogsheads of wine, glassware, dried and salted fish, spices and other domestic provisions from London or overseas.

Thames watermen were employed on the king's business before the Conquest, and Domesday Book recorded that those based at Wallingford did service for the king as far as Reading. Norman monarchs and noblemen chose to travel by barge whenever possible, for the journey could be faster, safer and more comfortable, and partly for that reason Windsor Castle was only one of several royal residences built at various times along the Thames near London. Even for the dead a journey by water could be safer and more dignified. In 1135 the body of Henry I, who had died in France, was brought by barge up the Thames for burial in Reading Abbey church. In 1219 the aged William the Marshall, one of the greatest statesmen and warriors of his time, and guardian of the young King Henry III, was carried by barge from London to his manor house in Caversham, where he had chosen to spend his last days; and after death his body was taken back by the same route for burial in Temple church.

The demands made upon the river were heavy, and throughout the Middle Ages there was conflict between the national interests of long-distance trade and the local interests of millers and fishermen. By the time of the Domesday survey there were mills at frequent intervals along the Thames, at least nine on the Berkshire side below Streatley alone, and as many on the opposite bank, as well as many fisheries. Millers constructed dams of timber and rubble across the stream to build up water power for their mills; fishermen set piles and nets or rows of hurdles into the river to catch fish in large numbers. When boats could not pass over these obstructions, part of the dam or weir was removed to allow a flash of water to carry the vessels through, a manoeuvre not only dangerous for boatmen and their cargoes, but one which often deprived the miller of his head of water for many hours. River navigation was of paramount importance and in one of many royal edicts Edward I, in 1274, ordered the Thames 'to be so widened that ships and great barges might ascend from London to Oxford, and descend, without hindrance from any weirs; as the Thames was so narrowed in divers places that ships could not pass'. Nevertheless, dams and weirs were continually heightened and extended, leading to further complaints from boatmen. Millers, on the other hand, complained that boats were increasing in size and burden, and made themselves more unpopular by demanding tolls from every boat passing through their dams, to compensate for the loss of power and wasted time. In 1348 a petition on the boatmen's behalf stated that there were so many obstructions along the river, set up by fishermen, millers and riparian landowners, that ships could only pass over them in a time of great abundance of water, and that so many 'ransoms imposed at will' were exacted at weirs that the carriage of victuals by ship was greatly impeded and victuals grew daily dearer.

Yet road transport was more expensive, and subject to worse obstructions and delays due to the appalling state of the roads and poor standards of repair. In dry weather, the roads were passable for those on foot or horseback, and for such goods as could be carried by pack ponies. In wet weather, mud and floodwater made rutted and potholed ways more dangerous, and impossible for wheeled vehicles. An additional hazard was the far from unlikely possibility of attack by robbers or outlaws. In 1285, Edward I's Statute of Winchester acknowledged that robberies, murders and arsons were increasing and, as a measure of protection for travellers and trade, commanded that highways between market towns should be widened so that there would be no ditch, undergrowth or bushes where anyone could hide with evil intent within 200 feet on either side of the road. Notably, this clearance was not to apply to any large oaks or other valuable trees. The lord of any manor who failed to fill up a ditch or cut down bushes would be answerable if a robbery was committed, and, in the event of murder, made to pay a fine at the king's pleasure. Even a lord owning a park bordering the road must reduce the area of his park to create the necessary 200 foot verge, or else erect a wall or hedge sufficiently high and strong to prevent malefactors from making use of it to hide or to make good their escape.

These orders applied only to roads directly linking the most important towns, and therefore affected only a small proportion of the road system. However, responsibility for maintaining minor as well as major roads was a public, and unpaid, duty of manorial lords, landholders, and townships, although the work of maintenance involved no more than cleaning drainage ditches and mending the road with loose stones and rubble. Complaints about bad or impassable roads were frequently brought to court by local juries, and those accused of negligence often showed their reluctance to accept responsibility for what was obviously an irksome and unrewarding chore. At Michaelmas assizes in Reading in 1387 the jurors of Kintbury Hundred pleaded that the road at Kintbury leading from the Kennet was stopped up and the surrounding meadows flooded by the rising river, by default of the Prioress of Amesbury, who was lord of the manor. The jurors of Theale Hundred pleaded that the road from Basingstoke to Abingdon, together with a bridge on this road, and the roads from Basingstoke to Reading, and from Theale to Reading, were all out of repair by default of the Abbot of Reading. Several similar complaints were brought against the Abbot, but in some instances he denied responsibility because they did not concern the king's highway. Lawrence Dru of Southcote was accused of neglecting to clean a ditch and repair the road from Stokyngbrugge bridge to Southcote, and consequently the road was stopped up and flooded. Lawrence appeared before the court and acknowledged liability for cleaning the ditch, which he said had now been cleaned, but as to the repair of the road, he disclaimed all responsibility. He was fined three shillings and fourpence for his neglect of the ditch and the sheriff was ordered to distrain. At the same session the townships of Enborne and Hamstead Marshall were found guilty of allowing the road between Newbury and West Woodhay to become ruinous and flooded, and the township of Church Speen guilty of neglecting to maintain the road from there to Newbury.

Obstructed roads could often be bypassed but broken down bridges, or bridges swept away in stormy weather, could cause more serious delays, and special measures were taken to keep bridges open and in a state of repair. As trade expanded and traffic increased in the 13th century, many new bridges were built, but ancient ferries were usually continued alongside the bridges to provide additional facilities, especially for the poor. Nearly all medieval bridges over the Thames were built of timber. Stone was only used at an early period along the upper Thames, where it was locally available. Five new bridges were built in the 13th century between Berkshire and Oxfordshire or Buckinghamshire.

Caversham Bridge may have been a joint enterprise between the Abbot of Reading and the second William Marshall, lord of Caversham. A ferry had operated for many years on this ancient route to Oxford, and a bridge was first recorded in 1231, when 'the Chapel of St Anne on the bridge at Reading' was referred to in the records of Henry III. A few weeks later, the king ordered the Keeper of Windsor Forest 'to deliver to Andrew, Sergeant of Caversham, one good oak to make a boat for ferrying poor people over the water of Caversham'. The cost of using the bridge was evidently above their means. It was customary for fixed tolls and, hopefully, voluntary donations, to be collected from travellers towards the expense of maintaining a bridge, and nearly every bridge had a chapel on it, where a hermit or chaplain was responsible for collecting these moneys. In 1240 Henry III sent an oak from Windsor Forest to Brother William, Chaplain of St Anne's on Caversham bridge, to make shingles for the roof, and in 1242, three more trees were supplied for repairs to the chapel.

Further downstream, bridges were built in the early years of the 13th century between Henley and Remenham, and between Bisham and Marlow, both linking Berkshire with routes through the Chilterns. The former bridge was maintained by the town of Henley, and the latter by 'the Bailiffs and Good men of Great Marlowe', although they were answerable to the Prior of Bisham.

Maidenhead bridge is known to have existed in 1255 and perhaps was built some years before that. It owed its existence to the straightening of the highway from London, which previously wound through Burnham to cross the Thames at Babham End and pass through Cookham before swinging south-west towards Reading. No doubt the old route was needed when Cookham was the centre of an important royal manor with a market, but later trade and the king's business demanded a shorter route, and a crossing lower downstream was adopted, where a new wharf had been established early in the century. By 1297 the bridge was in such a state that a petition to Edward I obtained a grant 'in aid of the bridge of Maydenheth, which is almost broken down, of pontage for three years, to be taken by the hands of two good and lawful men'. This grant of bridge tolls was renewed for six years in 1337, when a charge was specified of one penny for every cartload of merchandise passing over the bridge, and one penny for every boat laden with merchandise passing under it. The income from these charges may have been insufficient, for Maidenhead obtained additional sums from a chapel at the Berkshire end of the bridge, where a hermit solicited alms from travellers. Records have survived of the ceremony at the induction of a new hermit in 1423, when the chapel had just been rebuilt. On 29th October that year, John, Warden of the Collegiate Church of Shottesbrook, with the commission of the Bishop of Salisbury, came to Maidenhead to admit Richard Ludlow to the hermitage at the bridge. He was met by Andrew Sperling, steward of the manors of Cookham and Bray, John Mustard, the beadle, and the chaplains, bailiffs and other prominent men of the neighbourhood. At the bridge Richard Ludlow recited in their presence a lengthy oath concerning the duties of his 'profession of heremite', swearing to lead a life of abstinence and devotion, avoiding all taverns and 'other suspect placis of Synne', hearing mass every day and fasting on Fridays, while collecting such alms as people might give or bequeath for the upkeep of the bridge and common ways of the town, and to keep for himself only what he needed for his meat, drink, clothing and fuel.

At Windsor a bridge would have been needed when work began on the castle, and one certainly existed by 1172, when records show that Osbert de Bray collected on the king's behalf £4 6s. 6d. in tolls from vessels passing beneath it. In 1228 the Abbot of Reading successfully resisted a claim of the bailiff of Windsor to tolls on abbey vessels carrying goods up and down the Thames between Reading and London. The bailiff claimed arrears amounting to £52, but a search through the abbey charters proved that it was exempt from these tolls. Such charges were made to compensate for damage caused by heavy barges colliding with the bridge piles, and in 1523, for instance, William Webbe was fined for 'brekyng ye leg of ye bridge'. Henry III gave generously of forest oaks for the repair of Windsor bridge, but Edward I, who spent little time at the castle, allowed it to fall into decay. The townspeople, who needed the bridge far more than the king, petitioned him for permission to charge and retain tolls for its upkeep, and in 1277 Edward granted them a charter confirming certain market and other privileges they already enjoyed, and making Windsor a free borough, with a merchant guild responsible for the government of the town and the maintenance of the bridge. Monarchs did not often use the town bridge, having their own private exit from the castle by ferryboat across to Datchet. Traffic crossing by Windsor bridge used the road through Eton to reach the main London to Bristol highway, and where the roads met a hamlet grew up which developed into the village of Slough.

A great deal of traffic along medieval roads was generated by weekly markets and less frequent fairs, at which nearly all trading took place. They were important events and always well-attended. From the 12th century onwards numerous grants were issued by the Crown to lords of manors, bishops and abbots allowing them to hold a weekly market at which traders would pay various fees for the privilege of setting up stalls and conducting their business. By the beginning of the 14th century at least 17 markets had been granted in Berkshire. Cookham's was recorded as new in the Domesday survey, but Reading claimed that its market was even older, having been granted by Edward the Confessor. Newbury's market probably started about the time when the new town was developed in the late 11th century, while Thatcham's dated from the early 12th century. New Windsor's market is likely to have existed by 1130, when the town was first recorded as a borough. By 1204 a market had been started at Eton, and in 1271 a market was granted to help support Burnham Abbey. The Bishop of Winchester obtained a market charter for Wargrave in 1218, and the Bishop of Salisbury one for Wokingham in 1219. The countryside to the south of Reading probably offered scope for the market granted to Aldermaston in 1292. Further west along the Kennet valley, Speen was granted a market in 1218, and Kintbury in 1267. Hungerford's market is not recorded before 1296 but was probably much older. Lambourn's market was serving the upper Lambourn valley and the Downlands by 1227, and other west Berkshire villages to obtain market grants included East Garston in 1238, East Ilsley in 1232, Yattendon in 1258, Catmore in 1306, Basildon in 1309, West Woodhay in 1317. Little is known about the history of these village markets, and many may have been discontinued during the economic decline of the 14th century. East Ilsley's, however, was successful and became famous for trade in corn, wool and sheep. Its position on an important highway between Oxford and Newbury was a great advantage.

The rights bestowed by a market charter, and the success of markets which did thrive, were jealously guarded, and rivalry sometimes led to open conflict. Thatcham's market suffered from the hostility of the people of Newbury. When Henry I gave Thatcham to his newly founded abbey at Reading, he confirmed that its market should continue, thus providing a further source of income for the abbey. Apparently it showed little profit, for in 1153, Henry's grandson, the future Henry II, issued an instruction that the men of Berkshire should trade at the Abbot of Reading's market at Thatcham. A few years later he forbade the men of Newbury to interfere with Thatcham market, but in spite of continuing royal patronage this market did not thrive. It was declared of no value when the abbey was dissolved in the 16th century.

Newbury market drew trade from a wide area; for instance, in 1228 the men of Andover obtained the right to trade free of tolls at Newbury market. How welcome they were there is not known, but a similar right claimed by the men of Reading some years later certainly met with a hostile reception. At the assizes of 1261 four Reading bailiffs, representing the town's merchants, sued the bailiffs and men of Newbury because, in the previous year, they had exacted market tolls and stallage fees contrary to the royal charter held by the Reading men. The Newbury bailiffs declared that they had never heard of this charter, but were forced to acknowledge it when produced in court, and to agree that, in future, Reading traders should be free of tolls and other charges at Newbury. In the same year Reading bailiffs brought a similar charge against Windsor, claiming that John the Dyer and other Reading merchants had taken their goods to Windsor market but were set upon and their goods thrown down, torn and trampled in the mud. Once again they won their case and the Windsor bailiffs were fined and ordered to pay damages.

The right to hold a fair was usually granted to a place where a weekly market was already held. Fairs were much larger than markets, lasted longer, and provided opportunities for people to buy from a wider range of goods than was available locally at any other time of the year. Merchants and craftsmen travelled from far and wide to trade in rare and costly goods, fine silks and velvets, high quality leather articles, metal wares, ornaments and spices, as well as everyday necessities such as wool, salt, wax and hard-wearing cloth. Because of the travelling involved, and the duration of these events, fairs nearly all took place between April and October. They were all attached to the festival of a saint, sometimes the saint to whom a local church was dedicated. Fairs lasted from one to four, or even five, days, usually including the saint's day plus the vigil and a number of following days specified in the grant. By the middle of the 14th century a considerable number had been granted to towns and villages in Berkshire, although it is not known whether some of the smaller ones were very successful or long-lived.

April 22–23	Windsor, St George's Fair
April 30–May 3	Reading, St Philip and St James' Fair
June 10–12	Basildon, St Barnabas' Fair
June 10–12	Wokingham, St Barnabas' Fair
June 23–27	Windsor, St John the Baptist's Fair
June 28–30	Yattendon, St Peter and St Paul's Fair
July 6–7	Thatcham, St Thomas' Fair
July 6–8	Aldermaston, St Thomas' Fair
July 15	Wickham, St Swithin's Fair
July 19–21	Catmore, St Margaret's Fair
July 25–28	Reading, St James' Fair
August 10–13	Reading, St Lawrence's Fair
August 14–16	Datchet, Feast of the Assumption Fair
August 24–25	Newbury, St Bartholomew's Fair
September 7–9	Kintbury, Nativity of St Mary Fair
September 21	Lambourn, St Matthew's Fair
September 21–23	Burnham, St Matthew's Fair
October 27–29	Kintbury, St Simon and St Jude's Fair
October 31–November 2	East Garston, All Saints' Fair
October 31–November 2	Wokingham, All Saints' Fair

In addition, Hungerford's St Lawrence's Fair, first heard of in 1361, may have begun many years earlier. The distribution of fairs across the county was subject to change. St Lawrence's Fair in Reading, granted by Henry I, is believed to have died out before the end of the 14th century, perhaps because it was too close to St James' Fair; whereas Windsor's fairs were only instituted in 1350. The revival of trade in the 15th century encouraged grants for other fairs, including two at Eton, and others at Cookham, Finchampstead and Lambourn. Fairs and markets brought together large crowds of people and were useful not only for the exchange of news and gossip on an informal basis but for the publication of official information. A new law, such as the Statute of Winchester in 1285, concerning the widening of highways as a protection against robbers, and the duty of the public to assist in the pursuit and apprehension of thieves and felons, was commanded to be proclaimed and solemnly read in shire-courts, hundred-courts, markets and fairs and other places where people assembled, so that no-one could excuse himself on grounds of ignorance.

Through trade and the protection of their rights, towns eventually won independence from their overlords and gained powers of self-government. For some towns, it was a long struggle. The valuable royal charter used with such effect by Reading's merchants was obtained from Henry III in 1253 after a lengthy dispute with the abbot. The records of this dispute contain the earliest written references to the Reading merchant guild, already a body of great antiquity which claimed to date back to the reign of Edward the Confessor. The rights claimed by the guild conflicted with the manorial rights granted by Henry I to the Abbot of Reading, giving rise to considerable ill-feeling, and eventually to violent action on the part of the merchants. Their men were accused of coming armed into the town to hinder and threaten the abbot's bailiffs, and even of lying in wait for them by day and night to prevent them from carrying out their duties. When summoned to court before Henry III the merchants were unable to produce any written evidence for their claims but, not long afterwards, the king granted their guild a charter allowing them, among other privileges, the right to trade anywhere in England free of all customary tolls and dues. Disputes between town and abbey did not end there, for the abbot retained an irksome measure of control over the guild through his right to appoint, each year, the chief officer or warden. He could also exact fees from new members and for licences to trade within the borough. The abbot continued to administer justice in the town and manor, and was responsible for most other administrative matters, such as roads and bridges. The power of the guild was increased a little by Henry VII in 1487, when the warden was allowed to assume the title of mayor, and to be attended by two sergeants at mace; and substantially by Henry VIII in 1542, after the dissolution of the abbey, when Reading received its first charter of incorporation.

Windsor's close association with the castle was not always in the best interests of the town, which could not escape involvement in political

59

disturbances and wars between kings and barons. When the castle was besieged in 1193, 1216 and 1263 the townspeople must have suffered damage to property and livestock. But freedom from the administrative control of the castle was won with the charter of 1277, giving the merchant guild authority to supervise the crafts and trades of the town, and to elect its own bailiffs, who were empowered to preside over the borough court of justice. The guild was free to elect its own steward, who, in the 14th century, assumed the title of mayor. The security bestowed by firm and efficient government in the town must have been appreciated by its inhabitants for, in the forest roundabout, law and order were maintained with difficulty by the king's officers, and the area was a notorious refuge for robbers and outlaws.

In the 14th century Reading and Windsor were rated as boroughs for taxation purposes, and paid more than Newbury, which was rated only as a vill. Without a great castle or abbey to give it status, Newbury seems to have faltered after its promising start as the thriving new town of west Berkshire. For just a few years at the beginning of the 13th century it belonged to the king, and about that time a governing body seems to have been formed with the foundation of St Bartholomew's Hospital. Although established for the accommodation of the aged and infirm, the support of leading townsmen made the hospital the centre of corporate life. St Bartholomew's Fair, granted by King John to the hospital in 1215, helped the town's trade to expand, but it was slow to reach its 16th century eminence as a clothing town, and a merchant guild is not recorded before the reign of Henry VIII. Its first charter of incorporation was granted by Elizabeth I in 1596.

From 1295 certain cities and boroughs of England were called upon to send representatives to Parliament in addition to the two knights of the shire who already attended. Reading sent two burgesses continuously until the 19th century. Windsor and Newbury each sent two to the Parliament of 1302, but Newbury ceased to be represented after 1337 until modern times, while Windsor's representation was irregular until the end of the 15th century.

Among smaller towns, Hungerford began well, being recognised as a borough by the 1170s and, by 1241, it had its own bailiffs and jurors. But the loss of its early records means that little is known about its medieval history, although archaeological evidence suggests that it was slow to expand beyond the original burgage plots laid out in the 12th century. In the 14th century it seems to have declined and it was not then known as a borough.

At Wokingham the Bishops of Salisbury showed reluctance to relinquish their hold on the town. The market they had started in 1219

60

was successful, and two three-day fairs were granted in 1258, but Wokingham still had no parish church and the existing chapel possessed only limited rights. No charter is known before Queen Elizabeth's in 1583, which permitted the town to elect its own officers, but even then the Steward of Sonning retained overall control.

Maidenhead, on the boundary between Cookham and Bray, remained under their manorial jurisdiction until the 15th century. The primary concern of the community was the upkeep of the bridge, which provided an important source of income and brought traffic and trade which made it busier than either of its parent villages. By the 15th century its main street had grown through the establishment of several large inns as well as stables, smithies and other necessary services for travellers. A chapel-of-ease was built in 1270 for the community and for the use of travellers, and this was rebuilt in the 14th century and dedicated to St Andrew and St Mary Magdalene. A guild was formed around the chapel in 1452, when Henry VI gave permission for it to have an overseer, wardens, brethren and sisters, who were responsible for the maintenance of the chapel and the bridge; but this religious guild was dissolved by Henry VIII and it was not until 1581 that Elizabeth I granted Maidenhead a charter of incorporation, making it independent of Cookham and Bray, and empowered to own property and to hold a weekly market and fairs.

The pre-eminence of Reading and Newbury at the end of the Middle Ages was due to their clothing trade. The Berkshire Downs had pastured sheep producing fine fleeces for many centuries before clothmaking began to be developed as a large-scale industry, and roads across Berkshire from the Cotswolds had been used by trains of pack ponies carrying bales of wool to south coast ports. The woolmen of Reading and Newbury also sent their finest wool to Southampton and Portsmouth for shipment to continental weavers. Then, in 1258, at a parliament held in Oxford, the first of several measures was passed prohibiting the export of wool and encouraging clothmaking in England.

Clothmaking was a complicated process which was not confined to towns. Some of the initial stages, such as carding and spinning, could be carried on in the country, thus spreading a little of the wealth generated by this great industry. Originally, the fulling process also gave employment to large numbers of workers, but by the 13th century fulling mills had been introduced to perform this laborious task. The use of mills, instead of 'fulling by might and strength of man, that is with hand and foot', was bitterly opposed and various attempts were made to suppress mills, but inevitably the new method triumphed. Fulling mills could be set up wherever there was a sufficient supply

The old Cloth Hall at Newbury, built in 1626–7 to provide a workhouse for poor weavers, survives today as a memorial to the wealth of the clothing trade in the town in the 15th and 16th centuries.

of water, and around Newbury and Reading, streams were abundant. An early fulling mill is mentioned in a survey of Newbury in 1204, showing that clothmaking was already established there, although on a small scale. Some 50 years later another fulling mill was recorded at Benham, and two at Speen in 1279. Fulling mills are known from later records at Kintbury, Boxford and Thatcham.

By 1355 twelve clothiers were in business in Newbury, and fullers, weavers, dyers, kersey makers and associated craftsmen began to occur frequently in the town's records. Newbury's clothing trade reached its peak in the late 15th and early 16th centuries, when Jack of Newbury was an acknowledged leader of the industry in England. Much of his fame is derived from Deloney's romanticised history, which extols the sheer size and extent of Jack's operations. His workshop is said to have contained 200 looms employing 200 weavers, 100 women carding wool, and 200 girls spinning. One hundred and fifty children of the poor were given work picking wool for a penny a day, plus their meat and drink. Fifty shearmen were employed to trim the cloth and 80 rowers to smooth it with rollers. A further 40 men worked in Jack's dyehouse, and 20 in his fulling mill at Bagnor. Jack, or John Winchcomb, was one of the influential English clothiers who petitioned Henry VIII for greater freedom of trade with other countries at a time when the industry was suffering from the effects of foreign wars. If Deloney is to be believed, Jack entertained the king in his house in Northbrook Street, only a small part of which now survives. St Nicolas' church, which Jack and his son rebuilt between 1509 and 1532, stands as a memorial to his wealth and greatness.

The earliest known signs of a clothing industry in Reading date from the 13th century, when a fulling mill was recorded in St Giles' parish, and the charter granted by Henry III in 1253 to the merchant guild referred to weavers, dyers and drapers. The records of St Lawrence's church show that, among its many medieval altars, there was one dedicated to St Blaise, patron saint of wool staplers and wool combers. Staplers sorted and graded wool according to quality after shearing, and the existence of such an altar indicates that the trade was well-represented and wealthy before the 15th century. Records of the merchant guild surviving from the middle of the 15th century are studded with the names of fullers, weavers, dyers, drapers and mercers, who together must have formed an influential majority in the guild. About 1540 John Leland recorded his famous description: 'In the vale of the town of Reading, where the two arms of Kennet run near together, I marked divers armlets breaking out of the two streams and making medians, over which be divers bridges of wood. And these waters be very commodious for dyers, well occupied there; for the town chiefly standeth by clothing.'

7

KNIGHTS AND PILGRIMS

In the 14th century a succession of natural disasters, bringing hunger, disease and agrarian unrest, halted the economic progress made in the 12th and 13th centuries. A climatic change brought several bitterly cold years and severe flooding, causing failed harvests and widespread famine. Disease attacked sheep and cattle so badly that, in some places, horses, which were immune, had to be used instead of oxen to draw ploughs. At the same time the feudal organisation, which had controlled rural life and labour, was breaking down as the system of enforced services due to a lord in return for a small plot of land and a few basic rights of pasture gave way to a system of wage payment for labour and rent payment for tenements. Some peasants gave up their ties with the land altogether, in order to hire themselves out for the best wages they could get. Those who did not do so, grew discontented and unwilling to work as before. This process of change was accelerated by the Black Death, which created a shortage of labour, leading to higher wage demands and higher prices.

In the early 1340s another hard winter and the failure of spring crops brought hunger and distress to villages in the Thames Valley and on the Downs around Lambourn and Ilsley. When, in 1348, the Black Death swept into the country through the ports of Southampton and Bristol, the population had few reserves of health to withstand it, and little time to recover before the next outbreaks in 1361 and 1368–9. Little is known about the precise effects of these plagues in Berkshire but there is no reason to suppose that the county did not suffer the estimated national loss of between a third and a half of the population. Records which have survived show that there were many deaths among the monks and nuns of monastic houses, while the death rate among the clergy was so high that four times the usual number of new priests were needed in 1348, and three times the number in 1349. The outbreak of 1361 struck Windsor so severely that a large number of workmen at the castle died, and in 1362 the sheriffs of seven other counties were ordered, under penalty of £200 each, to send to Windsor able and skilful masons and diggers up to a total of 302.

However bad the miseries at home, knights, noblemen and their retainers could escape into the more exciting life of foreign warfare, feats of arms and, sometimes, plunder. In 1337 Edward III laid claim to the throne of France, thus beginning the intermittent Hundred Years War, and in 1346 English knights and longbowmen won a resounding victory at Crécy. Two years later, Edward celebrated his triumph by founding the Order of the Garter, the highest order of English chivalry. The first ceremony, honouring the chosen 25 greatest and bravest knights in the land, was held at Windsor Castle on St George's Day 1348. A 13th century chapel in the Lower Ward of the castle was dedicated to the order, and within the chapel a stall was allotted to each knight and overhung with his personal banner.

Among the knights of Berkshire were the De la Beches of Aldworth, lords of the manor of De la Beche, who, like many of their kind, spent most of their time in attendance upon the king or fighting in his wars. The management of their estates was left to their bailiffs, or sometimes to their wives. The silver seal of Isabella de la Beche, dug up on the site of their manor farm in the 19th century, suggests a lady very much in charge after the death of her husband, Sir John, c 1329, and during the minority of their son. Sir John had greatly increased the family estates in Berkshire, and, in 1318, had obtained from Edward II a licence to hold a fair and weekly market on his newly acquired manor at Yattendon. Of Sir John's five brothers, Philip served the county as sheriff, and Edmund as Archdeacon, but the most distinguished career was that of Sir Nicholas. Held in high esteem by Edward III, Nicholas was entrusted with the offices of Constable of the Tower of London and Guardian of the Black Prince during his childhood. In 1342 he accompanied the king to France and was rewarded for his services in battle by the Seneschalship of the rich land of Gascony; but in 1346 he died, leaving no direct heir. His effigy is therefore the last of the eight mutilated but still powerfully evocative De la Beche monuments in Aldworth church.

The archers who followed Sir Nicholas and his neighbour, John de Ferrers of Aldworth manor, to France learned their skill with the longbow at village butts, often situated near the parish church. This was the period when archery was practised by royal command, and idle sports such as football, hockey and cockfighting were forbidden. At Compton, another manor held by the De la Beches, the field to the west of the church was used for archery practice, and was still known as The Butts in the 19th century. Medieval archery butts were also the origin of the name of the street in front of St Mary's Church in Reading.

Edward III's victories at Crécy and Poitiers marked the most triumphant period of his reign. Within a few years the fortunes of war

The mutilated effigy of Sir Nicholas de la Beche in Aldworth church. Sir Nicholas was perhaps the most distinguished of the family, held in high esteem by Edward III.

turned against him. His son, Edward, the Black Prince, died; most of the territories he had won in France were lost; and towards the end of his life the king declined into senility. His successor, Richard II, inherited none of the martial qualities of his father or grandfather, so that the French were able to carry out with impunity a number of damaging raids on south coast towns. A full-scale invasion of England was threatened, and in the ensuing state of alarm, county levies were summoned to assist in the defence of the coast. In 1377, 1378 and 1380 Berkshire was called upon to 'array and equip all the men of the county and to keep ever arrayed the men-at-arms and archers to resist foreign invasion'. In 1385 invasion seemed imminent when it became known that the French king had gathered a huge army and was preparing to cross the Channel, and an urgent demand was sent for 200 archers from Berkshire to join the forces Richard was assembling for the defence of London. The invasion did not take place, but dissatisfaction with the young king increased, while support grew for his cousin and rival, Henry

Bolingbroke. It was during this period of political unrest that Sir Richard Abberbury was granted a royal licence to fortify and crenellate the castle on his manor at Donnington. Sir Richard, a knight formerly in the service of the Black Prince, had been one of the guardians of the king during his childhood, and remained in his household after Richard's accession to the throne. Donnington commanded the crossing of two important routes, from east to west and north to south, and it was vital to Richard II that it was held by a loyal subject. The principal addition to the castle in 1386 was the massive gatehouse flanked by sturdy round towers, much of which survive today.

In 1396 Richard confirmed a truce with France by his marriage, unpopular in England, with Isabel, eight-year-old daughter of the French king; and three years later he was deposed when Henry seized the throne. Political intrigue touched Berkshire in January 1400, when supporters of Richard plotted to murder King Henry IV at Windsor Castle during the Twelfth Night festivities. In the tradition of the Trojan Horse, armed men were to be concealed in covered wagons carrying armour and accoutrements into the castle in preparation for a grand tournament. Once inside, they were under orders to kill the king and all four of his sons, but the plot was discovered and the intended victims were able to escape before a large force of hostile barons, backed up by 400 archers and men-at-arms, arrived at the castle gates. In London, Henry speedily assembled an army and set off in pursuit of the rebels, who were making for the west country. At Maidenhead bridge some of them fought a desperate rearguard action, delaying Henry's forces, but eventually most of the rebels were defeated and captured near Cirencester. While these events were taking place, the young Queen Isabel was removed for her safety to the old palace of the Bishops of Salisbury at Sonning.

War with France was resumed by Henry V, whose victory at Agincourt again brought England vast possessions in France. But, again, all these were lost in the reign of his son, the weak and wilful Henry VI, so that by 1453 only the wool staple town of Calais remained in English hands. Henry VI was born at Windsor Castle in 1421, and throughout his life Windsor was one of his favourite residences. The royal hunting lodge at Easthampstead was also kept in readiness for his use. After 1437, when Henry took up the reins of government at the age of 16, he undertook an annual progress through parts of his kingdom, attended by a huge household. This included his confessor, his chamberlain, his wardrobe keeper, his master of horse, his cofferers, clerks, and a number of knights, esquires and yeomen of the chamber. One of the longest-serving of these esquires was John Norreys, builder of Ockwells manor house near Bray. Norreys was a Berkshire justice and involved in the notorious affair of Thomas Carver.

Carver was bailiff to the Abbot of Reading. Like many men of his time he was disappointed in the young king, particularly when comparing him with his predecessor. Now the dauphin of France was proving his mettle in command of an army in Gascony, while the English king stayed at home. In April 1444 Carver was overheard commenting to other abbey servants on the characters of the two young men; all they had in common, he said, was their age. He was also reported to have said, among other things, that it would have been worth more than £100,000 to England if the king had never been born. Reports of these treasonable statements brought out the vindictive streak in Henry's character. He determined that Carver should suffer an exemplary punishment, making sure that there would be no further outbreaks of discontent in an area so close to the royal court. Carver was arrested, a special commission of enquiry was set up, and in June he was sent for trial in Kings Bench. For lack of evidence he could not be convicted, but the king was not satisfied and ordered a second enquiry by commissioners carefully chosen from his household. Several were local men: William Staverton, yeoman of the chamber and lord of Strode manor in Bray, was foreman of the jury, John Norreys of Bray and Richard Restwold of Sonning, both esquires of the chamber, were members of the commission.

At a second trial in Reading in July Carver was found guilty of 'imagining the king's death' and seeking to accomplish it by inciting others. He was sentenced to be publicly exhibited through the streets of Reading, and then taken in a cart across Berkshire to the bridge end of Maidenhead, and thence drawn on a hurdle through the middle of Maidenhead and Bray to the nearest gallows. There he was to be hanged, thrown down alive and quartered, his head to be sent for display on London bridge and his quarters to high places in Reading, Maidenhead and two other towns outside Berkshire. In the event, not all the sentence was carried out. Carver suffered the journey and the hanging, but at the last minute the king sent a pardon ordering that Carver's life should be spared, and after hanging he was taken back to prison in Wallingford Castle.

John Norreys, who inherited estates in Bray, began to build Ockwells in 1446. The brick and timber house, regarded today as one of the finest surviving examples from that period, took over 20 years to build, and was not quite complete at the time of Norreys' death in 1467. He had served Henry VI for many years, both in the royal household and in the county as sheriff in 1442 and 1457, and he proclaimed his loyalty in the heraldic glass with which he emblazoned the windows in the great hall at Ockwells. This contained the coats of arms of Henry VI, Queen Margaret, and several noblemen who fought for the House of Lancaster in the Wars of the Roses (1455–85), and met their deaths on the field of St Albans or Tewkesbury. Norreys, however, remained in favour after the deposition of Henry VI in 1461, and continued to hold office under Edward IV. His son, William, fought for Edward and was knighted at the battle of Northampton in 1460. John Norreys added substantially to the family estates. By 1450 Yattendon and Frilsham were his, as well as Hampstead Norreys, which still bears the family name. In his will he bequeathed £100 to Bray church for 'ye newe makyng and edefying of St Nicholas Chapel', and a further sum for a marble tomb for himself within the chapel.

The Wars of the Roses affected Berkshire very little. As in other parts of the country, most ordinary people tried to keep out of these power struggles among the nobility. Only Newbury suffered during a brief occupation by Lancastrian forces because of its allegiance to the House of York. A medieval chronicle recounts that, in 1460, 'The Earl of Wiltshire, treasurer of England, the lord Scales, and Lord Hungerford, having the king's commission, went to the toune of Newbury, the whych longed to the duk of York, and there made inquisition of all them that in any wise had shewed any favour or benevolence or friendship to the said duk, or to any of his; whereof some were found guilty and were drawn, hanged, and quartered, and all other inhabitants of the foresaid town were spoiled of all their goods.' In the following year, when Yorkist control was restored, Edward IV bestowed the manor and town of Newbury on his mother, Duchess Cecily of York; and from that time Newbury remained a royal possession until the 17th century.

While Norreys was building Ockwells, his royal master was occupied with his new foundation at Eton. Henry VI wished to mark the beginning of his reign by making his own unique contribution to the number of monasteries and churches founded by his predecessors. In 1440 he decided that this would take the form of a magnificent church, to which would be attached a college of ten priests, four clerks, six choristers, and a school for 25 poor scholars, plus accommodation for 25 poor and feeble men whose duty would be to pray for the King's soul and the souls of his forbears and all the faithful departed. The site chosen was at Eton, within sight of Windsor Castle, and his first step was to purchase the existing parish church, which he declared he would raise from poverty to distinction, and two houses on the north side of the churchyard. He then began to draw up plans for the splendid buildings which were to replace them, but it was here that his ambition soared beyond the bounds of possibility. The church of his dreams was to be a minster

Henry VI, whose statue stands in the School Yard at Eton College, planned to build a church and college at Eton to rival the greatest in the land.

large enough to rival the greatest cathedrals of England. Winchester and Salisbury were carefully measured to ensure that this would be so, and work already begun at Eton was altered and enlarged at the king's command. Huge quantities of stone and other materials were brought to the site for the church alone; the college and other lay buildings were to be constructed more cheaply in brick. Bricks could be made locally from the abundant clays around the neighbouring village of Slough, and over 1½ million bricks were delivered to Eton between 1442 and 1444.

Eton itself, which had been a place of small importance until then, suddenly found that it was a centre of great activity, called upon to house and feed large numbers of stonemasons, carpenters, bricklayers, plasterers, tilers, plumbers, smiths and other workmen. Within a few years the situation was made worse by the arrival of pilgrims attracted by the availability of indulgences granted by the Pope, in response to Henry's request, to people visiting the church and college of St Mary the Virgin at Eton. These indulgences were eventually extended to full remission of sins, and the power, granted to the provost, to hear confessions and give full absolution within the college community. Henry's delight at receiving these spiritual privileges for his new foundation is said to have moved him to spare the life of Thomas Carver, and three years later, to free him from prison. To help provide for the massive influx of workmen and pilgrims into Eton, Henry granted the provost the right to hold two annual fairs, one following Ash Wednesday and the other at the Feast of the Assumption. In addition, in 1452, he granted Eton a weekly market to be held each Wednesday under the authority of the provost. This market was obtained only after a petition from the inhabitants, scholars, craftsmen and labourers complained that there was a shortage of bread, ale and other victuals for want of a regular market.

Meanwhile, construction of the church ran into difficulties as the huge expense emptied the royal coffers. In the event, only the choir of the projected minster was built, and survives today as the college chapel. The college buildings, unaffected by Henry's changes of plan, made steady progress, and the school proved so successful that its numbers were increased to 70 scholars, an extra usher to assist the schoolmaster, ten more priests, six more clerks and ten more choristers. The college buildings were completed by 1460, but the chapel was not ready for use until 1476, five years after Henry's death.

Eton College Chapel was soon surpassed in beauty and splendour by the new chapel of St George at Windsor Castle. Begun by Edward IV in 1475, St George's Chapel was planned as a royal mausoleum as well as the chapel of the Order of the Garter. Edward's own elaborate tomb, protected by iron gates of exquisite workmanship, was installed there in 1483. A year later, the remains of Henry VI were removed from their original resting place in Chertsey Abbey, where they had already begun to attract the devotion of pilgrims, and brought to St George's Chapel for interment near the altar. Ten years of seclusion made necessary by his increasing insanity, and the rumoured violence of his death in the Tower of London, had caused the pious Henry to be regarded as a saint. His relics brought pilgrims in their thousands to Windsor, and numerous miraculous cures and escapes from sudden death or disaster were attributed to him. Between 1484 and 1500 the cult of 'Good King Henry' was at its height, and Windsor profited hugely from votive offerings and the sale of pilgrim badges bearing his image. But, in spite of the efforts of his nephew, Henry VII, he was never canonised, and his cult died out in the 16th century.

8

THE END OF THE MIDDLE AGES

The great age of religious pilgrimage was almost over. The pious, the sick, the miracle-seekers, and the curious who went for the sake of travel, continued to visit holy shrines, but as early as the 14th century Chaucer had mocked the dubious authenticity and proliferation of holy relics, and shown that commercialisation was exploiting and undermining religious faith. On a more practical level, the power wielded by the Church over men's affairs, through ecclesiastical courts and the payment of tithes and other dues, had begun to breed antagonism towards the clergy, and as more people became literate and educated, they began to question the learning and ability of clerics. Most of all, people resented the great monastic houses, which had accumulated considerable worldly wealth and exercised extensive rights as landlords of vast estates. The growth of trade in the Middle Ages had nourished individual wealth and enterprise among the merchant classes, and such men were no longer willing to part with their money or lands to support communities of monks and nuns. Instead, their generosity was directed to worthy causes close at hand: the embellishment of their parish church, often the chief glory of their native town or village, the endowment of chapels or chantries, or of almshouses for the poor.

The 15th century saw parish churches all over the country enlarged and enhanced by the addition of aisles, chapels or towers, or the refurbishment of the interior through gifts of woodwork, ornaments and vestments. Many new towers, and new bells, were added, and older towers rebuilt and heightened. The churches of Hampstead Norreys, Farnborough, Bucklebury, Thatcham, Bray, St Lawrence in Reading, All Saints in Wokingham, Binfield and Warfield, all have towers dating mainly from this period. Some churches were rebuilt entirely; at Yattendon a 13th century church was rebuilt by Sir John Norreys c 1450, soon after he became lord of the manor. Monuments became more elaborate. At East Shefford, John Fettiplace, citizen and draper of London, left, on his death in 1464, money for the repair of the old church beside the river Lambourn, and to build an enclosure round the tomb of his parents, Sir Thomas and Lady Fettiplace, whose effigies were finely carved in alabaster. At Lambourn, the chapel of St Katherine on the north side of the church was rebuilt in the 15th century and, in 1502, a new chapel of the Holy Trinity was added on the south side at the expense of John Isbury, or Estbury, founder of the almshouses nearby. Isbury's marble tomb was placed in the centre of the chapel, where all the bedesmen in the almshouses were bound to assemble each day to hear mass and pray for the souls of their benefactor and his family.

One of the finest Berkshire churches was St Lawrence's in Reading, originally built to serve pilgrims to the abbey, but later the principal town church, upon which numerous gifts and endowments were lavished. John Kent, a prosperous mercer who died about 1415, was one of 150 subscribers towards the cost of reroofing the church, using timber from Earley. He also gave the church a cope of cloth of bawdekyn (a rich silk material) embroidered with birds and flowers of gold. This item was only one of a huge collection of copes, vestments and altar cloths given to the church by various donors, and their descriptions in the inventory illustrate, incidentally, the range of luxurious fabrics in which mercers traded, many of them imported from Italy, a principal market for English woollen cloth. As well as bawdekyn, silks, satins, velvets, damasks, sarsenets and cloth of gold are mentioned, many of them in brilliant colours and embroidered with flowers, birds, leaves, crowns, angels or images of saints. Around 1458 the original Norman tower of St Lawrence's was rebuilt and raised to its present commanding height, again by public subscription. At the end of the century its four bells were increased to five by the addition of 'the grete bell namyd Harry', given by Henry Kelsall, a clothier, in his will of 1493. Like many of his contemporaries, Kelsall left sums of money to other churches in Berkshire and to the Grey Friars, but nothing to Reading abbey.

In the 15th century, declining numbers of monks and nuns may have led to a decline in their charitable work among the poor and needy. Certainly, towards the end of this century, rich men began to provide for such people in more direct ways by founding almshouses to accommodate a limited number, or leaving funds for regular gifts of food and clothing. Among the earliest almshouses in the county were those built by John Leech, or A'Larder, in Reading, and endowed in his will of 1477, which directed that the original five houses should be increased to eight. Such institutions attracted many later gifts. Henry Kelsall, for instance, bequeathed 'to the Almshowses in Redyng which were of the foundacion of John of the Larder, to every of the same howses a coverlette, price of every of them iis viiid. Item, to every of the same howses a pair of Shetis, price of every pair xvid.' In addition, Kelsall left a sum of money to buy 100 other poor men in Reading a gown of black frieze cloth. Many more almshouses and charities were founded after the Dissolution of the Monasteries, to help cope with the rising numbers of the poor. St Bartholomew's Hospital in Newbury, which had been assisting the old and infirm since the 13th century, was not suppressed with other such religious houses during the Reformation, but converted into almshouses.

No great abbeys were founded in the late Middle Ages, and even Henry VI's plans for a minster and college of priests at Eton proved a dream out of time. Significantly, it was the lesser part of his project, the school, which proved acceptable to changing attitudes. The secluded life of abbey and nunnery no longer attracted many recruits, and by the 15th century most of the smaller monasteries were impoverished and underoccupied. Long before the enforced closure of such places in the 1520s, many of them had closed. Sandleford Priory, never very well endowed, survived for many years with some local support, notably from John Estbury, who, with others, gave it a substantial acreage of land in Newbury. But in 1440 the priory buildings were reported to be badly dilapidated, and the conduct of the prior so immoral that he was deprived of his office. Two more priors were appointed, but Sandleford continued to decline and, in 1478, was said to be deserted. Its buildings and possessions were given to the collegiate church of Windsor, whose dean and canons sent a stipendiary priest to hold services for the parish in the priory chapel.

The nuns of Broomhall Priory had always been poor but, in the early years, devout and hard-working. In the 14th century moral decline set in, erupting in a scandal at the beginning of the 15th century, when the nuns complained that one of their number, who had wrongfully assumed the rule of the house, had led an evil and corrupt life for 20 years. Following an enquiry in 1405, the usurper-prioress resigned, and the priory sank back into obscurity until 1521, when the Bishop of Salisbury was called upon to enquire into the conduct of the then prioress and two remaining nuns. His report found their behaviour so profane that the priory was suppressed. In 1522 its possessions were transferred to St John's College, Cambridge.

Poughley Priory appears to have maintained a good reputation to the end. Moderately well endowed with Chaddleworth church, Woolley chapel, Curridge manor in Chieveley, and other estates in Peasemore, Bagnor and elsewhere, the peaceful existence of the Austin Canons was rarely disrupted except by such common rural problems as the fire which destroyed their mills and granaries in 1313, and a dispute in

1428 with a landowner in Speen, who claimed that the Prior of Poughley had built a mill opposite his side of the river Lambourn, diverting the water and causing it to flood his meadows. The house from which the priory administered its Curridge estate has given its name to Priors' Court Farm, near Chieveley. Poughley was dissolved in 1524 along with a number of other religious houses of low value, and appropriated by Wolsey as part of the endowment of Cardinal College (later Christ Church) which he had recently founded in Oxford on the site of the former St Frideswide's Abbey. After the few remaining canons had been pensioned off, Wolsey used the priory buildings as accommodation for scholars while his college was being built. But after his fall from power, all Wolsey's possessions returned to the king, and Poughley was leased to Edward Fettiplace, treasurer to the Duke of Suffolk, who greatly increased his family's estates in Berkshire as a result of the Dissolution.

The closure of these three monasteries in the 1520s was a foretaste of events to follow in the next decade. In 1536, after an act was passed for the suppression of all religious houses with an income of less than £200 a year, Hurley and Bisham were surrendered to Henry VIII. Hurley had become increasingly impoverished during the 15th century. The king granted its site and buildings, manors and other sources of income to Westminster Abbey, but when that great monastery surrendered in its turn, Hurley passed into lay hands. Bisham Priory had never prospered, and in 1536 its annual income was assessed at little more than £185, making dissolution inevitable. But, surprisingly, another brief chapter was added to its monastic history. Henry, softened by grief after the death of his third queen, Jane Seymour, decided to re-establish Bisham as an abbey. Thirteen monks under the rule of an abbot were to pray for the king during his life, and for his heir, and for the souls of his late queen and his ancestors. Founded by charter in 1537, the abbey was endowed with all the possessions of the former priory as well as the lands of the late abbey of Chertsey. It lasted for six months. By June 1538 the king had ceased to grieve for Jane and was planning his fourth marriage. The abbot and monks were dismissed and the abbey's possessions sold, even the crops and hay harvest in its fields, and the copes, vestments and cowls belonging to the monks. Like Hurley Priory, Bisham passed into lay ownership.

Early in 1538, Abingdon Abbey had surrendered, and its abbot was rewarded with a pension of £200 and the manor house of Cumnor for the rest of his life. Most abbots were similarly bribed or bullied into surrender, but Reading was one of three great abbeys which held out against the king, and whose abbots paid for their stubbornness with their lives. Throughout 1538 Thomas Cromwell's agents were busy obtaining surrenders by one means or another. In Reading, both the wealthy abbey and the poorer house of Greyfriars remained to be dealt with. The latter offered little resistance and surrendered in September, when most of the friars were found to be very old men, and the friary to contain few possessions of any value. Cromwell's agent reported that the grounds at the back of the house contained a goodly walk with trees, pond, and an orchard, 20 acres in all, but concerning the interior furnishings, 'Household stuff coarse; what little plate and jewells there is I will send up this week. There is a great trough of lead at their well, and another in their kitchen, and the bell turret is covered with lead. Church ornaments slender. The inside of the church and windows decked with grey friars I have defaced, and yet made some money out of these things. On Monday I will pay their debts to victuallers and rid the house of them all.'

Reading Abbey was not so easily brought low. Abbot Hugh Faringdon had been on good terms with the king for many years, supporting his divorce and accepting the Act of Royal Supremacy, but he refused to surrender his abbey, even when, in April 1539, Parliament passed an act vesting all monastic property in the Crown. As a result he was attainted of high treason and taken to the Tower, where he was held prisoner while Cromwell's men went through the abbey, listing holy relics, plate, tapestries, vestments and anything else of value which could be sent immediately to London. In October, Abbot Hugh was brought back to Reading for trial and condemned to the traitor's death of hanging, drawing and quartering. The sentence was duly carried out, on 15th November in front of the Abbey gate.

The abbey church and monastic buildings survived empty but largely intact until 1548, when Henry had been succeeded by his son, Edward VI, and the young king's uncle, the Duke of Somerset, Lord Protector of the Realm, set about procuring for himself some of the possessions of the former abbey. Its buildings were surveyed and their value in terms of lead, timber and stone assessed. In 1549 church and buildings were stripped of these materials, which were loaded onto barges and taken away to London. Some stone and less valuable items of woodwork were sold locally and used for the repair of St Mary's church and various other purposes. The destruction of Reading Abbey was assisted by thousands of willing hands.

The fall of the monasteries made less immediate impact on the majority of the population than the despoliation of their parish churches. The reign of Edward VI saw images destroyed, altars and stained glass removed, church plate and vestments sold, and medieval wall paintings covered with whitewash. 'Paid for 4 boketts for the werkmen

The execution of the last Abbot of Reading, Hugh Faringdon, after his refusal to surrender the abbey to Henry VIII.

to whytelyme the churche ... 12d.', was a typical entry in church wardens' accounts in 1547, and in place of the familiar coloured pictures, instructive texts were written on the walls. In 1548 traditional church ceremonies were abolished, and in 1549 the First English Prayer Book was issued. Mary Tudor attempted to reverse all these changes and to restore traditional practices in a Church reconciled with Rome, but her fanaticism and the unpopularity of her marriage to Philip of Spain helped to increase support for Protestant reform. Both sides produced martyrs. In Mary's reign, Jocelyn Palmer, a Protestant master of Reading Grammar School, who had written a paper attacking the burning of Bishop Hooper, was arrested and, after questioning by the mayor, sent to Newbury, where he was brought before the chancellor of the diocese on 17 July 1556. The next day he was found guilty of heresy and, the same afternoon, burned at the stake together with two other men, Thomas Askew and John Gwyn, who refused to recant. Another brave Protestant was Sir John Baptiste Castillon, soldier and courtier, in the service of the

Princess Elizabeth when she was held, a virtual prisoner, under suspicion of plotting against her sister Mary. In an attempt to involve Elizabeth in Wyatt's rebellion in 1554, Castillon was imprisoned in the Tower and questioned on the rack, but he refused to incriminate the princess in any way. When Elizabeth came to the throne four years later, he was freed and given a post in the royal household. In 1565 she gave him the manor of Wood Speen near Newbury, and he was buried in 1597 in Speen church.

FROM REFORMATION TO CIVIL WAR

Elizabeth I began her reign in a spirit of reconciliation, endeavouring to re-establish the Protestant Church in England while tolerating more extreme opinions, so long as they posed no threat to the security of the realm. The demands of Puritans, on one hand, calling for radical reform, were firmly resisted; while, on the other, loyal subjects who declined to attend the new church services and celebrated mass in private were penalized only by the imposition of a shilling a week fine. Most people conformed, and there were many who welcomed the new Anglican services. The display of royal arms in parish churches emphasised the unity of Church and State.

The suppression of the monasteries brought many social and economic changes, among them new ownership of former monastic estates. Most of the land seized by the Crown was quickly leased out or sold at market prices, some changing hands several times in the next few years, some becoming the property of families who then settled there for generations. Bisham Abbey was acquired in 1553 by Sir Philip Hoby, who demolished some of the buildings in the process of converting it into a private residence. After his death in 1558 this work was continued by his brother, Sir Thomas. Both brothers represented England abroad, Sir Philip as the last legate to Rome in the reign of Queen Mary, and Sir Thomas as ambassador to France at the beginning of Elizabeth's reign. Sir Thomas died in 1566 but was outlived by his wife, Elizabeth, until 1609. She was sister-in-law to William Cecil, the Queen's great Secretary of State, and a considerable scholar who composed the Latin verses on the splendid Hoby monuments in Bisham church. The Hobys remained at Bisham until the end of the 18th century.

Hurley manor and the ruined priory were sold to John Lovelace in 1545. On the site of the priory he built a house (forerunner of the present house) and called it Ladye Place, in memory of the dedication of the priory to the Virgin Mary. His descendants played a prominent part

79

in the political events of the next century, but were forced by mounting debts to sell Ladye Place in the 18th century.

The lands of Reading Abbey were dispersed among several new owners. Immediately after the Dissolution, even before the execution of the abbot, the mayor and burgesses celebrated the end of 400 years of monastic rule by electing a new mayor, the first to be chosen without abbatial approval. They had already petitioned the king for permission to take over the church of the Grey Friars for use as a town hall, pleading that their existing one, beside the Kennet near High Bridge, was very small and so close to the common washing place of the townswomen that, on session days and court days there was so much noise from the beating of washing with battledores that no man could hear another speak. Although this request was made in 1538, it was not granted by Henry VIII until 1544, when the mayor and burgesses were given the use of the nave and aisles of the church for the nominal annual rent of one halfpenny. In 1540 the king, to whom all the abbey lands had reverted, appointed his own bailiffs of the borough, one of whom was Thomas Vachell, a local man whose family had been settled in the area since the 13th century, with a principal seat at Coley. Vachell, a zealous Protestant, was made overseer of the abbey properties and rewarded with a salary of 40 marks and substantial additions to his estates in Reading and Coley. His descendants remained leading figures in the town's history until the 18th century. Other abbey lands were granted in 1545 to William Grey, a London merchant whose marriage to a member of the Blagrave family founded that family's fortunes and began centuries of Blagrave influence in local affairs through their estates in Reading, Southcote and Bulmershe.

Battle manor was first granted by Edward VI to John Dudley, Duke of Northumberland, but after his execution for treason in 1552 Queen Mary gave it to Sir Francis Englefield, a devout Catholic who had served in her household before she came to the throne. The Englefields had held the manor of Englefield since the 12th century, adding Tidmarsh to their estates in 1522 and former abbey property at Tilehurst in 1545. Besides Battle, Mary gave Sir Francis the lease of Whitley manor, south of Reading, and made him a Privy Councillor. His career ended with the accession of Elizabeth. Soon afterwards he fled abroad to live in exile for the rest of his life. In Spain he corresponded with King Philip and the Pope on behalf of Mary, Queen of Scots, and was consequently attainted of treason under English law. All his manors were forfeit to the Crown, and the leases of Whitley and Battle were transferred to Sir Francis Knollys, a staunch Protestant.

Knollys was as faithful a servant of Elizabeth as Englefield had been of Mary. His father had held office under Henry VIII and established the family seat at Greys Court, a few miles north of Reading. Sir Francis married a first cousin of Queen Elizabeth and became a trusted friend and counsellor, holding office as treasurer of her household from 1572 until his death in 1596. Other Reading Abbey manors undergoing a change of ownership were Bucklebury and Thatcham, both acquired by Jack of Newbury's son, John Winchcombe, who was now in a position to set up as a country gentleman. At Bucklebury, he pulled down an old house which had been used as a country residence by the abbots of Reading, and built a new mansion which was to remain in his family for nearly 200 years. Beenham manor was granted by Henry VIII to Henry Norreys, a descendant of Sir John of Ockwells, while Pangbourne was given by Queen Elizabeth to Thomas Weldon, a cofferer in her household.

Of the former estates of Abingdon Abbey, Farnborough was purchased by John Winchcombe; Welford was leased to Thomas Parry, a treasurer to Henry VIII and the Princess Elizabeth; and Hurst to Richard Ward, who had served in a similar capacity in the households of Henry VIII, Edward VI, Mary and Elizabeth, and died in 1578.

A new and progressively more dangerous phase of Elizabeth's reign began in 1568 with the imprisonment in England of Mary, Queen of Scots. Encouraged by the Pope and Philip of Spain, various plots were devised to assassinate Elizabeth and put Mary on the throne, and by 1580 over 100 trained Jesuit missionaries had entered the country secretly in order to contact Catholic families and promote conspiracies. With the safety of Church and State as well as the Queen's life threatened, more severe laws against Catholics were bound to be passed, and after 1581, when Edmund Campion was captured in a secret room in a house at Lyford and subsequently executed, Jesuit priests were hunted everywhere. The shilling a week fine for non-attendance at parish church services was increased to a crippling £20 a month. The houses of all Catholics were watched and neighbours encouraged to report to local magistrates on the least suspicion that the occupants were celebrating mass or harbouring a priest. Informers were promised rewards if their allegations proved true.

Catholic families in west Berkshire included the Englefields of Englefield, the Moores of Fawley, the Wollascots of Woolhampton, and the Perkins of Ufton Court. In 1586 it became known that a priest named George Lingen, who was related to the Englefields, was visiting these families in the guise of a music teacher, giving lessons on the virginals. Ufton Court was most suspected as the centre of conspiracy. The timber and plaster house of many gables had been enlarged in the 1570s and contained a maze of passageways at different levels and a great many small rooms and dark closets, making it ideal for the concealment of secret hiding places within the walls and under floors. In 1586 Roger Plumpton, a tailor of Sulhamstead Abbots, who was employed in the house, reported to local justices that an unknown person was lodging there in a cock loft, or some other secret place, and was rarely seen abroad. Moreover, on certain days, he had seen members of the Perkins family slipping away in a secretive manner to a room at the top of the house, and listening as near as he could, he had heard a little bell and guessed they were hearing mass. Other suspected papists often visited the house at night.

Part of the timber-framed and many-gabled front of Ufton Court, built in the 1570s. Its small rooms and maze of passageways made it an ideal hiding place for fugitive Catholic priests.

The day after Plumpton had made his report, three local magistrates, armed with a search warrant, arrived at Ufton Court. Its master, Francis Perkins, was away from home, but his wife explained that he had gone hawking with a party of friends on the Downs near Ilsley. A messenger was sent to bring him back, and in the meantime a thorough search was made of the house, and particularly of his study, where all his books, letters and private papers in chests and cupboards were closely examined. All his servants were questioned, three being committed to prison, and the sum of £500 was taken in bond to ensure that Francis Perkins would appear in person before the magistrates. But in spite of every effort, no incriminating evidence could be found. The wretched Plumpton received no reward, but he continued to spy on the Perkins and to report every scrap of malicious gossip he could pick up in the neighbourhood.

Ufton Court was searched again in 1599, when a man named Gayler, brother of a former servant of the Perkins, alleged that he knew where a great treasure was hid in the house, and that it was the money of ill-affected persons, to be employed to some ill purpose. Warrants were sent to Sir Francis Knollys in Reading for the arrest of 'one Jarrett, a Jesuit escaped out of the Tower of London, and one Garnett, two notorious traitors supposed to be in the house of one Francis Perkins of Ufton, a place generally reputed to be a common receptacle for priests, Jesuits, recusants, and other such evil disposed persons', and also for the removal of any large sums of money found in the house to safe keeping. Another thorough search of the house brought to light two chests containing bags of gold and a quantity of plate, hidden in a cavity under a floor. This was loaded into carts and taken away to Reading. The chapel door, which was locked, was broken open and a few popish relics, pictures and half-burnt candles were found, but there was no sign of any priests. Once again the Perkins family was apparently innocent of any serious crime, but suspicion cost them dear. Their gold and treasure were only restored to them after a lawsuit lasting several years. Whether or not they were hiding priests in their house is not known for certain, but Ufton Court contains four cunningly concealed hiding places, apparently built in the 1580s.

The transfer of land from ecclesiastical to lay ownership in the earlier part of the century was followed by a significant increase in the power of towns. The stability and prosperity achieved in Elizabeth's reign owed much to her encouragement of trade and manufacture. In 1560 Reading was one of the first towns to receive an important charter increasing its powers of self-government. The merchant guild's long struggle against abbey domination had ended with Henry VIII's charter of incorporation in 1542, but the king's generosity had not extended so far as to bestow any of the abbey properties on the town, and he himself retained the income from judicial fines and other dues formerly payable to the abbey. The new corporation suffered from lack of funds until Elizabeth's charter gave it the income from courts, markets and fairs, together with certain lands and rents. These gifts were made on condition that the corporation accepted responsibility for the repair and upkeep of the roads and 19 bridges in the town, and full control and financing of the grammar school. The charter referred to the sorry state into which the roads and bridges had fallen since the abbey ceased to maintain them. The bridges were so dilapidated that crossing them was dangerous for men and beasts; and, as her contribution towards the cost of repairs, the Queen gave permission for 30 oaks to be felled on her manor of Whitley, and 200 loads of stone and other materials to be taken from the ruins of Reading Abbey. The charter defined the responsibilities of the corporation and its officers, the sergeant at mace, treasurers, market clerk, wardens and constables, who were to ensure the good government of the borough, control its trades and maintain law and order. Although most of the abbey was being used as a quarry, certain buildings, such as the abbot's lodging and stables, had been preserved for the accommodation of royal visitors, and there was no lack of these. Reading was on one of the regular routes for royal progresses, so that the mayor and burgesses were required to welcome every Tudor monarch to the town. Elizabeth visited on at least six occasions.

In Newbury, the 16th century saw the clothing trade reach its peak of success. Jack of Newbury, who had done so much to organise and promote the industry, died in 1519, but his factory continued to prosper under his son, John Winchcombe. In 1539 it supplied an order for 1,000 pieces of cloth for Thomas Cromwell, and in 1544 Winchcombe kerseys were said to make 'a great heap of money' at Antwerp. Several other local families grew rich on this industry. Blandy, Kystell and Holmes were all leading clothiers, while the Dolman dynasty, beginning with William Dolman, foreman to Jack of Newbury, was so successful that, by 1581, Thomas Dolman was able to retire to his new house at Shaw, the largest Elizabethan mansion in Berkshire. Newbury had a merchant guild by the beginning of the 16th century and a weavers' guild was founded probably in the reign of Henry VIII. Surprisingly, it was not until 1596 that the town obtained its first charter of incorporation, placing its government in the hands of a mayor and 30 burgesses forming a common council. This body may not have been popular. Its first act was to draw up a long list of minutely detailed ordinances regulating every aspect of trade, manufacture and employment. Every tradesman had to belong to one of five principal companies, each controlled by a master and wardens. The mayor had the right to enter the house of any craftsman or tradesman to examine his tools, wares, weights and measures. On Sundays, journeymen and apprentices must attend services at the parish church and engage in 'lawful exercise' afterwards. Games with dice and cards were forbidden, but shooting with the longbow was recommended as a healthful occupation for the youth of the town on holidays.

No such ordinances were in force at Hungerford, where there seems to have been a deficiency rather than a surplus of administration. The time-honoured right of free fishing in the Kennet was a considerable benefit to the inhabitants, the source of an excellent food supply as well as recreation. It was not a right they were prepared to surrender, in spite of attempts by the Duchy of Lancaster, in the 1570s, to deny its existence. Unfortunately, the townspeople could produce no proof of their claim; no copy of the charter said to have been granted by John of Gaunt in the 14th century could be found. The town's copy was alleged to have been stolen, and in 1573 two men were charged with its theft and put on trial, but nothing could be proved against them. To make matters worse, the court found that, as the burgesses of Hungerford were not incorporated, they were not qualified to plead their case. In 1574, they appealed to the Queen, who returned a gracious but not wholly satisfactory reply confirming that Hungerford's inhabitants 'should hereafter have, use

Shaw House, the largest Elizabethan mansion in Berkshire, was completed in 1581. It was built for the wealthy Newbury clothier, Thomas Dolman.

and enjoy without interruption all such liberties and profits and benefits as heretofore, time out of mind and remembrance of man, they had used and enjoyed'. She gave them no increased authority and named no particular rights, leaving room for years of legal argument between the town and the Duchy, and the matter was not resolved until 1617, when the government of the town and manor were placed in the hands of a Constable and 13 local men 'in trust for the inhabitants'. At the same time, their fishing rights within the manor were precisely defined. In the 17th century, Hungerford prospered as a small market town, with two annual fairs for cattle, sheep and wool. Many of its tradesmen were engaged in associated occupations, such as tanning, saddlemaking, fell mongering, weaving and dyeing.

Long before the 16th century, the main lines of trade and communication through Berkshire were well established, nourishing the old towns of Reading, Newbury and Hungerford, and promoting the growth of Maidenhead, but leaving Lambourn cut off, with little trade and no industry. Maidenhead enjoyed every advantage that Lambourn lacked: two major routes by road and river, a busy wharf, an important bridge, and consequently, numerous customers requiring food and accommodation, and the services of smiths, wheelwrights and harness-makers. But Maidenhead's position on the boundary between Bray and Cookham, and the jealous stewardship of these manors, delayed its progress towards independence. Leland's comments, c 1540, show that it was already a place of some importance. The town, he remarked, 'stondith a praty distance from the Tamise side and is meately well buildid', and he noted in particular, 'There is great warfeage of timbre and fier wood cummith out of Barkshir, and the great woddis of the forest of Windelsore, and the great Frithe'.

As the town increased in size, the need for an independent governing body became more urgent. In the 1570s the inhabitants sent a petition to the Queen, and in 1582 she granted a charter of incorporation under the style of 'the warden, bridgemasters, burgesses and commonalty of the town of Maydenheth'. The charter gave them the right to hold a weekly market and two annual fairs, and a new scale of tolls was laid down for merchandise passing over the bridge. Elizabeth's charter was confirmed in 1604 by James I, who granted a third fair to provide extra income for bridge maintenance, and three oaks every third year for its repair. These grants give some idea of the constant heavy use made of the bridge. The increased importance of the town was demonstrated by the appointment of two mace-bearers to walk in front of the town warden.

Windsor's development remained inextricably bound up with the castle. It had no other industry. Edward IV's creation of the Home Park, by the enclosure of 200 acres of land between the castle and the forest, and his new St George's Chapel, had improved the castle's attractions, while his charter of incorporation to the mayor and burgesses in 1466, and the grant of an additional fair, had partly compensated for their loss of common land. Queen Elizabeth was often at Windsor, and the town owed some improvements to her reign. In 1585 an act was passed ordering the paving of the main streets with cobble-stones, as they had been 'yearly impaired and made noisome and foul by reason of the great and daily carriage and re-carriage' to the castle. Elizabeth's liking for Windsor probably suggested to Shakespeare the setting for his comedy of *The Merry Wives*, thus placing a provincial English town alongside Venice, Verona, and other exotic locations. Datchet Mead, where Falstaff was tossed into the Thames with the dirty linen, the Garter Inn, and the legend of Herne the Hunter, would all have been familiar to the Queen.

Wokingham began its slow progress towards independence with Elizabeth's charter of 1583, although the Steward of Sonning still retained overall control. He presided over the borough courts, at one of which the town's officers were chosen each year. These were an alderman, two constables, two bailiffs and two aletasters. A weekly market was held and two fairs annually. Freedom from Sonning was not won until 1612, when James I granted Wokingham a charter of incorporation with a governing body of a mayor and 19 burgesses. Silk manufacture began in Wokingham towards the end of the 16th century. It gave a much-needed boost to the town's economy and remained one of its principal industries for 200 years. The knitting of silk stockings was a local speciality, and the borough byelaws of 1625 show that silk knitting was an occupation imposed on everyone who was not otherwise employed. The poor and idle who refused to obey were committed to the House of Correction. The cultivation of mulberry trees in large gardens became common in Elizabeth's reign, and there are records of a purchase of over 1,000 mulberry plants by Sir Henry Nevill, Sir Francis Knollys and Sir John Norreys, all three the owners of extensive estates. Nearly all raw silk continued to be imported but James I encouraged the breeding of silkworms in this country by ordering mulberry trees to be planted in many towns. Some trees survived in Wokingham until modern times.

Silk manufacture spread to Reading, and later to Twyford, and was one of several industries which helped to compensate for the decline of clothmaking in Berkshire. Reading's most notable clothier made his fortune in London at a time when the industry had begun to decline in his home town, and he is remembered for his efforts to revive it. John Kendrick is said to have kept 140 looms in use, not quite so many as tradition claims for Jack of Newbury, but still a very considerable number, giving employment to hundreds of workers. He died in 1624, by which time there were already many poor and unemployed people in the town. In his will he bequeathed over £7,000 for the purpose of building a factory (later known as The Oracle) on the south side of Minster Street, where the poor might be kept in work and supplied with materials for clothmaking. Sadly, the funds were mismanaged and The Oracle achieved none of its founder's aims.

Other local industries were pin-making and bell-founding. There were at least three pinners in 17th century Reading, making an article which had previously been imported in vast quantities. A bell-founder was working in Wokingham as early as the 14th century, and many bells were made there for churches in southern England before the firm moved to Reading about 1495. Bell-founding was an important industry in Reading from the 16th to the 18th century, the most famous founders being the Knight family.

Of all the expanding industries of that period the one which made the greatest impact on the landscape was brickmaking. In an area short of building stone, and which had made prodigal use of its timber supplies, the rediscovery of brick was much needed at a time when the growing population and increased wealth created a demand for more houses. From the 16th century brick was widely used for domestic buildings, combined with timber or flint at first, but later on its own. Ufton Court, in timber and plaster, and Shaw House, in brick with stone dressings, were almost exact contemporaries, but the first was built in the old traditional way and the second in the new fashion. In the 17th century, brick began to be used conspicuously for church towers, and there are examples at Wargrave, Winkfield, Hurst, Ruscombe and Shinfield. They stand in marked contrast to other east Berkshire towers, built in the local brown conglomerate, at Warfield, Binfield and All Saints, Wokingham.

THE GREAT REBELLION

10

The first notes of rebellion were sounded in Buckinghamshire with John Hampden's refusal to pay ship money, which he considered an illegal royal tax. Ship money, originally levied on seaports in time of national danger, had been demanded by the king from the whole country in peacetime, and for the third year running, in 1636. Most places paid up, although reluctantly, according to their assessment; Reading, for example, paid £260, Wokingham £50. Hampden was brought to trial and lost his case, but only narrowly. Five of the twelve judges decided in his favour. Resistance to ship money spread, adding fuel to growing discontent with the King's autocratic style of government and the High Anglican forms of worship introduced by Archbishop Laud. When war broke out, in 1642, most prosperous towns, whose citizens felt that they had been made to pay dearly for the luxury and extravagance of the court, and where Puritanism was strong, sided with the rebels. Reading and Newbury supported Parliament, and so did Windsor.

King Charles had moved with his family from an increasingly hostile London to Windsor in January 1642. But even there his popularity had sunk so low, and the mood of the country generally had become so threatening, particularly towards his Catholic queen, that in February he sent her for safety to Holland. He himself travelled north and, in August, set up his standard at Nottingham. After the opening battle of the war at Edgehill, in October 1642, the way was still open for him to return to his capital, but his march was too slow, and the Parliamentary army, commanded by the Earl of Essex, arrived there first. Windsor, too, was now cut off from the King. Parliament had taken steps to secure it as soon as war was imminent, and Reading was also in their hands. Hence, Oxford, where the King arrived six days after Edgehill, was chosen as the Royalist HQ for the rest of the war. In Oxford, although the town was inclined towards Parliament, the University favoured the King. There, too, he was closer to the western and northern parts of England which were to give him most support throughout the war. Parliament drew its support from the more economically advanced areas of eastern and southern England.

In Windsor, the townspeople welcomed the arrival of Parliamentary troops, who quickly occupied the castle. Its commanding position was once again appreciated, as was that of many another castle which had been slumbering peacefully since the Middle Ages. Throughout the war, Windsor was a Parliamentary stronghold, used as a supply base for operations in Berkshire and around Oxford. The castle served as HQ, barracks, and prison for Royalists; the park and forest as army training grounds. Like the town, the whole forest area was hostile to the King. Ancient forest laws, protecting the deer, had been revived in the 1630s, although the King rarely hunted. A petition on behalf of the inhabitants in 1640 complained of 'the unmeasureable increase of deer, which if they shall go on for a few more years will leave neither food nor room for any other creature in the forest'. Parliament appointed as governor of Windsor, Colonel John Venn, a Puritan, fiercely antagonistic to the King, who had played a leading part in the organisation of the London Trained Bands for the defence of the capital.

Reading had been in a state of alarm since the beginning of September, when the council met to discuss 'the greate dainger that this towne and the inhabitantes thereof are in by reason of the Caviliers abroad', and a decision was made to send out scouts every day to bring warning of any approaching. Before war broke out, Parliament sent a Berkshire MP, Henry Marten, to secure Reading for their cause; but work on the defences had barely begun when, little more than a week after Edgehill (the outcome of which was uncertain), a Royalist force was seen approaching the town. Marten abandoned it and fled to London.

On 4th November the council was obliged to welcome the King when he passed through Reading on a belated march towards London. While this was in progress, Prince Rupert and a small force arrived outside Windsor in the hope of recapturing the castle. Royalist cannon, set up in the grounds of Eton College, bombarded the town for several hours, causing considerable damage to houses but very little to the castle, which was ably defended by Venn's troops. At the end of the day (7th November), Rupert withdrew, having insufficient men and ammunition to continue the attack.

The failure of the King's march, and the humiliation of his repulse by the London Trained Bands at Turnham Green, brought him back to Reading by 19th November. He ordered the town's defences to be completed, and men were made to labour at digging and building them under pain of fine. A garrison of 3,000 men was encamped in and around the town and a cavalry commander, Sir Arthur Aston, was appointed governor. Other heavy demands were made upon the town. The council met to discuss the levying of a tax 'to pay the greate charges which are now layed upon the Borough concerning cloth, apparell, victuals, and other thinges for His Majesties armye'. This was to be only the first of many such charges, and was soon followed by a demand for £2,000 to be raised during December.

Returning to Oxford, the King held a council of war. That city, too, must be fortified, and a ring of smaller towns, including Abingdon, Wallingford and Faringdon, must be garrisoned as outposts of Oxford's defences. To the south, Newbury, with a strong Puritan element, welcomed Parliamentary soldiers into the town, but a Royalist stronghold was established later at Donnington Castle.

In the winter of 1642–3, east Berkshire began to suffer from its

The Earl of Essex, Parliamentary Army commander 1642–44, who directed the siege of Royalist-held Reading in 1643.

uncomfortable position between Royalist and Parliamentary forces. In January, sorties from Reading attacked Roundheads encamped near Twyford and Hurst, but in spite of some fierce fighting, failed to dislodge them. In the same month the Earl of Essex strengthened his position in the Thames Valley by occupying Henley. The large garrison at Reading placed an increasingly heavy burden on the town and surrounding parishes, whose inhabitants were ordered to provide food and other necessities for its support. When supplies grew short, corn, cattle, sheep and horses were taken by force. Both sides were equally ruthless. Twyford people complained to Parliament that they were pillaged by one side or the other almost every day. In a nasty incident in Wokingham, Royalist soldiers from Reading ordered the townspeople to supply eight cartloads of firewood and bedding, and when they failed to do so, four houses were destroyed and their occupiers told to take themselves off to Windsor.

The spring campaign of 1643 opened with a decisive move by Parliament to recapture Reading. In the town, the cost of the garrison together with repeated demands from the King for 'loans', had driven the council to petition His Majesty that they might be excused a loan of £2,000, 'by reason of their greate paymentes, burthens and losses which they have already and doe daily undergoe'. But the petition met with no success. Sir Arthur Aston, a stern and uncompromising governor, kept the townspeople hard at work on the defences. A line of ditches and ramparts enclosed an area which is now only the town centre, running from the abbey along Friar Street to Greyfriars church, and from there to a heavily fortified salient on Castle Hill, guarding the road from the west. On the other side of the Kennet, the earthworks continued from Katesgrove to a south eastern salient at the top of Silver Street, and from there northwards to the Kennet at Blake's bridge, which was guarded by redoubts on both banks of the river as it approached the town wharves. Around the Forbury, the construction of earthworks involved the blowing up of part of the remains of the former abbey church, stones from which were used in the defences. In Caversham, there were more earthworks to the north of the church, and part of the bridge over the Thames was replaced by a drawbridge.

All these preparations were severely tested during a ten day siege in the spring. The Earl of Essex, marching apparently from Windsor towards Oxford, turned unexpectedly south and, on 15th April, arrived on Caversham Heights with an army of 15,000 foot and 3,000 horse. By the evening of the next day he had taken Caversham bridge and encamped his men in fields on the Berkshire side of the river. All the western approaches were under his control, and he himself set up his headquarters at Southcote manor house, home of the Parliamentarian, Daniel Blagrave. Reading suffered several days of bombardment, inflicting heavy damage on buildings. On the third day, Sir Arthur Aston was struck on the head by a falling tile and so badly injured that the command devolved on Colonel Richard Feilding. Essex, meanwhile, had received reinforcements of men and artillery to help him cut off the eastern side of the town, and control traffic along the Thames and Kennet. By day he continued the bombardment; by night his men and guns moved closer to the town. Inside, the besieged were running short of food and ammunition. Feilding had sent a messenger to Oxford informing the King that he could not hold out much longer. His Majesty mustered a relief force, despatched a summons to Prince Rupert, who was besieging Lichfield, to join him, and set out for Reading. In order to let Feilding know that help and supplies were on the way, he sent ahead a messenger, who succeeded in making his way through the enemy lines at Caversham and swam across the river to deliver the King's message. But on his way back, he was captured and made to reveal the Royalist plan.

Essex quickly sent a cavalry force towards Oxford, to harass and delay the Royalist advance, and ordered a smaller party to ambush any supplies which reached Caversham. At Dorchester, his cavalry engaged the Royalist horse and fighting took place in the narrow streets and lanes of the town, leaving many dead and wounded. Essex's men returned to Reading in triumph, bringing prisoners and waving some captured Royalist colours, the sight of which spread alarm and despair among the garrison in the besieged town. On 24th April, a desperate sortie was made from the town resulting in more Royalist casualties before they were driven back. Still there was no sign of the promised relief, and Feilding decided that it would be better to save his remaining forces than let them be destroyed in a hopeless cause. On 25th April he ordered a white flag to be hung out and sent a drummer to beat a parley. Terms of surrender were actually under discussion when the delayed relief forces, led by the King and Prince Rupert, arrived on Caversham Heights. Under Rupert's command, the cavalry swept down the hillside and furiously attacked the forces guarding the bridge. The ensuing fight at Caversham, on a day of hail and rain, over difficult ground with heavily defended outposts, was a violent, brave and bloody climax to the siege of Reading. But it was in vain. By nightfall the Royalists were forced to retreat, leaving hundreds of dead and wounded lying in fields, barns and outhouses. The next day, Essex sent his own surgeons to attend to the wounded, and ordered the local people to bury the dead where they lay.

To the fury of the King and Prince Rupert, Feilding refused to renege on the truce terms he had agreed, and on 27th April the garrison marched out of Reading, with colours flying, carrying arms and ammunition, and taking 50 cartloads of baggage and wounded men, including Sir Arthur Aston in a litter. As the Royalists made their way across Caversham bridge on the road to Oxford, Essex led his army into the town from the west. He remained in occupation for several weeks.

During the summer of 1643, the war moved away to the West Country. The Royalists gained major victories at Devizes and Bristol, and laid siege to Gloucester. Essex took an army of 15,000 to raise the siege, and in September, with the campaign season drawing to a close, found himself faced with the task of getting the main part of the Parliamentary forces back to London through largely hostile country. Marching south west of Oxford, he was attacked by Royalist cavalry near Aldbourne, and only with difficulty beat them off. Abandoning his intended route to Newbury, where he hoped for much needed provisions for his hungry army, he made for Hungerford, hoping to put the Kennet between him and the enemy. But the King reached Newbury before him, and Essex arrived to find the Royalist army not only barring his way but commandeering all the available food and supplies.

The King's speedy move to intercept the Parliamentary army at this time gave him the opportunity to win a decisive victory, and perhaps to end the war. So far, his armies had done well, but he had neither money nor resources to prolong the war; while Parliament controlled the capital, many towns, and the wealthy eastern side of England, and was in a better position to do so.

The first battle of Newbury was fought on 20th September 1643 in the muddy fields and lanes between the Kennet and Enborne, and on the higher ground at Wash Common. At first light, the two armies were deployed in the customary manner, with infantry and artillery in the centre and cavalry on both flanks. The Royalist cavalry on the King's left was under the command of Prince Rupert and occupied what appeared to be the most dominant position on Wash Common. The Roundheads, however, reconnoitring during the night, had discovered the importance of Round Hill, between Wash Common and Skinners Green, and had moved their infantry to occupy this strongly defensive position. Numerically, the two armies were about equal at around 14,000, but the King's army had a preponderance of cavalry, while the Roundheads were more than two-thirds infantry. In the event, it was the difficult terrain for cavalry charges, and the tenacity of the Roundhead infantry holding Round Hill, that deprived the King of victory. The area was one of small fields surrounded by hedgerows, so that the fighting became confused. Again and again the Royalist cavalry attacked, driving the Roundhead cavalry from the field and almost dislodging their infantry from Round Hill. In one desperate assault, Lord Falkland, the King's secretary, and 100 of his regiment were shot down in their attempts to break through the hedges. At this point, Skippon, Essex's second-in-command, sent in the Trained Bands, many of them London apprentices, to hold the top of Skinners Green Lane, and it was their resolution under repeated assaults that saved the day. When fighting ceased at nightfall, both sides were exhausted and had suffered heavy losses. But the battle had not proved decisive. The King still held Newbury and barred Essex's way to London. Essex must have expected to resume the struggle next day, but to his great relief, when dawn broke, the Royalist army had gone. The King, appalled by his losses in men and horses, and worried by his depleted supply of ammunition, had decided to return to Oxford.

The old Guildhall and Market Place at Newbury. An imaginative view showing how it may have looked during the Civil War period.

Essex resumed his march towards London, keeping to the south of the Kennet because Royalists still held the bridge at Newbury and harassed his army on its way through winding country lanes. In a steep-sided gulley near Padworth, his rearguard was attacked, throwing it into disorder and killing many men. About 300 bodies are believed to have been buried in hastily dug pits in Padworth churchyard, where their bones were discovered more than two centuries later. Essex reached Reading that evening with all his cannon and the main part of his army, and rested there before moving on to London. Within a few days another Royalist garrison, under the command of Sir Jacob Astley, had moved in.

Before he left Newbury, the King had signed a commission to Colonel John Boys to garrison Donnington Castle 'for the defence of this part of our county of Berkshire'. The castle belonged to the Packer family, whose sympathies lay with Parliament, and in his preparations for its defence Boys was ruthless, ordering many trees to be cut down and houses in the village which might shelter the enemy to be demolished. The countryside around was scoured for food and provisions, and the castle's defences were strengthened all round by elaborate star-shaped earthworks. In October, Boys was ordered to send two of his cannon and a quantity of ammunition to Basing House, which was also preparing for a siege, and obeyed rather unwillingly. The enemy were expected every day, he wrote, and his security was threatened by having 'such ill neighbours as the factious town of Newbury'.

In the spring of 1644, two Parliamentary armies under Essex and Waller began to move towards Oxford. The King knew that the city was undermanned and against the advice of some of his Council, decided to withdraw the Reading garrison to Oxford, and ordered Reading's defences to be slighted. Thus the unfortunate town suffered a fourth change of garrison: on 18th May Essex's troops moved in, and on the 20th the town council, in obedience to Essex's command, ordered carpenters to repair Caversham bridge, broken down by the departing Royalists. Parliament held on to Reading for the rest of the war. They now controlled all of eastern and most of southern Berkshire. By June, Oxford was almost surrounded, but the King managed to escape to Worcester, leaving Essex and Waller in disagreement over their next move. In London, Parliament was busy appointing county committees for areas under their control. These committees were responsible for raising money and forces, collecting taxes, confiscating the estates of 'papists and other delinquents', examining ministers, schoolmasters and others in positions of authority, and seeking out any who were hostile towards Parliament. The committee for Berkshire included Sir Francis Knollys, Henry Marten and Daniel Blagrave.

In July, Donnington Castle came under attack when General Middleton arrived with 3,000 men to demand its surrender. Boys sent a defiant reply and remained defiant throughout the 20-month siege which followed. A twelve-day bombardment severely damaged the castle walls but did not discourage the defenders from sallying forth to attack the besiegers and inflict heavy losses. In October, the King, after some success in the West Country, hoped to raise the sieges of Donnington and Basing, but Parliament moved its armies to prevent him, and by 25th October had gathered a force of around 20,000 between Newbury and Thatcham, twice the number of the King's forces. Now Parliament, in its turn, had a chance to end the war with a decisive victory, but the second battle of Newbury, fought on 27th October, was as ill-managed as the first. The King took up a strong defensive position between Speen village and Shaw House, with some protection from Donnington Castle.

The Parliamentary forces were disposed on both sides of the Kennet, their command shared between Waller and the Earl of Manchester. After lengthy discussion, they decided that Waller should take 12,000 men on an overnight outflanking march, via Hermitage, Chieveley, Winterbourne and Boxford, and to attack from the rear; Manchester, meanwhile, must divert the Royalists' attention until he heard Waller's guns opening fire at Speen. This would be the signal for him to attack simultaneously from Clay Hill. The cross-country march probably took longer than anticipated, and it was not until three o'clock in the afternoon that Waller launched his attack, taking the Royalists by surprise and driving them out of Speen village. But, for some reason, Manchester delayed his attack until four o'clock, and Shaw House was so strongly defended by the Royalists that it withstood an assault by some 3,000 infantry and 1,200 cavalry. The battle around Shaw raged until nightfall, by which time Manchester had suffered heavy losses and the attack was abandoned.

Waller's success at Speen, however, had put the King in a dangerous position and the next day he made good his escape, having bestowed a knighthood on John Boys, and left most of his baggage and guns in Donnington Castle. Two weeks later he came back to retrieve them and then spent several days travelling through west Berkshire, visiting Royalist families such as the Brownes at Great Shefford House and attending divine service at Winterbourne church. The siege of Donnington Castle continued, and more damage was inflicted on the village. All the houses, including the almshouses, were burned down by Sir John's orders, and hundreds of people made homeless. But Donnington soon ceased to be of strategic importance, for the rest of the war was fought in other parts of England.

In the winter of 1644–5 Parliament deliberated on the indecisive nature of the war, and concluded that victory could only be won by a more efficiently organised fighting force. 'Till the whole army were new modelled', declared Oliver Cromwell, 'and governed under a stricter discipline, they must not expect any notable success in anything they were about'. By the Self-Denying Ordinance members of both Houses of Parliament, including Essex and Manchester, resigned their military commands and new officers were appointed. Cromwell, as Member for Huntingdon, also resigned but was soon given a new appointment as cavalry commander. The Captain-General of the New Model Army was Sir Thomas Fairfax, a man who was well liked and inspiring as a leader. Fairfax arrived at his headquarters at Windsor on 3rd April 1645, and organised a short but intensive period of training. Strict discipline was enforced to discourage theft, drunkenness, rape

The impressive remains of the 14th century gatehouse at Donnington Castle. The castle held out for the King under siege for 20 months beginning in 1644.

and pillage. Windsor townspeople were in the centre of things as the army was mustered, drilled and made to practise manoeuvres in the royal park. New regiments were formed and, for the first time, every man was issued with uniform clothing. The army numbered about 22,000 men, including about 14,400 infantry, 6,600 cavalry and 1,000 dragoons. Their departure from Windsor on 30th April to begin their summer campaign must have been a stirring sight; and so, too, their march across Berkshire through Reading, Theale and Newbury.

The New Model Army won its first decisive victory at Naseby in June, and after that the King's cause was lost. Pockets of resistance all over the country were overcome or surrendered, as did Donnington Castle, by command of the King, on 30th March 1646. The terms of surrender allowed Sir John Boys and his men to march out with full military honours, drums beating and colours flying. In 1647 the King became virtually a prisoner of the Army, and was moved with it from place to place. In July 1647 he was brought to Windsor Castle for a few days, and from there to Reading, while the Army held council. Because he was still their lawful king, the mayor and aldermen of Reading welcomed him formally as he entered the town, and he was comfortably lodged at Lord Craven's house at Caversham Park. There he was allowed to receive visitors, among them Elias Ashmole, who was to be Windsor Herald and founder of the Ashmolean Museum in Oxford in the reign of Charles II. From Caversham he was also allowed to travel under escort to Maidenhead for a brief reunion with his younger children, the Princess Elizabeth and the Duke of Gloucester.

Nearly two and a half years later, King Charles saw Windsor for the last time when he was held prisoner in the castle for a few weeks before his trial and execution in London in January 1649. Among the 59 signatories to his death warrant were two Berkshire MPs, Henry Marten and Daniel Blagrave. On 7th February, the King's body was brought back to Windsor, the journey being made at night to avoid popular demonstrations in his favour. Two days later, in the midst of a snow storm, his coffin was carried into St George's Chapel, and buried without ceremony in a vault beneath the choir.

11

THE LATER SEVENTEENTH CENTURY

The Civil War left its inevitable legacy of poverty and distress among all classes of the population; houses, mills and barns were damaged or destroyed, farms devastated, trade and industry depressed. But Parliament had won the war and hard work, thrift and discipline were Puritan virtues, aiding recovery. Parliament was in desperate need of money, and at one point even proposed to sell off Crown property, including Windsor Castle, but the sale did not take place, although in 1650 a survey was made of the trees in Windsor Great Park, and the number of those marked for the use of the navy totalled 2,604. Another way of raising money was by further punishing royalists. Those who had not already lost their estates were liable to have them sequestered and offered back by the Parliamentary Committee for Compounding at a price assessed according to the scale of the owner's delinquency. Sir Humphrey Forster of Aldermaston was involved in a lawsuit with the Committee for several years. He had mortgaged his estates shortly before the war for the large sum of £14,000, raised, so he claimed, to enable him to rebuild Aldermaston Court; but the Committee suspected him of using at least part of the money to support the royal cause, and considered that his was a serious case of delinquency. His estates were sequestered and not restored to him until 1660. One of the arguments that had been used in his favour was that his son had supported Parliament during the war and offered to pay his debt. Even more unfortunate was the Marquess of Winchester, who had defended Basing House throughout a siege lasting more than two years, and seen his property there plundered and reduced to rubble by Cromwell's soldiers. He was imprisoned in the Tower and other estates belonging to him at Englefield were sequestered and sold by Parliament. After the Restoration, Englefield was returned to him by a grateful Charles II, and the Marquess lived there for the remaining years of his life.

Other royalists were Richard Nevill of Billingbear, who had served with the King at Oxford and had to compound for his estates after

Aldermaston House, built by Sir Humphrey Forster in the 1630s. A Royalist, his estates were sequestered by Parliament after the Civil War and not restored to him until 1660.

the war; and Lord Craven, who had been created Baron Craven of Hamstead Marshall by Charles I in 1627, and was one of the King's most loyal and valuable supporters. His wealth enabled him to contribute huge sums towards the royal cause, but after the war he went into exile and all his estates in Hamstead Marshall and Caversham were sold. In 1660 he returned to England with Charles II and recovered his property. The new King loaded him with honours and made him Viscount Craven of Uffington and Earl of Craven in Yorkshire.

The value of friends in high places was well understood by Elias Ashmole, whose royalist sympathies were no secret, and who noted in his diary in November 1648 that his property at Bradfield had been sequestered. But not for long. Six days later he obtained the release of his lands through 'the interest of some friends among the godly', meaning on the Parliamentary side. Daniel Blagrave, MP for Reading and now Parliamentary Treasurer for Berkshire, was soon to be Ashmole's cousin by marriage. Ashmole's wife was Lady Mainwaring, widowed daughter of Sir William Forster of Aldermaston. She was 20 years his senior, but wealthy and was described by Ashmole's friend, William Lilly, as 'a lady very handsome, and of goodly structure'.

The sturdy tower of St Mary's, Shinfield, dates from 1664 and is a fine example of local brickwork. With the Restoration of Charles II the confidence to build returned to local landowners.

For many people, whichever side they had supported, the years of dictatorship and the imposition of Puritan forms of worship and strict morality became increasingly hard to bear, and everyone was burdened with heavy taxation. Nevertheless, the years of the Commonwealth were not ones of unrelieved gloom and certainly not of stagnation. An embryo civil service administered public affairs more efficiently than any previous government. Trade at home and abroad began to revive, agriculture recovered and became more productive as more land was taken into cultivation and new crops were introduced. The official postal services, which had been started in 1635 along the main highways out of London, and had proved their worth during the war, were developed for private and commercial use. The first public stage coaches began to run; two regular weekly services between London and Bath or Bristol were advertised in 1657. One was operated by Onesiphorus Tapp, postmaster at Marlborough, who added another service in 1658 for the journey between London and Marlborough, via Reading and Newbury, every Monday and Thursday. Road repairs were attended to more systematically after an Act of Parliament in 1654 empowered surveyors to assess the inhabitants of each parish for tax, and to hire labour and carts for repair purposes. Poor relief was maintained and education encouraged during the Commonwealth.

But after the death of Oliver Cromwell the question of who should rule became paramount, and was resolved by the restoration of the monarchy in 1660, albeit a monarchy with reduced powers. Henceforth, Parliament, not the royal court, was to be the seat of government, and administrative departments set up under the Commonwealth were retained. The return of Charles II was greeted with popular as well as official rejoicing; with him the Church of England was restored, and there was a general feeling of stability. Charles had promised freedom of conscience to all Nonconformists, the settlement of all long-running disputes over property, and the return to their rightful owners of church and private lands confiscated during the Commonwealth.

Thus, to a great extent, the old order of society was re-established. Heraldic visitations of the counties, carried out in the 1660s, compiled records of the upper layers of society based on proofs to title and ownership. Berkshire's visitation was carried out in 1665 by Elias Ashmole, who had been appointed Windsor Herald in 1660. His purpose was to enquire into the titles and honours borne by the baronets, knights, esquires and gentlemen of the county, and to ensure that the coats of arms they used had been granted by the proper authority. He was empowered to enter houses and churches to survey and record arms, and to pull down any not lawfully used. He could 'make infamous by proclamation' anyone using arms or titles (even that of gentleman) without due cause. In preparation for his visitation, warrants were sent to the constables and bailiffs of each district, requesting them to summon the persons named on a list to attend the herald at a specified place and date, bringing with them their pedigrees, arms, crests and other documentary evidence. Ashmole met them in one or other of the larger town inns; the Bear or the Ship in Reading, the Mermaid in Newbury, or the Three Tuns in Windsor. Altogether, representatives of 118 leading local families appeared before him, including Sir Thomas Rich of Sonning, Richard Harrison of Hurst, William Barker of Sonning, Richard Palmer of Wokingham, Sir Thomas Dolman of Shaw, William Packer of Donnington, Sir Henry Winchcombe of Bucklebury, John Blagrave of Southcote, William Kendrick of Reading, Sir Humphrey Forster of Aldermaston, Francis Perkins of Ufton, and the High Sheriff, Sir William Backhouse of Swallowfield. Those who were unable to attend had to send a sufficient excuse. John Hyde of Earley pleaded an attack of gout, while Mrs Kate Hoby of Bisham sent her husband's apologies for not appearing, as he had 'a greate Cold att present'. A certain Angell Bell sent a disclaimer saying that he thought it strange his name should be included among the knights and gentlemen living in Sonning, as he had no grounds for such a claim, and 'trewly Sir, I am no waies ambittious after any of those titles'. One of the aims of the visitation was to weed out upstarts who aspired to social status during the Commonwealth, a period when men had been rewarded for merit rather than privileged by birth and pedigree. However, Ashmole added at least one new entrant to his lists of gentlemen: Jethro Tull of Shalbourn, who had proved his descent to the herald's satisfaction.

In spite of the promise of religious toleration which Charles II made before his restoration, no Act of Parliament was passed to enforce it, and before long Nonconformists were made to suffer for non-allegiance to

103

the Established Church, and, by inference, to the State. Puritanism was no longer the powerful, united force it had been. Division into sects, Baptists, Presbyterians, Independents, and Quakers had weakened it, but all Nonconformists remained free-thinking and outspoken. Their services were intellectual rather than ceremonial, and their preachers exercised a powerful influence over their congregations. After 1661 a number of acts were passed designed to exclude Nonconformists from office, or any position of influence. Troublesome preachers were dealt with by the Act of Uniformity of 1662, which required all beneficed clergy to conform to the Prayer Book, and deprived of their livings any who refused to give their unfeigned assent to everything the book contained. This led to the departure of many popular and respected ministers. At Newbury, Benjamin Woodbridge, a highly esteemed scholar and speaker, who had been offered a canonry at Windsor provided he would conform, which he declined to do, was ejected. He had preached three times a week in Newbury, and it was said when he left that 'there was scarce a family in it where there was not praying, reading and singing of psalms'. At Hungerford, John Clark, 'a grave, serious and zealous preacher . . . of peaceable spirit and blameless life', was bitterly lamented and floods of tears were shed at his farewell sermon. Like Woodbridge, Clark did not go far away, but continued to preach in private houses in neighbouring villages. In Reading, Christopher Fowler, Vicar of St Mary's, and 'a busy, turbulent man', was deprived of his living but continued to hold meetings in his own house, as a result of which the congregations in the parish churches were much diminished. The violence of his opinions led to a term of imprisonment, and he was never again allowed to preach in Reading. Elsewhere in the county, Thomas Voisey lost his living at Thatcham, Rowland Stedman at Wokingham, and Thomas Woodward at Bray, while seven others were temporarily deprived but afterwards conformed.

The most troublesome Nonconformists were the Quakers, who refused to attend church services, or to pay tithes or take the oath of allegiance. Their movement had grown in the later years of the Commonwealth, and in 1655 their founder, George Fox, addressed a large meeting behind the Broad Face Inn in Reading. They became most numerous in that town and in Newbury, where their meetings, held in private houses, were often violently interrupted and those present fined or imprisoned. The courage and defiance of the authorities which characterised Quakers was illustrated by the life of Oliver Sansom, a farmer of Boxford, who endured many years of persecution, including several terms of imprisonment in Reading gaol. Sansom had been baptised into the Church of England but became a Quaker in his twenties and began to hold meetings in his own home. The vicar of Boxford, James Anderton, and other neighbours tried, quite kindly at first, to persuade him to return to the Church of England, but Sansom was nothing if not stubborn. Their efforts began with fining him for non-attendance at church and nominating him for the post of parish constable, for which he would have to swear the oath of allegiance, and which he refused. Then punishments grew harsher. At various times his horses, his hay, his winnowing fan and his harrow were taken away by force, and then his household pewter; all purportedly in lieu of the annual tithes which he refused to pay. His cows were put in the village pound and kept without food, the local miller was forbidden to grind his corn, his harvests were spoiled, his farm workers assaulted, and a horse on which he had ridden to Newbury market was taken and sold, while he himself was put in the stocks there. Neither Sansom, nor his long-suffering wife, ever gave in. Life for Quakers became somewhat easier after the Toleration Act of 1689 recognised their objection to judicial oaths and allowed them to make a statutory declaration instead. Sansom's reputation as a preacher increased and he was invited to speak at meetings in many towns and villages. He died in Abingdon in 1710 and was buried there in the Quaker burial ground next to the Meeting House.

Whatever people felt about Protestant nonconformists, their fear of popery was stronger and proved more inflammatory. The open Roman Catholicism of James II speedily united the opposition of powerful sections of the community, the landed gentry and the merchant classes, and resulted in the expulsion of James and an invitation to Protestant William of Orange, who had married James' daughter, Mary, to accept the throne. The Glorious Revolution of 1688 was a triumph for Parliament but was not achieved entirely without bloodshed. Some of the 3,000 Irish Catholic troops, which James had ill-advisedly brought into the country to defend him, clashed with some of William's Dutch troops in Reading. Berkshire lay on William's line of march from Torbay to London, and, on reaching Hungerford, he halted for several days to consult with the King's representatives and afterwards entertained them to dinner at Littlecote House. Meanwhile, a detachment of his army went forward to Reading, and found the town defended by Irish troops, much to the indignation of the townspeople, and the alarm of some who feared that the 'papishes' would murder them while they were attending church. A confused skirmish took place up and down the streets, ending in the Irish being driven out of the town, leaving about 50 dead, some of whom were buried in St Giles' churchyard. According to a tale told to Defoe some years afterwards, the Irish were so terrified that a mere 50 Dutch chased about 300 Irish as far as Twyford, where, the pursuit having drawn off, the Irish rallied and marched on towards Maidenhead, 'swearing and cursing after most soldierly a manner, that they would burn all the towns wherever they came, and cut the throats of all the people'. Luckily, no such atrocities took place, and the events in Reading that day were afterwards sung in a jolly ballad to the tune of Lillibulero:

> Five hundred Papishes came there,
> To make a final end
> Of all the town in time of prayer,
> But God did them defend . . .

The Declaration of Rights, accepted by William III, established Parliament's control over the throne; while the Toleration Act allowed freedom of worship to Nonconformists, although still excluding them from the universities and other influential bodies. The Church became more divided and less powerful, so that religious questions, which had contributed so largely to the upheavals and tragedies of the 16th and 17th centuries, ceased to dictate events. Politics became the absorbing interest of the ruling classes, and the two great political parties of Whigs and Tories came into being at the end of the 17th century. The ballad of *The Vicar of Bray*, probably written c 1720, lampooned the twists and turns of religious and political opinion demanded of the clergy over the past half-century. A High Churchman in the reign of Charles II, the legendary vicar was prepared to turn Jesuit under James II, but after the Revolution was able to adapt his conscience to serve William of Orange.

> When William our deliverer came,
> To heal the nation's grievance,
> I turned the cat in pan again,
> And swore to him allegiance.

Like him, few clergymen felt that, having sworn allegiance to James, they could not conscientiously accept the new king. In the reigns of Anne and George I, it was from Tory to Whig that he turned.

12

THE EIGHTEENTH CENTURY: TRADE AND TRANSPORT

In the 18th century, Berkshire was a county of numerous villages, hamlets and farms, where most of the population lived and worked, and half a dozen market towns, none of which was built up very far beyond its commercial centre. In west Berkshire, where the land was still largely unenclosed, farming was the principal occupation. In east Berkshire, timber remained the major product. The forest extended to the river Loddon, and the royal deer were sometimes hunted as far as the outskirts of Reading. The south-eastern tip of the county formed part of a vast area of sandy heathland stretching away into Hampshire and Surrey, a wilderness for which man, as yet, had found little use. Defoe condemned it as 'quite sterile, given up to barrenness, horrid and frightful to look on, not only good for little, but good for nothing . . . I was so far in danger of smothering with the clouds of sand, which were raised by the storm, that I could neither keep it out of my mouth, nose or eyes; and when the wind was over, the sand appeared spread over the adjacent fields of the forest some miles distant, so that it ruins the very soil.'

Berkshire's clothing industry was almost extinct. Clothmaking was still fairly prosperous in Wiltshire and survived in a small way in Newbury, where coarse-quality cloths were still made for sacking, sailmaking and the linings of men's coats. In Reading, in the 1690s, Samuel Watlington, a clothier whose handsome house survives in the street named after him, attempted to revive the manufacture of cloth at the Oracle for making gowns for the boys of Reading Blue Coat School, but the experiment was short-lived. In 1716, the Oracle was fitted up anew for the accommodation of the poor, who were kept usefully employed in pinmaking or spinning flax for sailcloth or cotton for candle wicks. The 18th century saw increasing diversity. The most important product of the county was malt. Good quality barley was widely grown, particularly in west Berkshire, where brewing and malting were principal trades in all the towns. A great deal of malting was carried on outside breweries, and malthouses were common in country villages. The total production of malt far exceeded local demand, so that huge quantities were sent by barge to London brewers.

Maltsters paid duty on their produce, which was weighed and checked by a local exciseman before it could be sent to London. Navigation of the Thames was then so dangerous in places that it was not unusual for a barge to founder, losing a valuable cargo. If this happened, the maltster could reclaim the duty paid through the court of Quarter Sessions. In one such case, in 1726, Benjamin and Joseph Tomkins claimed that they had lost 130 quarters of malt when their barge sank in the Thames near Purley, while carrying a load from Abingdon to London. They were granted a refund of three shillings and sixpence for each quarter, totalling £22 15s.

Timber as well as malt was despatched in great quantities from Reading. At Maidenhead, too, the scale of trade along the Thames in malt, meal and timber was what most impressed Defoe.

Wheat was extensively grown in west Berkshire, and large quantities were sold at East Ilsley corn market, then at the height of its success. From there, wheat was taken by cart to Streatley, to continue its journey by barge to London.

In a countryside which looked much busier then than now, mills were important centres of activity. Watermills were working at frequent intervals along the Thames, Kennet, Loddon and Pang, and a few were driven by the Enborne, Emmbrook and Blackwater. Windmills, introduced towards the end of the 12th century, were working on the Downs. The growing demand for food meant that watermills which had served as fulling mills, in the heyday of the clothing industry, had been able to convert to flour milling. Other mills were engaged in quite different activities. Near Bisham, Defoe was interested to see that Temple Mills, otherwise known as the Brass Mills, were turning out kettles and pans of all kinds. 'They have first a foundry, where by the help of lapis caliminaris, they convert copper into brass, and then, having cast the brass into large broad plates, they beat them out by force of great hammers, wrought by the water mills, into what shape they think fit for sale.' Of two other mills nearby, one engaged in pressing oil from rape-seed and flax-seed, and the other in making thimbles, 'excellently well finished', and no doubt much in demand at a time when everything was hand-stitched. Papermaking was a growing industry. There was already a great demand from London printers, and later in the century, from provincial printers. Paper had been made in the 17th century at

Wraysbury and Horton but, tragically, rags collected for its manufacture had brought the plague to Horton during the severe epidemic of 1636–7, causing many deaths. But that disease was now extinct, and papermaking continued at Horton. By the end of the 18th century, papermaking had begun at Burghfield and Thatcham.

Berkshire's landscape was still one of open fields and commons, where farming was carried on according to traditional methods, and changes took place very slowly. But this century saw significant advances in farming practices, and one of the earliest innovators was Jethro Tull, who did most of his work at Prosperous Farm near Shalbourn. Tull was born at Basildon in 1674, into an old-established Berkshire family (acknowledged as gentry by Ashmole), and trained for the law; but ill-health obliged him to live in the country, and he took up farming. He soon began to deplore the wastefulness of the traditional practice of heavy seeding and ordered his men to make channels into which smaller amounts of seed could be sown. But the rustic mind was resistant to any change in customary procedure, and the men refused to obey him. Tull, therefore, set himself to design a mechanical drill to sow seed in rows as he wished, thus inventing the first agricultural machine with internal moving parts. Later, he studied plant growth and soil nutrients; and travels on the continent convinced him of the benefits of intensive hoeing. His later inventions included a horse-hoe, the subject of his famous book, *The New Horse-Houghing Husbandry; or, an essay on the principles of tillage and vegetation*, first published in 1731, and followed by several later editions. Tull died in 1741, and was buried at Basildon.

Although many of Tull's theories proved wrong, his experimental work contributed to a widespread movement to improve farming practices, in order to produce better crops and fatter, healthier animals. One important development was the more general use of crops such as clover and turnips, which had been introduced in the previous century, and which made it possible to keep more farm animals alive through the winter, instead of slaughtering them and salting the meat. As the 18th century advanced, improved farming became a fashionable interest among wealthy landowners, not least King George III. 'Farmer George' experimented with many new ideas on his model farms in Windsor Great Park.

The King, of course, was fortunate in having his own private park in which to farm. Elsewhere, experimentation was difficult as long as the open field system continued, making every farmer dependent on his neighbours. Only when his land was enclosed into smaller, hedged units could he experiment satisfactorily to find the best ways of improving his crops and cattle. A few enclosures had been effected by private agreements between landowners from the 16th century onwards; notably at Waltham St Lawrence, Lambourn, Chaddleworth, Welford, Inkpen and Earley; but these were rare cases, and Berkshire remained largely unenclosed. In the later part of the 18th century, the process accelerated as many more applications for private enclosure acts were passed through Parliament, but, even so, the majority of Berkshire parishes were not enclosed until after the General Enclosure Act of 1801 had simplified the procedure. Enclosures brought about far-reaching changes in the countryside. The ordered pattern of field and hedgerow began to take shape; the area of common land was greatly reduced, depriving the cottager of rights to pasture and firing, but increasing food production by extending the acreage under cultivation; old footpaths disappeared and roads were confined between hedges; many new lengths of road were built.

The 18th century was a period of rapid expansion in trade and commerce, and demanded improvements in means of communication by land and water. By the beginning of the century, London was the centre of world trade. The Bank of England and the Stock Exchange had both been founded in the 1690s, and the introduction of new business methods, such as the use of paper money, facilitated transactions. Even before enclosures became widespread, the landscape had begun to change more rapidly as mankind altered it to serve his own ends. In the interests of speed and safety, roads were widened and straightened, often at the cost of felling fine trees and demolishing buildings; canals were cut across the countryside, to shorten river navigations, or introduce waterways where none existed. The predominant east-west movement of traffic across Berkshire had already begun to influence the development of the county. Increasing trade with America had made Bristol the chief western port; and, consequently, the highway linking it to London was one of the most important in England. The volume of commercial and private traffic passing along it stimulated trade in Maidenhead, Reading, Newbury and Hungerford, and encouraged the growth of intermediate staging places at Slough, Twyford, Theale and Woolhampton. Traffic along this road was swollen further as a result of the rise of Bath as the premier English pleasure and health resort, made fashionable by Stuart monarchs and favoured by society throughout the 18th century.

The legions of innkeepers, inn servants, smiths, wheelwrights and other tradesmen who made a living from travellers were needed because of the slowness of journeys along badly maintained roads, and the numbers of accidents to people, horses and vehicles. No roads, except perhaps those which had been in use since Roman times, had been planned overall or maintained in entirety. Most roads had simply developed through use, and were maintained at a parochial level. Repairs had hardly progressed beyond the medieval practices of clearing drainage ditches and filling ruts and holes with loose stones; work which was undone all the more speedily as traffic increased. Every main highway placed an unfair burden on parish authorities; and, as early as the 1660s, the idea of setting up gates at which to levy tolls on road users had been tried and failed. But, after another half-century, bad roads were the cause of such serious delays and expense to commercial and private concerns that the turnpike system was revived in earnest. Landowners, local businessmen and gentry formed trusts for the purpose of obtaining private acts of Parliament authorising them to raise money for improving a specified length of road, and to set up gates at which charges on a fixed scale were levied on travellers, vehicles and animals. The first trusts were formed to improve the worst sections of road, usually the badly worn approaches to busy towns. Roads entering Reading from the south and west were built over deep clays along river valleys, and were sometimes rendered impassable by mud and floodwater. In 1714, the road from Reading to Theale was adopted by a trust; and so, in 1718, was the road from Reading to Swallowfield, on the way to Basingstoke. The first of these was therefore one of the earliest sections of the Bath and Bristol highway to be turnpiked. Other sections subsequently adopted by trusts were: Maidenhead to Twyford, 1718; Newbury to Hungerford and Marlborough, 1726; Maidenhead to Slough and Cranford, 1727; Theale to Newbury, 1728; Twyford to Reading, 1736. The dates demonstrate how slow and disjointed road improvement was, even along a nationally important highway. The whole route from London to Bristol was not completely turnpiked until the 1750s. In 1784 the Bath Road was acknowledged the finest and smoothest in the country, and was chosen for the trial run of the fast mail coach services.

After 1760, other main roads across Berkshire were turnpiked. In the west, the road from Reading to Streatley and Wallingford was adopted in 1763; the Hungerford to Wantage road in 1772; and the Newbury to Oxford road in 1776. In south-east Berkshire, communications were improved by the Windsor Forest Turnpike Trust, set up in 1759. Before that, the way through the forest was no more than a narrow, ill-defined track. The new, wider road ran from the Old Gallows on the boundary between Reading and Sonning, through Wokingham, New Bracknell and Sunninghill to Virginia Water, and the whole length was marked by milestones and direction posts. Tolls were collected at three gates: Loddon Bridge, Copped Beech (a name recently adopted for a huge motorway roundabout near Binfield), and Blacknest. Charges ranged from one shilling for a coach and six horses, to one penny for a single horse or beast of burden.

Some private acts of Parliament enabled a landowner to provide a better road for the public and, at the same time, improve his estate or enlarge the park around his house. In 1771 such an act concerned the road from Pangbourne to its junction with the main highway near Theale. Originally this was a narrow, twisting lane running to the west of Cranemoor Lake and thence through Englefield village street, close to Englefield House. Paulet Wright, owner of the estate, agreed to give some of his land for the construction of an entirely new road, further from his house and the village, provided that the old road was discontinued and enclosed within his park. The new, straighter road, continued through Tidmarsh, where the only tollgate along it was erected, to the Elephant and Castle in Pangbourne (now the Copper Inn).

From the beginning of the century, ways had been sought to speed water transport and extend the navigation system. Around the coast, shipping carried a thriving trade in coal, timber, building materials and other commodities, making goods available more cheaply in and around seaports. Inland, navigable rivers bestowed similar benefits on certain towns; but there were many other towns, with no navigable river, which were anxious to increase their trade. One such town was Newbury. The Kennet was navigable for barely a mile from its confluence with the Thames, and therefore served only the wharves of Reading. In 1708, a bill to extend the navigation was presented in Parliament, supported by Newbury, Hungerford and towns further west. It was opposed by Reading, which feared a loss of trade in the large area it served as market and distribution centre. The bill was passed in 1715, authorising its promoters to make the Kennet navigable from High Bridge wharf in Reading as far as Newbury. After an unsuccessful start, due to a lack of canal building experience at the time, a new engineer and surveyor, John Hore of Newbury, was appointed and instructed to prepare a new plan. Hore tackled the previously unconsidered problem of reducing the meandering course of the river to a more direct route, and achieved this by making cuts for $11\frac{1}{2}$ miles and following the natural stream for only seven, thus linking the two towns by only $18\frac{1}{2}$ miles of navigation. Twenty locks were required to overcome the rise in ground level from Reading of 134 ft.

Construction could not begin until 1719, but the canal was ready for opening in June 1723. In Newbury it had involved the demolition of all that remained of a small Norman castle, in order to create a canal basin and wharf large enough to deal with ten 100-ton barges at a time.

The remains of a small Norman castle were demolished in order to build the canal basin and wharf at Newbury. Water transport was vital for the movement of heavy and bulky goods in the 18th century and Newbury had no navigable river, making the canal essential if the town was to grow.

Newbury enjoyed the benefits of its enterprise from the start. The canal carried local cornmeal, flour, cheese and other produce to London, and returning barges brought coal, timber, bricks, iron, groceries, wines and spirits. Cheaper coal was particularly welcome. As the population of towns and villages grew, and supplies of wood for fuel dwindled, coal became a prime necessity for domestic heating and cooking. The use of coal, the demand for materials to build more houses, and the consumption of more luxurious foods, were indications of a general rise in provincial living standards.

Water transport remained vital for the movement of heavy and bulky goods until the middle of the 19th century and competition from canals caused river authorities to review and improve their own navigations. In 1751 an Act of Parliament set up a body of Commissioners to survey and regulate the whole of the Thames above Staines. Their initial survey produced abundant evidence of the need for improved locks and weirs to control the flow of water, and to put an end to the age-old conflict between boatmen and millers. In 1770 Parliament empowered the Thames Commissioners to purchase and discontinue all flash locks, and to acquire land to create a continuous towpath. All the old locks were to be replaced by safer and more efficient pound locks, built along a new navigation channel, bypassing mill weirs and enabling

Boats and barges on the Thames at Windsor bridge, from a print published in 1793. Competition from the new canals encouraged river authorities to improve their own navigation.

boats to pass more speedily and with less waste of water. By 1773, eight new locks had been built between Maidenhead and Reading: Boulter's, Marlow, Temple, Hurley, Hambleden, Marsh, Shiplake and Sonning. Mapledurham lock followed in 1777, Caversham in 1778, Whitchurch and Goring in 1787. The locks, said to have been designed by Humphrey Gainsborough, brother of the painter, were built of timber, with sides containing only spaced piles to prevent barges grounding on the river bank. In the course of time they were all replaced by the solid masonry pound locks familiar today. The new locks necessitated the employment of lock keepers, for whose accommodation wooden huts were at first provided, but the keepers were so unwilling to live in them that, in 1796, the Commissioners decided to replace the huts with proper houses, and compel the keepers to occupy them.

These improvements to the Thames navigation were carried out all the more speedily because the Commissioners anticipated a large increase of traffic after the opening of the Thames and Severn canal in 1789, and the Oxford canal in 1790, bringing trade from the Midlands and the potteries.

In the event, Berkshire's other major waterway, the Kennet and Avon, linked the West Country with the Thames by a far more direct route than the Thames and Severn canal, and soon rendered the latter of small importance. A link between the Avon and the Thames had been an unfulfilled dream since trade with the New World had increased the importance of Bristol and other West Country ports. By the 1780s the Avon and Thames navigations had both been improved, and the techniques of canal building were sufficiently far advanced to bring the dream within the realms of possibility. The people of Hungerford had long wished for an extension of the Kennet navigation from Newbury through their town and westwards as far as was practicable, but at a meeting held there in 1788, of interested people from a surrounding wide area, and chaired by Charles Dundas of Barton Court, Kintbury, it was decided that nothing less than a canal from the Kennet to the Avon would be of material benefit to the town or to the country at large.

A bill was got through Parliament in April 1794, and work commenced later that year at Newbury and at Bradford-on-Avon. The Berkshire section was opened to Kintbury in 1797, and to Hungerford in 1798. One of the first beneficiaries was Mr Pearce of Chilton Lodge, for whom a very handsome staircase of Portland stone, brought round by sea and river, was delivered to Hungerford wharf. After the completion of the canal in 1810, stone from the West Country began to be used in Berkshire canalside towns and villages. The inland waterways enriched the county with many other products from the Midlands and the West Country, as well as from London.

Improved communications brought new vigour to old towns. The inauguration of the fast mail-coach service between Bristol and London in 1784 introduced, through its objectives of speed and strict time-keeping, a note of urgency and a quickening of daily life never achieved, nor aspired to, by stage-coaches or postboys. With easier travelling, more people visited towns, and civic authorities were stirred into improving amenities. Reading, Newbury and Hungerford all built new or enlarged town halls in the 18th century, providing more space for administrative functions as well as assembly rooms for social events. Towns were still primarily marketing centres and because their principal industries of brewing, malting and milling were dependent on agricultural produce, traditional links with the countryside were maintained. But the offices of newer trades, such as printing and bookselling, and of people providing professional services were multiplying, increasing the need for country dwellers to make use of towns. Lawyers, land-agents, surveyors and architects made livings out of the property and business concerns of the upper and middle classes. The first three banks in Berkshire were started in the 1780s at Windsor, Newbury and Reading.

Reading was already twice the size of Newbury, as it was also of Abingdon, the town with which it then disputed the honours of county town. The populations of these three at the first census in 1801 were recorded as 9,742, 4,275 and 4,356. Reading's growth in the previous 100 years showed in the great extent of its wharves, and in the ribbons of new houses along the main highways leading into the town. But it remained separated from the Thames by an expanse of meadowland so subject to flooding that the road linking the town with Caversham bridge was justly known as Watery Lane. The river Kennet, upon which it had been founded, was still vital to its livelihood, and trade along it reached its peak after the completion of the Kennet and Avon canal. Wharves, tanneries, timberyards, boatyards and breweries occupied its banks to the east and west of High Bridge. The Kennet drove the town mills near St Giles, and its tributary, the Holy Brook, still drove the former Abbey mill. Kennet valley clays supplied several brick and tile works in Katesgrove and Tilehurst. Five breweries were active at the end of the century, the largest being Stephen's in Mill Lane, producing 25,000

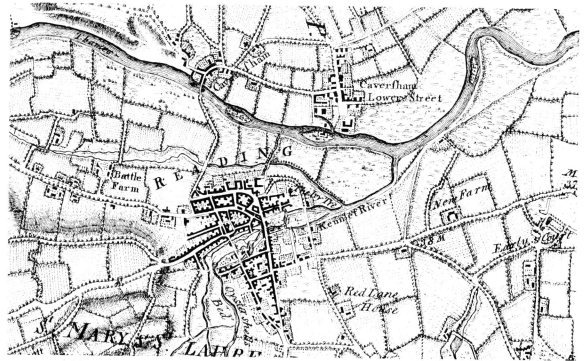

A Map of Reading, taken from John Rocque's *Survey of Berkshire*, published in 1761.

Simonds' Brewery was founded in the 18th century and became the largest in Reading. This view of the Bridge Street premises was taken in the 1920s.

barrels of beer and porter annually; but Simonds', founded in the 1760s, was set fair to overtake it. In 1790 William Blackall Simonds moved to a new site beside the canal at Seven Bridges, which gave him the space and distributive facilities he needed to expand. A leading architect, Sir John Soane, was commissioned to design the brewhouse and family residence on the site. An iron foundry was started in Katesgrove by Benjamin Williams in 1790, in anticipation of the growth of demand for iron in agricultural and industrial machinery. Reading's earliest bank was opened in 1788 by Marsh, Deane & Co. in Friar Street, followed by a competitor, opened in 1791, in Market Place by Micklem, Stephens, Simonds and Harris.

Newbury exhibited many proofs of its long history as a manufacturing and marketing centre. The 17th century Cloth Hall and Guild Hall, the fine parish church, the unusually generous provision of almshouses, and the grammar school dating back to the 15th century, all bore witness to its past prosperity. Great efforts were made to keep alive its historic connection with the clothing trade, culminating in the celebrated wager of 1811 which resulted in the Newbury Coat. But trade in corn and malt was now the principal source of wealth. Its corn market was one of the largest in the south of England and the reason for the large grain stores beside the wharf. Two corn mills produced quantities of meal which, as well as malt, was sent by barge to London. The Kennet navigation was capable of carrying barges of 110 tons burden, and so impressive was the scene at the canal basin when filled with barges loading and unloading that William Mavor remarked upon the 'maritime appearance' of the place, to which another important local industry, barge building, no doubt contributed. The renewed buoyancy of trade encouraged a linen draper and a timber merchant to open the town's first bank, Vincent & Co's, in 1782. Surrounded as they were by rich farmlands, the townspeople lived well.

At the beginning of the 18th century, Hungerford town was separated from the Bath Road by the river Dun, crossed only by a ford, but in 1740 land was purchased from the Bear Inn to allow a new street and bridge to be built. The Bath Road through Charnham Street was improved as a result of the Newbury to Marlborough turnpike act of 1744, but the road to Salisbury remained a narrow track, winding through Sanham Green until the 1770s, when it was widened and its course changed to a more direct route. Like Newbury, Hungerford was a place of many inns enjoying the trade brought by the Bath Road, but it was not until the end of the century that it could benefit from waterborne trade along the Kennet. Its weekly market, mainly in corn, was successful, and some malting and tanning were carried on, but there was no large industry.

At Maidenhead there had been a decline in timber traffic since the great 'warfage of timbre' observed by Leland in the 1540s. Forest oaks were not so plentiful as they had been. By the end of the 18th century, Maidenhead was primarily a thoroughfare town, depending on the trade of its inns and other services to travellers. William Mavor's description of it as 'a town nearly a mile long' suggests that it had found no cause to grow in other directions. Its bridge was one of the busiest across the Thames and provided the town with a useful income until the early 18th century, when takings became barely sufficient to cover the increasing costs of maintenance. There was considerable local resentment when Queen Anne built a free bridge at Datchet, thus reducing further the income at Maidenhead. A petition to the Crown in 1732 brought a generous grant of 20 oaks for the repair of Maidenhead bridge, but the days of timber bridges on busy highways were numbered. The wear and tear caused by traffic passing over it was aggravated by the damage inflicted by barges passing underneath, and in 1750 the old bridge was repaired for the last time. Between 1772 and 1777 a handsome stone bridge, designed by Robert Taylor, was constructed at the cost of nearly £19,000. Tolls continued to be charged for using it until 1903. Shortly before its opening was celebrated in August 1777, another civic ceremony had seen the laying of the foundation stone of a new town hall in the High Street.

Wokingham differed from other Berkshire towns in that it lacked the advantages of communication by river or canal, but in its own forest area it was the centre of commercial and social life. A guidebook of 1748 described it as 'a pretty large and well-frequented market-town. It has three Fairs, and contains several streets, a Free School, an Hospital and a Market-House.' Whatever 'pretty large' meant, the census of 1801 showed it with less than a quarter of the population of Reading. Its several streets included Rose and Peach Streets, and Down (later Denmark) Street, converging on the Market Place, where stood the ancient Market House or Town Hall, built c 1585 soon after Wokingham gained borough status. At Shute End two annual horse fairs and a June hay fair were held until 1711, when the council decided to move the horse fairs to Rose Street. The manufacture of silk stockings and cloth, important since the mid-17th century, was dying out by the end of the 18th century. The Lucas Hospital at Luckley Green was founded in 1663 by Henry Lucas to provide almshouses for 16 old men, 'inhabitants of the forest of Windsor', and consisted of a fine two-storey brick building with wings containing a chapel and master's house. A school for poor boys was started in the 17th century and well-supported by later endowments. Poor girls were not neglected. In 1713, Martha Palmer founded a free school for twelve girls, where a school mistress, for £5 per annum, taught them to read, sew, knit and spin until the age of twelve. The number of pupils was increased in 1795.

The market at this time was chiefly noted for fatted fowls, by which many poor people gained a living. The unfortunate fowls were confined in the dark and forcibly fed with barley meal, suet and treacle for a fortnight, after which they were either sold or they died from the effects of the treatment. Three silk manufacturers were still in business, making hatbands, ribbons, watch-strings, shoe-strings, sarsenets and figured gauzes for ladies' dresses. These firms provided employment for 100 people of all ages, men earning up to 30 shillings a week and women 8–10 shillings. The brewery of James Webb was also flourishing.

13

SOCIAL LIFE IN THE EIGHTEENTH CENTURY

The progress of trade, commerce and transport brought wealth and a higher standard of living to more people. Money, better roads and more comfortable carriages made travel easier, while intellectual and social life were stimulated by the spread of education through endowed schools, private academies and home tutoring, and by the growing volume of reading matter put out by the printing presses. Books, pamphlets, newspapers and engraved prints were a primary source of information and amusement, holding a monopoly in a world in which the media did not exist in any other form.

The success of newspapers in London encouraged printers, who were then also publishers, to start newspapers in leading provincial towns. Publication of the *Reading Mercury* began in 1723, when two printers, William Parkes and David Kinnier, set up in business in High Street, where they proclaimed, 'all manner of Printing Business is handsomely done, as Books, Advertisements, Summons, Subpoenas, Funeral-Tickets, &c. Shop-keepers Bills are done here after the best manner, with the Prints of their Signs, or other proper Ornaments. Also Gentlemen may have their Coats of Arms, or other Fancies curiously cut in Wood, or engrav'd in Mettal.' For many years the *Mercury*, whose original subtitle was *Weekly Entertainer*, contained only four pages of closely packed London and foreign intelligence, with a few items of local news and a great many advertisements. Often, it was the advertisements giving information about local events, race-meetings, assemblies, concerts and theatres, which were the most valuable part of the paper. The *Mercury's* circulation depended heavily on subscribers, and was distributed by newsmen on foot or horseback, each covering many miles in circuits around villages, hamlets and large country houses. In remote areas, its arrival was a welcome link with the outside world.

Books of all kinds – travel, philosophy, science, agriculture, poetry and novels – were read avidly. Anyone who could afford to do so collected books for a private library, which formed an essential room in

The house at Binfield where Alexander Pope lived with his parents from c1698 to 1716. Pope's presence attracted London coffee house society into Berkshire.

every gentleman's house. In the second half of the century, circulating libraries made reading even more popular.

The mid-18th century saw the publication of the first children's books. The publisher was John Newbery, who was born at Waltham St Lawrence in 1713, and in the 1740s became a partner in the firm then publishing the *Reading Mercury*. Newbery did not stay long in Reading. He was ambitious and keen to set up as a book publisher in London. From his shop at the sign of The Bible and Sun, in St Paul's Churchyard, he published many small volumes written and illustrated especially for children, thus opening up a huge market by making reading more attractive to the young. Newbery was a man of restless energy. His friend, Oliver Goldsmith, whose novel, *The Vicar of Wakefield*, was first published by Newbery, described him as, 'a red-faced, good-natured little man who was always in a hurry. He had no sooner alighted, than he was in haste to be gone, for he was ever on business of the utmost importance.' John Newbury died in 1767, and was buried at Waltham St Lawrence.

Increased readership made it possible for authors to make a living by writing. Among those who made quite a good living was Alexander

Pope, who spent most of his youth at Binfield in Berkshire, and became the most famous and influential poet of the century.

John Gay, the future writer of *The Beggar's Opera*, was one of Pope's earliest friends and was often visiting at Binfield. Pope's residence there attracted London coffee house society into Berkshire. According to tradition, on one occasion when Pope, Gay and other companions were detained by bad weather at the Rose Inn in Wokingham, they whiled away the time by writing a ballad to the landlord's daughter, *Molly Mogg, or the Fair Maid of the Rose Inn*.

Another member of Pope's circle was Henry St John later Viscount Bolingbroke, who married Frances Winchcombe, a descendant of Jack of Newbury and heiress to the Bucklebury estate.

The Bucklebury parish register recorded in 1718, 'The Right Honble. Frances Viscountess Bolingbroke was buried in linnen, October 28th'. Her husband made himself very unpopular in the village by ordering all the trees in the grove around Bucklebury House to be cut down.

The Georges remained on the throne for the rest of the century, a period in which commerce and the arts flourished and fashionable society was able to indulge its tastes for travel, pleasure and amusements. Outside the London season, the most popular destinations for society on the move were the health and pleasure resorts at watering places. The success of Bath and Tunbridge Wells had given rise to dozens of spas, some quite small but usually providing a comfortable inn or two as well as other attractions. Belief in the curative properties of health-giving springs for a variety of complaints had replaced the medieval pilgrim's blind faith in the power of holy wells. The water was seldom pleasant to drink; indeed, Defoe described that at one northern spa as 'fetid and nauseous to the smell, so that those who drink it are obliged to hold their noses'; but however horrible the medicine, it was helped down by liberal doses of delight in the form of balls, concerts, card parties, theatrical performances and other entertainments. Berkshire, too, had a spa at Sunninghill Wells. The spring here began to be exploited in the 1680s, and its success was boosted in the early years of the 18th century, when racing began nearby at Ascot. Sadly, neither Defoe nor Celia Fiennes sampled the water here, but modern investigations on the site revealed that it was yellow in colour and tasted of iron and sulphur. Sunninghill Wells was a flourishing resort by the middle of the century, and was reputed to be more select than some other places, so that many people of great rank and fortune visited it. Kingswick, and other large houses in the neighbourhood accommodated a constant flow of guests. In 1765, a lady who confessed herself a martyr to gout and rheumatism declared her firm belief in the efficacy of the Sunninghill waters; while in 1766, Horace Walpole wrote to a friend staying there, 'Pray, madam, continue your waters and, if possible, wash away that original sin, the gout.' By the 1780s its reputation had slipped and it had become more raffish. Public breakfasts, with music, were held every Monday, and balls two nights a week, while occasional concerts were given by military bands from Windsor. Military reviews and exercises on Ascot Heath attracted undesirable crowds.

Eighteenth-century people were as preoccupied with horses as 20th century people are with cars. The rich spent large sums to obtain the fastest, strongest and best-looking animals, and a great deal of money went into horse-breeding. This interest fostered the sport of racing and new race-meetings were started. Races had been held at Datchet for the amusement of Charles II, and were resumed for Queen Anne and her consort, Prince George of Denmark, who were both 'mightily given to racing'. The Queen was herself a keen horsewoman. Horse-racing began on Ascot Common in August 1711, encouraged by the Queen with the prize of a plate worth 100 guineas. Races were held at Ascot each year until the Queen's death in 1714, after which meetings were only held occasionally until the 1740s. In the reign of George II the course was moved to its present site on Ascot Heath, and this was assigned to the Crown on condition that it was 'kept and continued as a race-course for the public use'.

Racing soon acquired a bad reputation because it encouraged excessive gambling, and in 1740 an act was passed to control the number of race-meetings and to establish standards for horses and events. In 1744 regular meetings were resumed at Ascot due to the influence of the Duke of Cumberland. As Ranger of Windsor Great Park, the Duke occupied Cumberland and Cranbourn Lodges, and also leased training stables at Kates Gore, near East Ilsley.

Race-meetings were held at several other places in Berkshire. By the 1780s three-day meetings were held at Maidenhead, on a course adjoining the Thicket, and on Bulmershe Heath, on the eastern side of Reading. In west Berkshire, meetings were held at Lambourn by the 1750s. In this area the Earl of Craven was a notable patron of the sport, both as owner and steward of courses at Lambourn and Wantage. Near Newbury, racing took place on Wash Common until a new course was started on Enborne Heath in 1805, again under the patronage of the Earl of Craven.

Race-meetings, theatre and assemblies all contributed to the social life of towns, and attracted the custom of local gentry. The theatre became immensely popular in the 18th century but, although the first provincial theatre had been opened in Bath as early as 1705, elsewhere, for much of the century plays continued to be performed by troupes of travelling players in barns or rooms in some of the larger inns. In the eyes of the law, strolling players were rogues and vagabonds, and there was considerable resistance to them in many towns on grounds of morality. Performances, therefore, tended to take place on the outskirts. In 1786, Mrs White, who had already had some little success with a similar venture at Maidenhead, opened a theatre at the Marquis of Granby inn along the London Road to the east of Reading. Advertising in the *Reading Mercury* she promised that the theatre was fitted up in a 'warm and commodious style', and equipped with new dresses and scenery. The theatre enjoyed no little success for about a month but then thieves broke in and stole most of the costumes, including 'a stone-coloured three-caped silk coat, a brown cloth coat edged with gold lace, a striped green coat edged with silver, a pair of black satin breeches, a brown silk gown, and three pairs of silk stockings'. The theatre was closed and did not reopen.

Mrs White's misfortune only served to encourage Henry Thornton, an enterprising theatre manager who built up a large circuit of theatres in the south of England. By 1787 he had already started theatres in converted buildings in Newbury and Henley, and planned to open one in Reading. In 1787 after a season at Henley, he placed a notice in the *Mercury* designed to convince the public of the good character of his company. 'It is not unworthy [of] remark that the Company of Comedians who lately quitted this place has left the most respectable character; their very genteel appearance, behaviour and conduct during their stay gained them the patronage and countenance of the first families of distinction in the neighbourhood, who severally bespoke an evening's performance which never failed to bring a most crowded and splendid audience.' A year later he opened the first theatre in Reading; only a small building between two houses at the west end of Friar Street, but nonetheless a foothold in the town centre. His company opened there in May 1788 with a performance of *The School for Scandal*, a play then only eleven years old.

Thornton's first theatre in Newbury was in Northcroft Lane, but in 1802 he opened a superior, purpose-built theatre in Speenhamland. This was an imposing building with a classical portico of four columns and a pediment containing the royal arms. Although measuring only 75 ft by 35 ft, it contained a pit, gallery and boxes, and was well fitted up, the boxes being lined with crimson velvet. The delicately moulded ceiling survived to be admired long after the building ceased to be used as a theatre.

It was 1791 before Thornton was established in Windsor, where plays

Henry Thornton's purpose-built theatre at Speenhamland in 1802, from a print published in 1803. Thornton had enormous success with his theatres in Berkshire, attracting Royal patronage.

had been performed for many years in a barn at the bottom of Peascod Street, grandly known as the Theatre Royal. Thornton's success in other towns, and his growing reputation, were rewarded by his appointment as manager, and by 1793 he had moved his company into a new theatre in a better situation in the High Street. George III, Queen Charlotte and their family were regular patrons, and one side of the lower tier of boxes was reserved for them. The King and Queen were provided with comfortable armchairs and presented with playbills specially printed on silk.

These theatres were open only for a few short seasons each year, one of them coinciding with the local race-meeting, when the nobility and gentry were likely to visit the town. Local authorities, the churches, and people concerned with public morality remained hostile, and in Windsor Thornton had to cope with the opposition of Eton College, which feared that the theatre might corrupt its pupils. The Windsor theatre was allowed to open during the college vacations, but only by special permission of the Windsor magistrates and the college Provost could it open during Ascot races.

Hungerford Town Hall, built in 1786 to replace a 17th century predecessor. Berkshire's towns were beginning to assume some civic dignity during the 18th century.

Enthusiasm for plays extended to private theatricals. At Wargrave, the eccentric and extravagant Lord Barrymore, who was a keen amateur actor, put on plays in a barn near his house which, in 1792, he rebuilt as a private theatre large enough to seat 700, and lavishly equipped with dressing rooms, scenery and costumes. Here his lordship entertained his friends, who included the Prince of Wales and most of the county's nobility and gentry. Until his bankruptcy and death in 1793, while still in his twenties, Barrymore was an energetic organiser of social events, not only producing plays but arranging masked balls and stewarding race-meetings. His grand masked ball at Wargrave in January 1790 was attended by over 400 guests in fancy dress, including Mr and Mrs James Leigh-Perrot, Jane Austen's uncle and aunt, who lived at Scarlets in Hare Hatch. Among the crowds of guests appearing as gipsies, witches, shepherdesses, fairy queens, and eastern princes, these two were more

126

soberly dressed, Mr Leigh-Perrot as 'a counsellor' and Jane's redoubtable aunt as 'a strikingly elegant Pilgrim, in an Irish stuff gown bound with ermine, and a rich diamond cross in her high crowned hat'.

Towards the end of the century towns began to be a little cleaner and smarter. Streets in the centre were paved and lighted, houses and inns given new fronts of brick, stucco or stone, often concealing an old timber-framed building behind a symmetrical Georgian facade. Along main thoroughfares leading out of towns more houses were built, all in the neat, formal style so well suited to street architecture, lending the town an air of dignity and importance. All the principal inns were popular venues for social and convivial occasions, but the official centre of social life was the assembly room at the town hall. In nearly every town a new or enlarged hall and assembly room was built, where regular balls, concerts and card parties took place.

Reading began to shed some of its more deplorable buildings. In 1760 the accession of George III was marked by the demolition of a row of tenements dividing the lower end of Broad Street into two narrow lanes, and allowing King Street to be laid out. In 1785 the corporation obtained an act of Parliament empowering it to levy a rate for the purpose of paving the footways and providing for better cleaning, lighting and watching in the streets. As a result, the town centre was cleared of numerous obstructions, such as projecting buildings, posts and rails, while ruts and potholes in the roadway were mended. In 1785–6 a new town hall was built, containing a council chamber and an elegant assembly room for balls and concerts.

In Newbury, a new market house with assembly rooms on the upper floor was built in 1742. The streets were later paved and lighted by voluntary subscription.

Windsor was the next most populous town but without a strong commercial base its fortunes rose and fell according to the favour of the royal court. The Stuarts had spent much time there, and to their reigns belonged the fine town houses and guildhall which had so impressed Celia Fiennes at the beginning of the century. But neither George I or II cared for the place, so that trade stagnated and the castle was largely disused, although open to curious visitors. Eton College also drew visitors. Vitality returned to Windsor after the accession of George III. Both he and Queen Charlotte liked the town and came to live there with their 15 children and numerous attendants; at first in a house on Castle Hill, then, from 1778, in the castle.

The seats and mansions of the nobility and gentry were prominent features in the landscape. Wealth was invested in country estates and fine houses were prized possessions. Berkshire was not a county in which great noblemen held vast estates or built enormous houses. Lord Craven's estates in west Berkshire were the largest and his house at Benham one of the finest. More typical were estates of moderate extent and houses of unpretentious size, combining elegance with comfort.

Owners of many old-fashioned houses updated them. At Ufton Court, for instance, the garden side was very much enlarged by a brick extension in a style directly contrasting with the timber and plaster of the Tudor front. By the end of the century, Berkshire contained examples of every architectural fashion of the age, ranging from the plain early Georgian of Hall Place to the more elaborate design of Calcot Park, the grand classical manner of Basildon Park, and the fanciful Gothick of Donnington Grove or Sandleford Priory. Berkshire's pleasant wooded scenery made it attractive to wealthy people in search of a country residence not too far from London. Situations on rising ground or overlooking the Thames were particularly sought after, and became more feasible when ways had been found of controlling water supplies. Sites such as those of Park Place, Basildon House or Padworth House, enabled an owner to survey his rolling acres with pride, as well as effectively displaying the building.

The term 'park' had taken on a new meaning, and now indicated a fine house in a landscaped setting. Originally it had meant a tract of land fenced in for the protection of beasts of the chase. Berkshire had contained about 50 such parks, mostly in Windsor Forest and the wooded areas of the Kennet and Thames valleys. The Home and Great Parks of Windsor, as well as Sunninghill, Foliejon, Easthampstead and Ditton parks were all of medieval origin; and so, too, was Whitley Park, once a perquisite of the abbots of Reading. Parks had become civilised, their former wildness tamed by the imposition of artificial landscapes. By the 18th century, not every park was stocked with deer, although all were well stocked with valuable timber. Early in the century, art had directed that trees should grow in formal avenues leading to the house, as at Hall Place and Billingbear, but later, a more natural arrangement became fashionable under the influence of the great landscape gardeners. Benham Park was laid out for Lord Craven by Capability Brown in 1772–5.

Country house society mingled old-established families, such as the Perkins of Ufton Court or the Blagraves, who owned Calcot Park and much of Reading besides, with the newly-rich, such as William East, the wealthy city merchant who built Hall Place, or William Silver, the Westminster tallow-chandler who purchased Bear Place, Wargrave, in 1758. Nabobs who had made fortunes in the East India Company brought back with them an unsavoury reputation as looters and oppres-

Benham Park, the elegant house and grounds designed by Capability Brown, 1772–5. Benham, owned by Lord Craven, was one of the finest houses in 18th century Berkshire.

sors of the Indian people; and behaved besides in an over-ostentatious and ungenteel manner. Francis Sykes, the builder of Basildon Park, had to live down the nickname of 'Squire Matoot', derived from an Indian tax he had administered in Bengal. Yet he went on to a respectable 30-year career as a Member of Parliament, being created a baronet in 1781. He was a close friend of Warren Hastings, who lived a few miles away at Purley Hall whilst awaiting his trial. Major Charles Marsack, of the Bengal Army, bought Caversham Park from Lord Cadogan in 1783, and made himself the talk of Reading by his Indian style of living, his foreign servants and the drastic changes he made to the house and grounds. John Walsh at Warfield Park lived there scandalously with a succession of mistresses.

Other nabobs who settled in Berkshire were George Vansittart who bought Bisham Abbey from the Hobys in 1780; Stanlake Batson who purchased Winkfield Place, and William Watts who built South Hill Park, Easthampstead in 1760. Watts was an oriental linguist and was sent by the East India Company as envoy to Siraj-ud-daula, Nawab of Bengal. John Holwell, a surgeon and magistrate with the Company, was one of the few survivors of the Black Hole of Calcutta. He returned to England and lived for a while at Chilton Lodge, near Hungerford. Edward Golding invested his fortune in landed property in Berkshire, and spent lavishly on his estate at Maiden Erleigh.

Whatever demands the management of their estates might make on them, country landowners had public duties and obligations towards their neighbours and tenants. Those who were appointed Justices of the Peace were responsible for local government in rural areas until county and district councils were created in the late 19th century. In their own parishes they wielded considerable administrative and judicial powers. They supervised the Overseers of the Poor and the parish constables, as well as dealing with local problems and minor offenders. More serious matters were dealt with at the Court of Quarter Sessions, where all the magistrates of the county met together. At these gatherings, they discussed national as well as local politics, and deliberated on such questions as the selection of Parliamentary candidates for the county.

Principal links between the gentry and the villagers were the farmers, who employed most of the labour, and the parish overseers. The latter had been appointed by magistrates since the Poor Law Act of 1601, and were empowered to levy a rate from property owners to relieve the sick and aged, and help find work for the able-bodied unemployed.

By the 1790s the condition of the poor, and their increasing numbers, had become a cause of national concern and the subject of more than one official enquiry. The wealth enjoyed by the upper and middle classes had not spread downwards to the lowest level of society, that of agricultural labourers. Their working conditions were hard, their home lives wretched. Charity might be fairly generous in prosperous times, but when times were hard – as in the Napoleonic wars, when prices rose steeply – charity was less plentiful, and more people were dependent on the parish.

David Davies, rector of Barkham 1782–1819, collected material for his study of poor families in his parish over a number of years, and his findings were published in 1795 in *The Case of the Labourers in Husbandry*, addressed to the newly formed Board of Agriculture. 'The bulk of every nation', he wrote, 'consists of such as must earn their daily bread by daily labour. It is to the patient industry of these that the higher ranks are everywhere indebted for most of their enjoyments . . . . But of all the denominations of people in a state, the labourers in husbandry are by far the most valuable. For these are the men who, by being constantly employed in the cultivation of the earth, provide the staff of life for the whole nation.' Yet, he argued, far from enjoying their just deserts, they suffered continual hardships, very little relieved by the poor rate. In his parish he found labouring families indifferently fed and badly clothed, children without shoes and stockings, and very few sent to school. Most of them were in debt to small shopkeepers, not through sloth or wastefulness but because of the high price of necessities. He quoted case studies of individual families.

A labouring man in his parish might earn seven shillings (35p) a week, and his wife another sixpence (2$\frac{1}{2}$p) at bean setting, haymaking or harvest time. His older children might also earn a few pence: a boy of 16 could get two shillings and sixpence (12$\frac{1}{2}$p) a week. This meagre income was spent mainly on food. Flour for making bread, which formed the bulk of the family diet, might cost six shillings and threepence (31p) a week; tea one shilling (5p); and other items such as yeast, bacon, sugar, butter or lard, soap, candles, and thread for mending clothes, a few pence each. Other expenses included rent for the cottage, about £2 a year, and clothing. Fuel was usually turf from the common. A man could increase his wages during certain months of the year by piece-work at reaping, threshing, turnip hoeing, hedging and ditching or coppice work. He got no wages if he was ill or laid up with rheumatism, as often happened when he had been out working in wet weather. Some wives tried to better their lot by taking in washing or sewing, or keeping poultry. Some families kept a pig, but very few could afford a cow, and if they could, they had nowhere to pasture it. 'The commons were so covered with rich farmers' herds and flocks that the poor man's cow would soon starve there.'

The poor rate undoubtedly saved many people from starvation and destitution, but it was a wretched substitute for wages. A man with a wife and six children under the age of 16 could receive five shillings (25p) a week from the poor rate, but many deserving families preferred to suffer privation rather than incur the ill-will of their superiors by applying for poor relief. Davies suggested ways of keeping the poor independent of the poor rate but, in 1795 a new system was introduced which, unintentionally, made them more dependent on it.

In May 1795, Berkshire magistrates met at the Pelican Inn, Speenhamland, to consider the worsening plight of the poor, and it was agreed that some further assistance should be given. It was not thought appropriate for them to regulate labourers' wages, but farmers were earnestly recommended to increase pay in proportion to the price of food. Along the same lines, the magistrates proposed that future allowances for poor relief should be calculated in relation to the price of a gallon loaf of bread (weighing 8lbs 11ozs) and the number of children in the family. For every penny by which the price of the loaf rose above one shilling, the poor rate allowance should rise by three pence, plus a penny for each child. These benefits were only to be given to the industrious poor who endeavoured as far as they could to support themselves. The Speenhamland system was widely adopted in southern England and became as widely unpopular. In practice, it encouraged farmers to underpay in the knowledge that their labourers would receive additional benefit from the parish. The numbers of poor people applying for relief increased, and their morale was lowered. Year by year the cost of poor relief placed a heavier burden on the parish, and was the cause of bitterness and resentment among property owners who had to contribute to it.

14

MEN VERSUS MACHINES

The great technical advances achieved by the industrial revolution in the north of England spread slowly to the south. A county such as Berkshire, without resources of coal or iron, could play no part in the development of the new technology and had to wait for the introduction of iron working, steam power and mechanisation by its more progressive manufacturers and farmers.

The new method of producing iron in large quantities made this the leading material of the 19th century, and iron came to be used extensively in place of wood or stone. Iron working was made profitable in this area by the easy transport of pig iron along the inland waterways. Benjamin Williams' foundry, established in Reading in 1790, probably owed its supplies to the newly opened canal from Oxford and the Midlands. After the completion of the Kennet and Avon canal in 1810, supplies were also brought from South Wales; and within a decade or so, small foundries were working along or near the canal at Hungerford, Kintbury, Newbury (where there were at least five by the 1830s), Bucklebury and Reading. Soon after 1810 Thomas and Joseph Perry started a foundry in Katesgrove, Reading, which flourished from the 1830s under the partnership of Barrett, Exall and Andrewes, and was renamed Reading Ironworks in 1864. To begin with, this firm specialised in ploughs at a time when farmers were abandoning their old-fashioned wooden ploughs in favour of lighter metal ones designed to cope with a variety of soil and working conditions. Later, they made threshing machines and steam engines. Their business expanded hugely after 1838 through the production of iron work for the construction of the Great Western Railway; and from the 1840s through the manufacture of machinery and ovens for Huntley and Palmer's biscuit factory.

In Newbury, William Plenty, who had started in 1790 as a millwright and agricultural engineer, began experimenting in iron and invented an improved plough in 1800 and a lifeboat in 1816, both of which were very successful. The lifeboat, named *The Experiment*, was launched on the canal at West Mills and sailed down the Thames to London. The design was approved and subsequently adopted for lifeboat services around the coast. The growing number of uses for iron was demonstrated by the variety of Plenty's output: pumps, gates, fences, feeding troughs, water carts and parts for lock gates and sluices were just a few of their products. At Bucklebury, although three miles from the nearest wharf, the family firm of Hedges the blacksmiths, who had been shoeing horses and mending farm implements since the early 18th century, started a foundry about 1820 and produced a vast amount of decorative as well as useful ironwork, such as railings, gates, garden troughs, gearwheels and graveyard memorials.

Steam power provided a means of enormously increasing production and, potentially, of making basic industries such as flour milling independent of water power, a development which took place later in the century. But its introduction required considerable capital outlay and, for this reason, it was first adopted by the wealthiest of local industries – brewing. In Berkshire, the Windsor Brewery led the way with the installation in 1797 of a four horse-power Boulton and Watt engine, and soon succeeded in trebling its output to around 30,000 barrels a year. In Reading, in 1799, William Blackall Simonds purchased a two horse-power engine for his Seven Bridges Brewery, where it replaced a horse-driven wheel for pumping and grinding malt and provided steam for heating coppers and cleaning barrels. Simonds paid £224 for his Boulton and Watt engine, plus 10 guineas for installation. He was not yet the largest brewer in Reading but he was determined to be the most advanced.

In other applications steam made slower progress. A nine days' wonder was the steam barge which travelled along the waterways from Bath to London in 1813, covering an average eight miles an hour and consuming two bushels of coal a day. In London it was not a welcome sight for the capital's numerous boatmen, and the Lord Mayor declared that such vessels would put a great many watermen out of work. In 1829 a carriage drawn by a steam tractor made a trial journey from London along the Bath Road, but met with a very hostile reception at Melksham, where a crowd of labourers, shouting 'Down with machinery', stoned the vehicle and its driver, putting them temporarily out of action.

In agriculture, steam-driven machines were not widely introduced until the late 1840s. The early threshing machines, which caused so much resentment, and provoked such violent reactions from labourers, were powered by horses. The agricultural writer, William Mavor, reported in 1809 that, 'within the last two or three years, a considerable number of threshing machines, on different principles and of different powers, have been erected in Berkshire'. They were powered by two, four or even six horses but, as Mavor remarked, the work was very bad for the horses, which were made to trot round in a circle, pulling a bar which rotated the gears, for several hours a day. Each machine required the attendance of a varying number of men, women or children. At Sulhamstead, a machine turned by four horses employed two men and six women or boys: 'the work is performed very perfectly and even the labourers seemed pleased'. At Chieveley, Mr Rogers had a large machine worked by six horses, but it was not satisfactory. At Thatcham, Mr Tull of Chamberhouse had a hand machine turned by four women which employed ten persons in all, although only one man was needed: 'It was not much saving'. Mavor urged the advantages of machines for threshing. 'The flail is an instrument only fit for the savage state; a person using it constantly is sooner exhausted by ten years than one following any other branch of agriculture.'

> 150 Guineas Reward. Whitehall, September 3, 1811. Whereas it has been humbly represented to his Royal Highness the Prince Regent, that Two Anonymous Threatening Letters have been received by Mr. William Shackel, of Early Court, and Mr. James Fuller, of Loddon Bridge, near Reading, in the County of Berks, of which the following are copies, viz., "Blood and vengeance against your Life and your Property for taking away our Labour with your threshing machine; Seven of us near your dwelling House have agreed that if you do not refrain from your threshing Machine We will thresh your Ricks with fire, and Bathe your Body in blood. How will the People of Reading Gase to se Early Court all in a Blase. (Here follow the marks of the signatories.) You may believe it so Heip Mr. Shackel! Early Court, to be left at Marquis Granby.
> "A Warning, Whereas we are informed that you are about to have a Thershing Machine to take away our Labour and If you do there is a PLOTT laid among Us, the Labourine People in this neighbourhood to set your Rick and Barnes afire, and the first Opportunity to give you the Leaden fevour Mr. Fuller Lodden Bridge Farm Berks."
> His Royal Highness, for the better apprehending and bringing to Justice the persons concerned in writing and lending the said letters, is hereby pleased in the name and on the behalf of his Majesty, to promise his Majesties' most gracious pardon to any of them, (except the person or persons who actually wrote the same) who shall discover their accomplice or accomplices therein, so that he, she, or they may be apprehended and convicted thereof. And as a further encouragement, a reward of One Hundred Guineas is hereby offered by the said Messrs. Shackel and Fuller, and Fifty Guineas by the Directors of the Sun Fire, and Royal Exchange Insurance Offices (in which the respective premises are insured) to any person making such discovery as aforesaid.

Letters threatening violent action against William Shackel of Erleigh Court and James Fuller of Loddon Bridge Farm, *Reading Mercury*, September 1811. Unemployment and hunger fuelled discontent in the Berkshire countryside in the first decades of the 19th century.

Flailing also confined a number of able-bodied men to the barn when they might be doing other important work on the farm; and machines could be used at seasons when no other work was possible, and could provide work for women and boys as well as men.

Against a background of growing rural discontent and hardship among the labouring poor, experiments with threshing machines continued and more efficient models were evolved. Very soon farmers and landowners were receiving anonymous letters threatening the destruction of their machines and the burning of their ricks, while insurance companies offered rewards for information on the authors of the letters. But machines were only one among several causes which, over a long period, had contributed to the condition of the rural poor. During the Napoleonic wars (1793–1815) there was a boom in agriculture which was highly profitable to landowners and farmers but not to labourers. Prices had gone up, but not their wages; and the end of the war was followed by a prolonged recession, made worse by the return of thousands of men from the armed forces to swell the numbers of the unemployed. The accelerating process of enclosure had deprived the cottager of the few rights and small properties he had once enjoyed, widening the gap between the poor and the gentry, who now owned everything and enjoyed every privilege and pleasure of country life. The well-intentioned Speenhamland system had succeeded only in making the poor more dependent on poor relief, and as the greater part of the country's growing population belonged to the labouring classes, the poor were becoming so numerous that they placed an increasingly heavy burden on ratepayers.

In the autumn of 1830 the harvest was poor for the third year in succession, putting up the price of bread. The winter of 1829 had been long and bitterly cold, a time of unemployment, hunger and deprivation for many labouring families. Faced with the prospect of another such winter, labourers rioted in many parts of southern and eastern England. In Berkshire, the troubles began in mid-November in two separate areas: at Thatcham in the west and around Bray, Windsor and Holyport in the east. In the latter, where the rioters were more effectively brought under control, farmers possessing threshing, or 'thrashing', machines received threatening letters and fires were started at Holyport and Hurst. Farmers around Windsor offered rewards for tracing the culprits, and associations were formed to protect property. At a meeting in Wokingham Town Hall a Forest Association was set up, each parish agreeing to form its own force of special constables to apprehend incendiarists setting fire to ricks, barns or other buildings. When riots broke out at Binfield and Waltham St Lawrence, the trouble-makers were quickly taken into custody, but arson attacks and protest meetings continued throughout the area.

On 15th November, 1830, labourers gathered at Thatcham with the intention of persuading employers to raise their wages, and a large crowd of them, led by a man blowing a horn, marched around all the neighbouring farms compelling other labourers to join forces with them. By mid-day, between 200 and 300 had returned to Thatcham, where a vestry meeting had been called, and spokesmen for the labourers demanded that they should all be given work and that their wages should be increased. They received no very favourable reply and, after waiting two days, the men reassembled and with their numbers swelled by others from Bucklebury, Bradfield and Stanford Dingley, went from farm to farm, demanding higher wages, pressing men to support them, and destroying machines in several places. A Bradfield farmer, who was visited between one and two in the morning, reported that they demanded food and drink and wages of two shillings a day, and was told that if he did not agree to their terms they would have blood for supper. Like many threatened farmers, he had taken the precaution of putting his threshing machine out of action, so, having taken his money and some hammers and an axe from his workshop, the men went on their way to Beenham. There they visited three farms and destroyed three machines. The next day they concentrated on Aldermaston and the adjoining parishes, destroying machines, demanding money and forcing men at work to leave their masters' horses at the plough. Mustering in Aldermaston Park in the afternoon they boasted of having destroyed 33 machines in as many hours. At Colthrop they broke machinery in a paper mill before going on to Brimpton Common. But there, at last, they were confronted by a determined magistrate, backed up by a substantial body of constables and angry tradesmen. The Riot Act was read and, after a struggle, eleven men were arrested and taken to Reading Gaol.

At Speen, on the following day, unemployed men with some support from local farms made a successful demand on their vestry without resorting to violence. The vestry agreed to raise wages from nine to ten shillings a week and to pay the price of a gallon loaf for each child over the second. But at Hungerford and Kintbury, on 21st and 22nd November, another wave of violence broke out. Hungerford men marched around the countryside, destroying machines at Avington, Boxford, Welford, Chieveley and other places, and when they got back to Hungerford, found a mob from Kintbury rioting in the streets. Trouble had started at Kintbury on the preceding day, when a beggar had been committed to the lock-up for abusing a magistrate who had refused to give him poor relief. After rescuing the beggar the Kintbury men had made a round of local farms, as well as those further afield at Inkpen, Hampstead Marshall and West Woodhay, demanding money and breaking machines. Then they went to Hungerford and destroyed all the machinery and wrought iron at Richard Gibbon's foundry. Magistrates, endeavouring to restore order, invited representatives from both places to come to the town hall to discuss their grievances. The Hungerford men asked for an increase of wages to twelve shillings a week, a reduction in house rents, and the destruction of all machines. When the wage demand had been agreed and placatory replies received on the other points, they dispersed to their homes. The Kintbury men, however, were far more aggressive. They arrived at the town hall armed with hammers and bludgeons, and their spokesman, William Oakley, addressed the magistrates in an intimidating manner. 'You have not such damned flats to deal with as you had before. We will have two shillings a day till Lady Day and half a crown afterwards for labourers, and three shillings and sixpence for tradesmen, and as we are here, we will have £5 before we go out of the place or be damned if we don't smash it.' They were given £5 and departed.

The next day they joined up with men from other villages and there was more trouble at West Woodhay, Inkpen, Enborne and Hampstead Lodge, Lord Craven's house. Usually sums between £2 and £5 were demanded from landowners, but Craven was made to give £10. In Kintbury a manufacturer saved his machinery from destruction by giving them £4 in silver to buy beer at the Red Lion and the Blue Ball, their regular meeting places in the village. By this time the Kintbury men had got themselves organised and had appointed a treasurer, Francis Norris, a bricklayer, who, when he was arrested later, was found to have £100 in his possession. Their leader was 'Captain' William Winterbourne, another bricklayer, while their spokesman, William Oakley, was a carpenter and wheelwright. Here, as in other places, farm labourers had been joined by local craftsmen whose lives were bound up with the village community, and by others, such as paper workers, who saw their livelihoods threatened by machinery. Such men were often more intelligent and articulate, and came to the fore naturally as leaders.

Meanwhile, unrest was spreading. Rioters broke ten machines at farms in Lambourn, East Garston and Eastbury, where there was a running battle with special constables. At Yattendon, Frilsham, Hampstead Norreys and Ashampstead mobs were in action, demanding money, machine breaking, knocking on cottage doors by day and night and compelling the occupants to join them. At Burnt Hill near Yattendon they drank 40 quarts of beer in each of the two public houses before going on to Aldworth and Streatley. By that time, a good many had turned back but a pot-valiant few went on to Basildon, where a farmer from whom they demanded money for more beer refused to give them more than half-a-crown, saying derisively that they were no more than half a mob. Shortly after this they were rounded up by a troop of soldiers sent from Reading, and eleven were taken prisoner.

Disturbances in various counties were now so serious that the Home Secretary sent a letter to those in authority urging them to take decisive action. On 24th November, local magistrates assembled at Newbury a large body of special constables and former members of the Berkshire Yeomanry, including Lord Craven, and made a clean sweep of the affected villages. Dozens of trouble-makers were arrested and hundreds more cautioned and dispersed. At Kintbury, all the leaders and many of their supporters were captured at the Blue Ball and sent to gaol in Reading. As the Government recognised that there was considerable sympathy for the rioters, and that local magistrates might be too lenient, a Special Commission was appointed to try the prisoners in counties where the riots had been most violent. Berkshire was one of these. On 27th December the trial opened at Reading of 120 prisoners, half of whom, as the law then stood, were liable to the death penalty on charges of robbery, riot, arson or machine breaking. The judges proceeded with the utmost severity against the Kintbury men, 26 of whom were given capital convictions. Of these, 23 sentences were commuted to transportation, and only Winterbourne, Oakley and another named Alfred Darling were left for execution without hope of reprieve.

Public sympathy for the condemned men was strong. It was widely felt that, however violent and abusive their language, and however much damage they had done, no person had suffered serious bodily harm from them. Petitions for mercy were signed by thousands of local people, among them the Rev Thomas Fowle, vicar of Kintbury, who did all he could to get their lives spared. January 11th was fixed for their execution, and on the 10th Fowle visited the men in Reading prison. He found all three in the same cell, engaged in roasting some potatoes on a stove, so that they could eat their last meal together. They were humble and grateful to him for all he had done, he reported afterwards. At the last hour before the executions were due to take place, a reprieve came for two of them, and Winterbourne alone was hanged. His body was brought back to Kintbury and buried the next day in a quiet corner of the churchyard.

After 1834 the poor found themselves up against a different kind of machinery – that of the new Poor Law administration. Poor Law reform had been made inevitable by the mounting pressure of the poor rate, which kept wages down and, together with the allowances introduced by the Speenhamland system, tended to encourage pauperisation. Another difficulty was that the distribution of the poor was uneven, so that some parishes carried a heavier burden than others. Corruption among Overseers was common. In Reading, one ratepayer appealed against the poor rate on the grounds that the Overseers had spent £19 on a dinner at the George Inn out of money collected for the poor.

The Poor Law Amendment Act of 1834 was designed to introduce an entirely new system, with more efficient and economical management. It was intended to reduce the numbers of paupers and to encourage the able-bodied to find work wherever they could, rather than to seek relief. For those who were too old or sick to work, or for orphaned or abandoned children, shelter and assistance would be provided, but it would not be generous. The law insisted that it must no longer be possible, as had formerly been the case, for people receiving relief to be better off than some who were not. For, as the Poor Law Commissioners declared, 'Every penny bestowed that tends to render the condition of the pauper more eligible than that of the independent labourer, is a bounty on indolence and vice.' Poor law relief was taken out of the hands of local justices and parish vestries, and passed to elected Boards of Guardians, each of which administered a group of parishes combined into a Poor Law Union. In each union there would be one central workhouse, and for those who were driven to seek shelter there, conditions were made as unattractive as possible by poor diet, strict discipline, the separation of husbands from wives and children, and unpleasant occupations. All able-bodied inmates were expected to work to help pay for their keep. Stone-breaking, bone-crushing and oakum picking were occupations assigned to men. Women laundered, cooked and cleaned. The Master of each workhouse was expected to be married, and preferably to an experienced nurse who could serve as Matron. The Commissioners had hoped to be able to abolish outdoor relief altogether, but in practice this form of assistance was continued in many cases where allowances of money or food, distributed by Relieving Officers, were the most economical way of helping families in distress but not homeless.

In Berkshire the new Unions were centred on Hungerford, Newbury, Bradfield, Reading, Wokingham, Easthampstead, Windsor, Cookham and Slough. Many old parish workhouses were made redundant when the new Union houses were built, although in some places this took several years. In Hungerford the old workhouse in Charnham Close was replaced by a large new one in Park Street, described in Kelly's Directory of 1847 as 'in course of erection; it commands rather an elevated, and at the same time most healthy, site in the town; the Board sits every Wednesday.' In Bradfield, the largest Union comprising 28 parishes in west and central Berkshire, the Guardians acted quickly to build a new workhouse in 1835. In the grounds there was 'a neat Gothic chapel erected at the sole expense of the Rev. Thomas Stevens, for the use of the inmates'. In Reading, which together with the hamlets of Whitley and Southcote formed one Union, St Giles' parish workhouse was closed, St Mary's was converted into a poorhouse for the accommodation of the old and sick, and St Lawrence's was retained as the workhouse. Two corn mills and a grain dressing machine were installed to provide work for the men. Strict discipline was maintained by the Master, minor offences being punished by a term in a refractory ward and more serious ones by a sentence of hard labour in prison, imposed by magistrates.

In Easthampstead, the Union Workhouse was built on the site of some almshouses built in 1760 by William Watts, in return for some common land which he enclosed when he laid out South Hill Park. These had

Bradfield Union workhouse, built in 1835 to serve 29 parishes in west Berkshire. This early 20th century photograph shows the handsome front entrance rather than the accommodation for the paupers at the rear.

been rebuilt by the Marquis of Downshire in 1826, and were again rebuilt and enlarged after 1834 to accommodate the poor, sick and aged of Warfield, Winkfield, Binfield, Sandhurst and Crowthorne as well as Easthampstead. The first Master had to cope with 120 inmates with a staff of four. Wokingham Union at first used Wargrave parish workhouse, but this proved inadequate and, in 1850, a larger purpose-built house was erected in Barkham Road, Wokingham, at a cost of over £6,000. It was designed by John Billing, a well-known Reading architect. The building provided every accommodation considered necessary for the inmates, staff and the Board of Guardians, who held their meetings in a room facing the front entrance. At the rear, were separate entrances for incoming men and women, who were taken into separate receiving wards and given a bath. The sick were placed in the adjacent sick wards or fever ward, where a nurse and surgeon were in attendance. Able-bodied men and women had dormitories, work-places and exercise yards on opposite sides of the building, the women's work area being occupied mainly by wash-houses, drying grounds and kitchens. The centre portion of the building contained the dining room. Each sex had its own day room, and there were accommodations for aged men and women separate from those for the able-bodied. The Master's room and clerk's office adjoined the Guardians' meeting room. Inmates were rarely allowed to go out except to look for work, but if they were successful in this, and were able to support themselves, they were released. The numbers of orphaned and abandoned children left in the care of the Guardians posed a problem of education, and each Union had either to provide a small school or send the children to local National Schools. In 1850 Reading and Wokingham Unions combined to provide a district school in the old workhouse at Wargrave, where children up to the age of 14 were given an elementary education and training to fit them for the humble positions they would presumably hold in society. As many as possible were placed in service with selected local families.

15

THE GREAT RAILWAY AGE

In 1844 Turner exhibited at the Royal Academy his famous painting, *Rain, Steam and Speed – The Great Western Railway*. It showed the dynamic image of a new power emerging from a mist of rain and steam to forge ahead into the future; and, like the smoke-blackened tug towing a ghostly sailing ship in his *Fighting Téméraire*, the steam locomotive, with its fiery heart, was the symbol of a new age. The setting for *Rain, Steam and Speed* was Brunel's railway bridge across the Thames at Maidenhead, a place in itself evocative of the dying age of horse-drawn coaches, while the new bridge was a masterpiece of contemporary engineering.

Across that bridge the Great Western Railway first entered Berkshire, bringing a new concept of speed and opening up possibilities of travel and transport beyond anything hitherto achieved by roads or waterways. A century of improvements had brought roads, canals and river navigations to their highest level of efficiency, but they remained dependent on the speed and strength of horses and the clemency of the weather. Canal engineers had accomplished great works to facilitate the movement of raw materials and manufactured goods, yet severe frosts could close a canal for many days, delaying supplies and raising prices. A Reading diarist recorded in February 1814 that barges had been held up by frost for six weeks, and during that time unemployed bargemen had dragged a boat round the town begging, or had been put to work clearing snow from the streets. Dry weather, too, could cause delays by seriously reducing the water level. Between Reading and London, the Thames, although better controlled than it once had been, could still be so dangerous in wet and stormy weather that goods were sometimes unloaded at Reading wharves to be sent on by road, at vastly increased expense.

Such problems were matters of urgent concern to businessmen, merchants and tradesmen, and in the 1820s experiments with steam locomotion in the north of England were followed with close interest. The initial decision to build a railway between their city and London was made by the merchants of Bristol, who appointed I K Brunel as engineer and instructed him to survey the route. Brunel presented his survey and proposals at a public meeting in Bristol Guildhall in July 1833, and it was decided that a company should be formed to make application to Parliament for powers to build a railway. The Great Western Railway Company's prospectus, published in September, stated that the cost of the 120-mile line was estimated at £2,805,330 and construction would take four or five years. The railway would 'multiply the number of travellers, improve the conveyance of goods, encourage manufactures, diffuse the advantages of the vicinity of towns over the country intersected by the railway, improve the supply of provisions to the metropolis and extend the market for agricultural produce, give employment to the labouring class, both during construction and by its subsequent effects, and increase the value of property in its neighbourhood'. Opposition to the proposed line came from several quarters. It would pose a threat to existing transport concerns: the Thames Commissioners, the Kennet and Avon Canal Company, and many turnpike trusts, coach and barge owners. The line would cut across rich farmlands and wealthy estates, and it would bring noise, dirt and destruction to certain towns and villages which would prefer to remain unpolluted. Landowners against it included Lord Stowell, a retired High Court judge, who complained that the view from his windows at Erleigh Court would be spoiled, and Robert Palmer, MP, who objected to its interference with the preservation of game on his estates at Sonning and Woodley. The two county newspapers were at loggerheads: *The Reading Mercury* supported the scheme and *The Berkshire Chronicle*, a Conservative organ founded in 1825, campaigned against it. In Windsor, residents and tradesmen were inclined to favour the railway, which at that stage included a branch to their town, but their wishes were over-ridden by the Provost of Eton College, who declared that the railway would be ruinous to the school because it would enable boys to put themselves too easily beyond the reach of the school authorities. 'It is therefore a subject for the serious consideration of the tradesmen of Windsor and Eton, who depend mainly on the prosperity of the school for support, whether they will promote a project which must have the effect of impairing the prosperity of the school, and thereby their own.'

Reading was decidedly in favour. At a crowded meeting in the Town Hall in March 1834, Charles Saunders, Secretary to the GWR Company, spoke of the benefits the line would bring to the town: the comfort of travel to London in one-and-a-half to two hours instead of four-and-a-half to five hours; the influx of visitors, the growth of trade, the rise in the number and value of properties. At the end of the meeting only five hands were raised against a proposal that the Mayor and Burgesses

144

should submit a petition to Parliament in favour of the railway. This was duly presented by their MP, Charles Russell, at the introduction of the GWR bill in the House of Commons, but although passed in the Lower House, the bill was rejected in the Lords. In 1835, a revised bill with modified plans was successful, and the news was greeted by *The Reading Mercury*, and no doubt many of its readers, with great rejoicing. In the revised plan, the branch line to Windsor had been dropped, and the Provost of Eton mollified by a clause prohibiting the erection of a station at Slough or anywhere within three miles of the college. Another change had been made at Sonning, where Brunel had proposed to take his line on level ground through the village, but luckily Robert Palmer had succeeded in getting it moved to the south, where a cutting would have to be made through higher ground.

In the event, this cutting, nearly two miles long and, in places, 60 feet deep, proved to be the most difficult section of the line between London and Reading. Work began there as early as October 1836, when the hitherto peaceful farms between Ruscombe and Sonning were disrupted by the arrival of hundreds of tough, work-hardened navvies, who with the aid of picks, shovels, horse-drawn trucks and wheelbarrows were to labour for more than three years to shift and carry away millions of tons of compacted clay and gravel. Conditions were often appalling. Landslides were a constant danger, the gravel making embankment difficult, while frequent heavy rains turned the clay into a perilous sea of mud. There were many accidents in which men and horses were injured or killed by falling earth, or in explosions when gunpowder was used to shift veins of hardened clay. So many casualties were taken to the Royal Berkshire Hospital after its opening in May 1839 that the directors of the GWR Company sent a donation of 100 guineas, plus an annual subscription of ten guineas.

Other sections of the line progressed more speedily, and by May 1838 it was completed as far as Taplow. There the first Maidenhead station was opened on 4th June, when large crowds gathered to see the first train set out for Paddington at eight o'clock in the morning. Many people had come from considerable distances to experience the novelty of the new mode of transport. A coach proprietor in Reading started a special service through Twyford to Maidenhead to meet the trains, and in Speenhamland, 30 miles away, another coach firm advertised 'First rate travelling to London, through Woolhampton, Reading and Maidenhead, and thence on the Railway'. This was to be the pattern of long-distance travel for some years, with road coaches covering shorter and shorter distances to the nearest station, until they gave up routes served by railways altogether.

Between Maidenhead's first station and the town the railway was carried across the river by Brunel's famous bridge. The railway company hoped to benefit from the impressive amount of traffic using the road bridge, and a census carried out on its behalf over a two-week period recorded nearly 7,000 horses passing over it, drawing a variety of public and private coaches and carriages, gigs, market carts, and wagons laden with coal, grain, hay, straw and many other commodities. The probable loss of bridge tolls from a large proportion of this traffic caused the town council to view the approach of the railway with some hostility. Nor were the Thames Commissioners inclined to be helpful. They had stipulated that the railway bridge must in no way obstruct the navigation, so that only one pier was permitted to stand in the river, and, moreover, the bridge must be built in brick. Construction began in 1837, and when the centrings were in position, Brunel's design was seen to incorporate two of the longest and flattest arches ever built in brick, causing sceptical observers to predict disaster as soon as, or even before, a train passed

Brunel's famous flat-arched brick railway bridge at Maidenhead. Part of the 18th century road bridge can be seen in the distance.

over them. In April 1839 the bridge was completed and tested and proved sound, although Brunel gave orders that the centrings were to be left in place until the following spring. They were not needed. In January 1840 a violent storm blew them away and, in spite of subsequent high winds and floods, the bridge remained standing firm.

By then, trains had been passing over it for six months, ever since Twyford station was opened in July 1839. The railway company had hoped that the opening of Reading station would soon follow, but Sonning cutting was still some way from completion. As many as 1,220 men and 196 horses were now working there, and two locomotives had been sent to assist them to move the remaining 700,000 cubic yards of earth. As a result, it was the middle of March 1840 before the line was ready, and the official opening of Reading station was announced for the 30th of that month. Preparations for the great day were marred by the death of one of the workmen, whose name, like those of other railway casualties, would have been long forgotten had it not been for the extraordinary manner of his going. On 24th March, Henry West, a journeyman carpenter, was working on a raised lantern in the roof of one of the station buildings, when a violent gust of wind tore off the roof of the lantern, with West clinging to it, and hurled it over the station house to the ground on the far side. West's body was found some distance away and was carried to the Boar's Head Inn in Friar Street, where an inquest was held the same evening. On the following Sunday he was buried in St Lawrence's churchyard, his funeral procession from the inn being preceded by two mutes and followed by over 40 of his fellow workmen. The memorial board erected over his grave recorded that he lost his life in a whirlwind.

On the opening day, every vantage point in and around the station was filled with sightseers cheering every one of the 17 trains as they arrived and departed, and especially the train bearing their former MP, Charles Russell, who was now Chairman of the Great Western Railway Company. Train watching and engine spotting became popular pastimes. Just as the old familiar stage coaches had been known by names, so were the new engines, these embodiments of speed and power, emitting impressive quantities of smoke, sparks and steam, having been given such inspiring names as *Morning Star*, *Evening Star*, *Fire Fly*, *Ajax*, *Atlas*, *Mars*, *Tiger*, *Sun* and *Leopard*. Within three months it was possible to travel westwards as well as eastwards, for work had already been completed on cuttings through chalk hills at Purley and Pangbourne, and the necessary bridges had been constructed over the Thames near Basildon and Moulsford. In June the directors travelled down the line to Steventon with a new engine 'of extraordinary power and velocity' named *Charon*, which accomplished the 57¼ miles in one hour and ten minutes. A year later, in June 1841, the railway was opened to Bristol.

Most people had cause to welcome the railway. Businessmen could travel to the City and back within a day and arrive home comfortably in time for dinner; merchants and manufacturers were delighted that goods could be transported more speedily and cheaply over greater distances. People in search of employment found their horizons widened, while those who travelled for pleasure could visit places and people without the tedium and expense of road transport and accommodation at inns. News travelled faster, for the Post Office quickly transferred its business to the railways, and so did newspaper publishers. There were, inevitably, many losers among those engaged in old-style travel and transport industries; and many people who mourned the old ways of life and the damage done to the landscape. The view from Reading's Forbury Hill across the river meadows towards Caversham was spoiled forever, and the line through Goring Gap cut through one of the loveliest reaches of the Thames Valley. Such considerations were swept aside by the rising tide of 'railway mania', and the authors of new guidebooks dwelt upon the new vitality the railways brought to the rural scene. 'Through the peaceful Vale of Thames that gigantic result of human skill and enterprize, the Great Western Railway, has taken its undeviating course – amidst green trees, and over brawling rivulets – its mighty machines (the automaton elephants of modern science) alarming the quiet denizens of the pastures, and filling the minds of the rustic tillers of the soil with wonder.'

The advantages to Reading's trade and manufactures were quickly felt, and set in motion the vigorous expansion of the town which took place in the second half of the 19th century. Reading became as important a junction of railways as it was of roads and waterways. Great Western branch lines reached out to Newbury and Hungerford in 1847 and Basingstoke in 1848, while the South Eastern Railway Company opened a line from Guildford in 1849. Maidenhead did not lose as much as it feared, although the council had to reduce its bridge tolls considerably to retain a dwindling number of road users. In the long run, its attractive location combined with the improved accessibility provided by the railway, brought many new residents, and the town found a new role as a fashionable riverside resort. In 1854 it was linked by rail to the Chilterns when a line was opened from High Wycombe, including a station at Cookham. A new main line station was built in the town in 1871, and the first Maidenhead station was renamed Taplow. Twyford also found that the railway brought compensations for the loss of the coaching trade, and its station was enlarged in 1859 when it became the

The Provost of Eton College opposed the building of a railway station at Slough, believing it would be too easy for the boys to travel beyond the reach of the school authorities. However, pressure from the public and the GWR company resulted in a station opening at Slough by 1840.

junction for a branch line to Henley.

Slough had wanted a railway station and resented the opposition of Eton College. The railway company also wanted Slough to have a station and although, as the GWR Act allowed, it had built a station three miles away at Langley, when the line opened Langley station remained closed, in spite of the annoyance of residents in that area. The curious custom developed whereby trains stopped in Slough to set down and pick up passengers without the aid of a platform or other facilities. The Crown Inn acted as booking office and, later, so did a new inn named the North Star after one of the locomotives. Public and company pressure obtained a station at Slough by 1840, confirming the status of the village as the most important community in the parish of Upton-cum-Chalvey. In the 1850s Slough began to expand into the town which, eventually, engulfed the ancient parish and parts of those around it.

In 1842 Queen Victoria and Prince Albert made their first journey by rail to Paddington. The Queen was delighted, finding it smoother and more comfortable than travel by road. It also had the advantage of greater privacy, separating her from the noisy crowds which often gathered around the royal carriage on road journeys. The Royal Hotel, an impressive building in the Italianate style, was put up opposite Slough station and used by the Queen as a waiting room, but Her Majesty let it be known that she would welcome a branch line into Windsor. Two companies, the Great Western and the London and South Western, were eager to win the prestige of royal patronage, and so it came about that two lines were built into the town, terminating almost at the foot of the castle walls. The Great Western branch from Slough just won the race, being opened in October 1849. The London and South Western line from Staines, with intermediate stations at Wraysbury and Datchet, gained royal permission to cross the Home Park into its terminus at Windsor and Eton Riverside station, and was opened in December of the same year. This dual service strengthened the ties between the town and the capital which had always existed, and assisted its growth as a residential and tourist centre.

Wokingham had no rail service until 1849. In that year the South Eastern Railway Company's line from Guildford to Reading gave Wokingham a station and a useful link with Reading, but it was not until 1856 that the town benefited from a line to Waterloo via Staines, operated by the London and South Western Railway.

Railways brought improved communications to south-east Berkshire at a time when the area was being developed for residential and institutional purposes. Houses for the wealthy, many set in extensive grounds, had been a feature of the landscape since the 18th century, and in the 1820s had come under attack from William Cobbett, who disapproved of this kind of high-class occupation of rural areas. 'All the *useful people* become less numerous,' he growled, and although admitting that the land was 'as barren, and as villainous a heath as ever man set his eyes on,' he condemned Sunninghill as 'a spot all made into "grounds" and gardens by *tax-eaters*. The inhabitants of it have beggared twenty agricultural villages and hamlets.' Sunninghill, and other places in the Forest, remained unabashed and their rising populations were happy to make use of the new rail facilities. More custom for the railways came from the institutions which took over the 'villainous heath' along the Berks-Surrey border. Two army training camps were established at Aldershot in 1854. The Royal Military College had already been at Sandhurst since 1812 and acquired a station at Blackwater when the Reading to Guildford line opened in 1849. At Crowthorne, Wellington College for the education of the sons of deceased army officers was founded in 1853 as a memorial to the great Duke. When it opened in

1859 a station named 'Wellington College for Crowthorne' was added for the convenience of staff and pupils, the village being of little significance at that time. In 1863 this remote woodland area was chosen as the site of Broadmoor Asylum.

Elsewhere in east Berkshire, the railway from Waterloo to Wokingham served Bracknell and Ascot, encouraging the spread of brickmaking as a local industry. Ascot racecourse proved a profitable source of income and the station was much enlarged in 1878 by the addition of extra platforms and a subway for the convenience of race-goers. On the outskirts of Reading, another new station was provided in 1863 at Earley, a rapidly growing residential area.

While railways were playing a vital part in the development of east Berkshire, the want of them contributed to the decline of the western part of the county. When Brunel had made his survey for the Great Western main line in the 1830s, he had chosen a route offering the easy gradients and wide, sweeping curves necessary for fast movement in the early days of steam. West of Reading, he had abandoned the historic Kennet valley route across Berkshire and turned his line away to the north-west to benefit from the open levels of the Vale of White Horse. In so doing, he left stranded towns and villages such as Newbury, Hungerford, Thatcham and Woolhampton which had been served by, and had derived considerable trade from, the London to Bristol highway and the Kennet and Avon canal. Now their inns and wharves and tradesmen were no longer required to the same extent. So far as long-distance trade was concerned, both road and canal were redundant, although local traffic kept them alive for many years. The branch railway which linked these places to Reading and rural Wiltshire after 1847 brought small compensation for what they had lost.

To make matters worse, the north-south traffic through Newbury was also adversely affected by the new pattern of communications provided by railways, which weakened the town's ancient links with Oxford, Winchester and Southampton. In the 1850s and 1860s hopes were raised, only to be disappointed, by various schemes to build railways from the industrial north and midlands to the port of Southampton, putting Newbury on the map once more. Hope lay in such large schemes, for it was obvious that no plan for a line through Berkshire could expect to succeed unless it formed part of a major through route. The sparsely populated farming areas through which it must pass could contribute little towards its viability. Eventually, the circuitous nature of the existing rail route from Oxford to Southampton via Didcot, Reading and Basingstoke, gave credibility to a scheme for a Didcot, Newbury and Southampton Junction railway, to which Parliament gave

Hermitage was one of the villages served by the Didcot-Newbury line, originally envisaged as a link between Didcot and Southampton, although it was only completed as far as Winchester.

consent in 1873. The line would provide a direct link between the Great Western at Didcot and the London and South Western line at Winchester; and from there it was hoped that an extension might be built to Southampton to compete with the LSWR Company's existing line. The scheme was promoted enthusiastically by the town of Newbury and altruistically by influential Berkshire and Hampshire landowners, who hoped that the railway might revive local agriculture and find new markets for produce. Various difficulties, not least the heavy capital investment required, delayed construction for six years. The engineer confirmed that the line would be costly to build, involving deep cuttings through chalk downlands in both counties, as well as numerous bridges and embankments across rivers and streams. It was just the kind of terrain which earlier railway engineers had been anxious to avoid. Further expense was called for by the insistence of the Great Western Railway Company, which had agreed to operate the line once it was built, that it must meet main line specifications in order to compete with existing lines.

In 1879 construction commenced on the northern section between Didcot and Newbury. The 17 miles of track took two-and-a-half years to build, the longest delay being caused by the mile-long cutting through the Berkshire Downs at Upton. The official opening took place, amidst scenes of triumphant celebration, on 12th April 1882, when all the principal streets of Newbury were dressed with flags and flowers, and banners wishing 'Success to the New Railway' and 'Increased Prosperity to Newbury'. At village stations along the line, children were on holiday to welcome the inaugural train, so that Hermitage, Hampstead Norreys and Compton were crowded with old and young, waving flags, cheering and throwing flowers onto the line. In her speech at the official ceremony in Newbury, Lady Loyd-Lindsay, wife of the Chairman, declared: 'The two valleys of the Thames and Kennet, so long separated by the barrier of the Berkshire Downs, are now united. This portion of the new railway is, I trust, but the first step towards an extension which will cause the direct line of communication between the commercial and manufacturing districts of Liverpool and Birmingham, and the seaport of Southampton, and pass through Berkshire, thereby developing the resources and increasing the prosperity of our county.'

The southern section, from Newbury to Winchester, was opened in May 1885, but owing to mounting debts and wrangles with the LSWR Company the projected extension to Southampton was never built. Sadly, the Didcot, Newbury and Southampton Railway was never able to fulfil its purpose as a through route. Earnings were low right from the start, and the GWR Company persisted in using it only as a branch line, providing no fast trains and no convenient connections at Didcot. Disgruntled Newburians complained that it was easier to get to Oxford or Winchester via Reading, while Swindon could be reached more speedily by bicycle.

The final fling of railway mania in Berkshire was a less ambitious and, on the whole, more successful venture: the Lambourn Valley Railway. Almost to the end of the century, Lambourn's nearest station was at Hungerford, while its only communication with Newbury was a narrow road winding down the valley through a succession of pretty, but very quiet, villages – Eastbury, East Garston, Great Shefford, Welford, Boxford and Bagnor. Local people hoped that a light railway would serve as a lifeline to these remote communities, and allow Lambourn to prosper as other Berkshire towns were doing. It would provide better access via Newbury to Reading and London, improving work prospects and providing cheaper goods transport. The Lambourn Valley Railway Act, authorising the LVR Company to build a single-track line between Lambourn and Newbury, and allowing five years for completion, received Parliamentary consent in 1883. Financial problems beset the company from the beginning; there were troubles with contractors; and further delays were caused by landslips in cuttings and

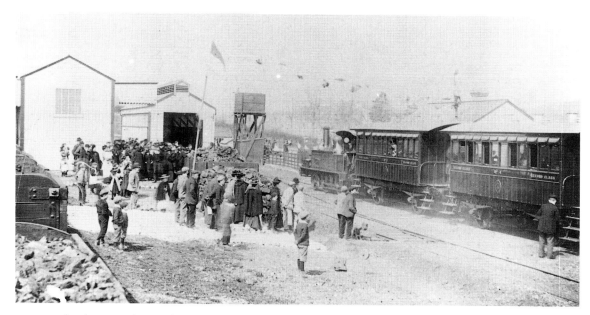

Lambourn station at the opening of the Lambourn Valley Railway in 1898. The 12-mile line was supported financially by Colonel Archer-Houblon of Welford Park, who wanted it to remain independent.

the discovery of a major Saxon burial ground near Shefford. But after an extension of time, the 12-mile line was opened in 1898.

Colonel Archer-Houblon, owner of Welford Park estate and Chairman of the Company, was so determined that the line should be run independently that he had personally paid £1,300 for four coaches, for which the Company agreed to repay him by instalments, but an engine had to be hired from the GWR for the opening run on 2nd April. Later that year, Colonel Archer-Houblon's generosity was extended to the purchase of two engines, which were named, appropriately for such a notable area of Saxon settlement, *Alfred* and *Ealhswith*, after the West Saxon King and Queen. Facilities along the line were basic to start with. Stations were merely lighted platforms, although seats and shelters were provided later, together with the assistance of a lad-porter responsible for everything from tickets to parcel delivery and goods movements to station cleaning. Lambourn's was the only station of any size, having a station master and staff, booking office, waiting rooms, engine sheds, loading bay and cattle pens.

Traffic receipts were satisfactory, covering running costs, but the company soon realised that there was no hope of repaying debts incurred before opening. Nevertheless, the Lambourn Valley Railway fulfilled many of its aims. People living in the area benefited from lower prices of goods, particularly coals, the carriage of which was only a tenth the cost of carting by road. Passenger traffic was not heavy but farmers kept the line busy with the dispatch of regular supplies of milk and other produce, and with the movement of livestock to and from markets. A valuable boost to revenue came from trainers, who quickly adopted the railway for transporting horses to race-meetings and bloodstock sales. This business was greatly increased after the opening of Newbury racecourse in 1905. But, in that year, the Lambourn Valley Railway Company gave up the struggle to remain independent and sold out to the Great Western Railway. Happily, the new owners carried out many improvements and modernisations, and the railway survived until after the Second World War.

16

CHANGE IN THE COUNTRYSIDE

This extract from a contemporary review of *Jude the Obscure*, published in 1895, reflects Hardy's dislike of the bleak downland area where his grandmother had been born and where his novel opens at 'Marygreen', his name for the village of Fawley:

'Berkshire is an unpoetical county, "meanly utilitarian", as Mr Hardy confesses; the imagination hates its concave, loamy cornfields and dreary, hedgeless highways. The local history has been singularly tampered with in Berkshire; it is useless to speak to us of ancient records where the past is all obliterated, and the thatched and dormered houses replaced by modern cottages . . . . In Berkshire, the change which is coming over England so rapidly, the resignation of the old dreamy elements of beauty, has proceeded further than anywhere else in Wessex.'

Even in Fawley there had been changes. Old cottages, even the parish church, had been pulled down and replaced by new ones; a school had been built; trees had been felled; leaving, as Hardy points out, the village well as 'probably the only relic of the local history that remained absolutely unchanged'. The well was essential to the life of the community. Every downland village and farmstead depended for its water supply on wells sunk deep into the chalk – Fawley's is said to be 250 feet deep – and failure of these wells in a dry season brought hardship to people and animals. Their dependence then was on water carts carrying supplies from rivers and streams; and throughout the period when roads were maintained by turnpike trusts, these were among the few vehicles allowed to pass freely through turnpike gates. On the Downs, the lack of running water had always discouraged large settlements, and, of course, had deprived the area of the benefits of water power and waterborne transport.

West Berkshire had always lived by farming, mainly the production of corn, so that the working population of the region was immediately affected by progressive mechanisation and other changes in farming

Aldworth, showing the village well, an essential feature of most downland villages where a lack of running water had historically discouraged the growth of larger communities.

practice as labour-saving devices were introduced; and, in a larger context, by the countrywide change taking place in the 19th century, when agriculture gave way to industry as the principal source of the nation's wealth. Conditions of employment for agricultural day labourers had always been uncertain, varying from season to season, and often the cause of discontent. Towards the end of the 1840s the labourers' old enemy, the threshing machine, appeared in a more powerful form driven by steam, and its use soon became common. After 1850, not only brewing and malting but flour milling became increasingly industrialised by the use of steam power. Windmills, such as those at East Ilsley, Compton and Lambourn, ceased to grind, and in the river valleys many smaller mills were closed. Some of the larger mills on the Thames, Kennet and Loddon were adapted to modern machinery and continued to work well into the 20th century, when flour milling has become centralised in towns. Although the repeal of the Corn Laws in 1846 brought British farmers into competition with foreign imports, corn remained a profitable crop until the 1870s, and the acreage under corn was steadily enlarged. But disaster struck when a succession of

157

Haymaking at Sulham in the 1880s. A picturesque scene, but the agricultural depression was to lead to migration from the villages towards the towns.

bad harvests in that decade resulted in the import of huge quantities of cheaper grain from the American prairies, and began a long period of depression in British agriculture. Land was returned to grass and, from the 1880s, farmers began to convert to livestock and dairy farming in response to the demand from urban areas for fresh milk, butter, cheese and meat, all of which could be carried quickly by the railways.

Throughout the second half of the century the population of west Berkshire declined as labour migrated overseas or into towns, where employment in factories, shops and other trades was more regular, better paid, and more secure. Census returns from 1841 to 1901 show a dramatic change over the whole region. Some sample figures are:– East Ilsley: population down from 733 to 482; Kintbury: 1,881 to 1,648; Inkpen: 743 to 658; Chieveley: 1,936 to 1,471; Fawley: 194 to 155. Even in Newbury the population increased very little, from 6,379 to 6,983, and in Hungerford from 2,323 to 2,364; and these figures include the inmates of the Union workhouses, drawn from surrounding parishes. Bradfield, the centre of another Union, but also containing the boys' college founded in 1850, was one of very few places in west

Berkshire to show a substantial increase, from 1,042 to 1,526. The decline is all the more remarkable in comparison with east Berkshire, where nearly every parish showed some increase of population in the same 60-year period. There was very considerable increase in areas of residential and institutional development; for example:– Earley: 471 to 10,196; Maidenhead: 3,315 to 12,980; Easthampstead: 627 to 4,243; Wokingham: 3,342 to 6,002; Sunninghill: 2,062 to 4,274; Sandhurst: 562 to 5,571; Winkfield: 2,178 to 4,243. These figures emphasise the different ways in which the two regions were developing. East Berkshire had a high proportion of wealthy and professional residents, many commuting to London, and a busy rail network. West Berkshire had little diversity of occupation and a high proportion of low-wage labour. Railways had been introduced late into the area, with no great success.

West Berkshire had suffered more severely in the labourers' revolt of 1830, and continued to suffer from rural unrest. Bitter memories of that time remained, particularly among relatives of men who had been transported. The failure of the uprising had widened the gulf between landowner and labourer, and further undermined the authority of the Church of England, whose clergy, although often sympathetic, had sided with the landowners and gentry. As a result, large numbers of the poor turned for help and spiritual guidance to nonconformist sects, in whose chapels they were among their own kind, and, notably, many of them turned to Primitive Methodism. This evangelical movement had begun early in the 19th century among the poor communities of the industrial midlands and had been brought by itinerant preachers into Wiltshire. From there it had been introduced into Berkshire by two men, John Ride and Thomas Russell, who at first made very little progress in this county. Their open air meetings, at which preaching alternated with bouts of 'fervent agonizing prayer', were sparsely attended, while their attacks on immorality and drunkenness were greeted with derision, unseemly interruptions and missiles. But slowly, in a troubled countryside, small congregations began to form. In April 1830, after Russell had preached at Kintbury, six persons 'decided to begin a religious life', and at Hoe Benham '16 others were convinced of sin and turned to the Lord'. By December, Russell was able to report 300 members and the establishment of 50 preaching places in west Berkshire. In the following years Primitive Methodism took hold in almost every rural community, and particularly in those where the rioters had been most active. In due course, open air preaching places were replaced by simple chapels, often situated well away from the parish church. In the then undivided parish of Thatcham, chapels were built at Cold Ash, Greenham and Newtown; in Chieveley parish, at Oare and Leckhampstead; in Yattendon, at

Burnt Hill. Other places where chapels were built included Kintbury, Bradfield, Burghfield, Stratfield Mortimer, Ashampstead, Aldworth, Compton, Hampstead Norreys, Peasemore, Weston in Welford and Wickham Heath. Many of the original chapels were enlarged and rebuilt later in the century. In Hungerford there was a chapel as early as 1830, which was rebuilt in 1864, shortly before it became the centre of a circuit. Primitive Methodism reached Reading in 1835, and from there preachers, or ranters as they became known, were sent out to evangelize east Berkshire. They made headway more slowly in an area where Wesleyan Methodism was already well-established and rural poverty less prevalent, but they had some success among the poorer communities in Maidenhead, Windsor and Wokingham, where they later became associated with the Temperance Movement and Trade Unionism.

Alarmed by its declining influence all over the country, the Church of England instituted wide-reaching reforms. Clergymen became more conscientious, more actively involved with the welfare of their parish-ioners, and at the same time less closely associated with the squire and his circle. Mounting criticism of clerical participation in recreations such as hunting and card-playing gradually weaned them away from these pursuits, and, as the century wore on, new recruits tended to come from lower levels of society. One of the old-style clergymen was the Rev James Edward Austen-Leigh, nephew of Jane Austen and Vicar of Bray from 1853 until his death in 1874. Austen-Leigh was an enthusiastic rider to hounds and a member of the Vine for many years, but public pressure obliged him to give up. He found consolation, however, in writing a book, *Recollections of the Vine Hunt*, which was published in 1865 with considerable success.

Church reforms, begun in the 1830s, were followed by a revival of interest in church architecture and ceremonial. Architects of new churches went back to medieval styles for inspiration, and numerous existing churches were 'restored' by the removal of post-Reformation additions and a return to the furnishings and layout of a more devout age. Some parishes saw the ancient, perhaps crumbling church with which they were familiar, completely demolished and replaced by a startling new one. At Burghfield, the old church was replaced in 1843 by one in the Neo-Norman style, designed by J B Clacy, and built in blue brick with stone dressings. But the most commonly revived style was Early English Gothic, of which G E Street and Sir Gilbert Scott were leading practitioners. Street was the architect employed in 1865–6 at Fawley, where, according to Hardy, 'the original church, hump-backed, wood-turreted, and quaintly hipped, had been taken down, and either cracked up into heaps of road-metal in the lane, or utilised as pig-sty walls, garden seats, guard-stones to fences, and rockeries in the flower-beds of the neighbourhood.' It had been replaced on a different site by 'a tall new building of modern Gothic design, unfamiliar to English eyes'. Street also rebuilt, wholly or in part, the parish churches at Brightwalton, Purley, Tilehurst, Warfield and Winkfield, and designed new churches for Eastbury, Boyn Hill and Sandhurst. Scott rebuilt the churches at Bradfield and Englefield, while another well-known architect, Henry Woodyer, was employed at Sonning, Greenham, Wokingham and Woodley. Very few churches escaped some degree of restoration in the mid-Victorian period.

A notably energetic vicar was the Rev Robert Milman who arrived at Lambourn in 1851 and, according to his biographer, 'passed 11 years toiling night and day to reform one of the wildest and most neglected parishes in the diocese of Oxford. One of his brothers described him, when he first went there, as being policeman as well as parson.' When he arrived 'the Dissenters practically had the command of the place', but Milman built a new church in the hamlet of Eastbury, consecrated in 1853, and followed this with a school, also designed by Street; while in Lambourn he saw to the completion of the National School, restored the chancel of St Michael's, founded a choir, and put new life into the church. All these buildings were erected at the sacrifice of his own small private fortune, but he was repaid by the rapid improvement in the parish. Although keen on outdoor sports, 'he was deeply convinced of the abuses of the turf, and having racing stables in the parish, he knew only too well to what evils it led. On one occasion, soon after he came to Lambourn, when he had refused permission for the church bells to be rung in honour of the victory of a Lambourn horse, the ringers obtained access to the tower, and locking themselves in, rang a peal. Mr Milman could not restrain his indignation; he summoned the ringers before the magistrates, and on the following Sunday preached so vehemently upon the abuses of the turf that no-one ventured to trifle with him again.'

Village schools were closely associated with the parish church, and Milman was only one of many clergymen who, together with other people in the middle and upper classes, became increasingly concerned with the mental and moral welfare of the labouring poor, and made great efforts to improve elementary education. At the beginning of the century there had been very few schools for the rural poor, although some parishes were lucky enough to have a charitable foundation such as Piggat's School at Shinfield, founded in 1707 by Richard Piggat, a local boy who had made his money as a cutler in Westminster. Piggat built and endowed the school for 20 poor boys, where they were to be educated up

161

to the age of twelve and receive each year a new suit of clothes and new shoes. In other villages there might be a school supported by the poor rate or by subscriptions from well-to-do patrons, but such schools rarely had a proper building and teaching often took place in the church or the vestry room. At Warfield, for instance, in 1783, the vicar had reported to his bishop that there was no free school in the parish, but one that charged threepence or sixpence a week for instruction. This sum was paid by charitable gentlemen for children of the poor. In 1810 the north aisle of Warfield church was let to a Mr Gerrard for two guineas a year for use as a school, and in 1816 Lord Braybrooke gave a plot of land in the parish to the vicar and church wardens for a building for 'the voluntary education of Poor Infants'. Throughout the early decades of the 19th century poor children continued to be dependent on the philanthropy of landowners or incumbents for what little schooling they had. At Brimpton the Earl of Falmouth gave a small piece of land on which a school was built and supported by voluntary subscriptions; at Easthampstead there was a school in the park supported by the Marchioness of Downshire; at Shaw a school was built by Mr Eyre of Shaw House and largely supported by him; at West Ilsley a free school was supported by William Morland Esq.; at Sulhamstead a school was endowed by the Misses Thoyts of Sulhamstead House. At Purley, Sulham, Bradfield and Stanford Dingley, the rector had built a school at his own expense and continued to be its main support.

By the 1840s about two-thirds of the parishes now in Berkshire had a school of some kind, mostly set up by local benevolence or parish enterprise. A few had National Schools (Aldermaston, Beenham, Burnham, Chieveley, Cookham, Datchet, Hurst, Greenham, Knowl Hill, Sunninghill, Thatcham, Tilehurst, Waltham St Lawrence, Welford) founded by the National Society for the Education of the Poor in the Principles of the Established Church, an organisation set up in 1811. The Society had made slow progress at first, but after 1834, when the Government began to give grants, the number of National Schools began to increase rapidly. These schools depended for their continuance on subscriptions and donations, and children attending contributed a penny a week, but they were at least taught in purpose-built schools, usually with a head teacher's house attached. Standards of instruction began to improve from the late 1840s, when formal teacher training and the award of certificates was introduced. Conditions in National Schools varied from place to place, depending still on the level of local support and interest. By 1864 more than half the village schools in Berkshire were National Schools, and a directory of that year shows that they were seen to be playing a worthy role in village life. At Hurst the National School had been built in 1843 'on a large scale in the Elizabethan style' and was well supported by subscribers. Sunninghill's, too, was 'liberally supported', while Earley's was described at unusual length as 'a handsome school with a master's house attached, in connection with the church, and supported by voluntary contributions, in which upwards of 100 boys and girls receive a sound, plain education at the trifling cost of one penny per week.'

National Schools, as the name of the Society made plain, were intended for Anglican children. Nonconformists attended schools established by the British and Foreign School Society, started in 1808, but British Schools were far fewer in number and were founded only in places where there was sufficient financial support. Compton and Thatcham were among the few villages with a British School, although there were others in Newbury, Reading, Wokingham, Windsor and Slough.

The Education Act of 1870 legislated for an undenominational school within reach of every child in the country and parish ratepayers were empowered to elect a School Board for the purpose of building and maintaining a school in places where there were none or the existing provision was inadequate. In Berkshire, School Boards were found to be most needed in the deprived areas of towns, but in the country they took over a few of the National Schools, such as those at East Ilsley, Inkpen and Chieveley. At East Ilsley the National School, built in 1832, was converted into a Board School in 1872 in order to provide for 100 children. At Inkpen, where an architecturally attractive school in the cottage style had been built by G E Street in 1850, a School Board was formed in 1875 and a new school, capable of holding 127 children, was built within two years. In Chieveley a School Board was formed in 1873 because provision in this large parish was inadequate, but a new school for 180 children was not built until 1896. In some places there was considerable local opposition to the setting up of a School Board. A notable opponent was John Walter III, proprietor of *The Times*, who built and supported at his own expense a school at Sindlesham on his Bearwood estate, and also built a two-room school and teacher's house at Finchampstead, and allowed the parish to use them rent-free so long as the expenses were defrayed without the aid of a School Board.

The majority of National Schools were either found to be satisfactory or hastened to become so, and continued to function until the end of the century. After school attendance up to the age of ten was made compulsory in 1880, and elementary education was made free in 1891, some schools had to be enlarged. Theale's National School (which is still standing) was built in 1833 for 175 children and enlarged in 1893 to hold 200, although average attendance was reported well below capacity.

Truancy was a serious problem everywhere.

Up to 1856 law and order in rural areas had been maintained in much the same way since Tudor times. Unpaid parish constables, under the direction of local magistrates, provided an amateur, uncoordinated, and sometimes biased service to their own communities, and were given to calling on the military for assistance in times of serious trouble, as they had done during the riots of 1830. In towns, the situation was better, but only Reading had set up a professional police force in 1836, as boroughs were empowered to do by the Municipal Corporations Act of the previous year. Country magistrates had been empowered to establish police forces and to build police stations after 1839, but the decision had been left to their discretion and, in Berkshire, as in many other counties, the proposal was defeated on the grounds of expense. There was, in fact, considerable support for a rural police force in east Berkshire. At a magistrates' meeting, Colonel Vansittart recalled that when he was living in Cookham in 1849, there were in that year alone six cases of arson and over 30 of attempted burglary. Few residents of the parish went to bed without providing themselves with loaded firearms, and some planted 'explosive balls' around their premises. Four constables had been appointed to the parish but none of the malefactors had been caught. In Bray, such was the feeling of insecurity that a public subscription had raised £180 towards establishing a police force, but funds were insufficient to maintain it. Along the south-east border Surrey County Police (established in 1851) complained that Berkshire thieves crossed the boundary to steal horses, sheep and chickens, but could not be caught because of the apathy of Berkshire parish constables.

The Police Act of 1856 made it obligatory for every county to establish a police force, and Berkshire County Constabulary was set up in that year. The Home Office exercised an effective measure of control through the authorisation of a government grant only to those forces certified efficient in terms of numbers and discipline by HM Inspectors of Constabulary. Berkshire County Constabulary headquarters adjoined the Assize Courts in Reading and divisional stations were built at Windsor, Maidenhead, Wokingham, Newbury and Hungerford. Within 20 years more than 50 of the larger villages also had police stations. There was no shortage of recruits for, in addition to a steady wage, each constable was issued with a full uniform topped by a coat and cape with badges, and a staff and handcuffs. If his beat was considered sufficiently dangerous, he was also issued with a small cutlass to be worn at night or in times of serious public disturbances. Discipline was far stricter than it had ever been for the old-style constables, and the turnover in the first few years was high, more than half of those recruited either resigning or being dismissed, many for drunkenness. The danger inherent in rural police work was unpleasantly demonstrated one night in December 1876, when Inspector Drewett and PC Shorter were brutally murdered by poachers near Folly Crossroads, barely a mile from Hungerford. Two brothers, Henry and Francis Tidbury, were found guilty and subsequently hanged at Reading Gaol. Theirs was the first execution to be carried out in private within the gaol, public executions having been abolished in 1868. Nevertheless, a large crowd gathered outside to wait for the hoisting of the black flag, indicating that the sentence had been carried out.

Throughout the 19th century the steady improvement of transport facilities, together with the growing efficiency of postal services, helped to break down rural isolation by keeping country people in touch with the outside world and making more of the world's products locally available. Village shops, which had formerly been rather small and specialised, were able to enlarge their stocks with a wider range of manufactured products and packaged foods which could now be brought more expeditiously from towns and country railway stations. As living standards rose, the lists of country tradesmen also increased. In 1830, for instance, Aldermaston had five general shops, two bakers, a butcher, a shoemaker, carpenter, glover and breeches-maker, toolmaker, miller and maltster, smith, painter and glazier. The rustic character of local requirements reflected in this list may be contrasted with the more genteel style of living suggested by tradesmen at Binfield in the same year: two butchers, three grocers and tea dealers, a baker and general shopkeeper, linen draper, tailor and straw-hat maker, boot and shoemaker, two smiths and farriers, saddler and harnessmaker, plumber, painter and glazier, surgeon. Here, superior food shops are indicated, as well as greater use of riding and carriage horses, providing work for shoesmiths rather than the general ironworking undertaken by the smith in Aldermaston. By 1847 Aldermaston also had a tailor and a plumber, and there was a coal merchant at the wharf. After food trades, clothing trades showed the largest increase during the century, with tailors and dressmakers becoming more numerous.

In less prosperous parts of the county multiple occupations were necessary to make a living. At East Ilsley, Joseph Badcock was 'draper, mercer, grocer, chemist and agent for Guinness's stout'; while at Lambourn, John Hutchins was 'grocer, linen draper, provision dealer and undertaker'. At Fawley, the sole tradesman apart from the blacksmith was Charles Edlin (a name borrowed by Hardy), who was shopkeeper, carrier, parish clerk and postmaster.

Post offices were only rarely part of a village shop. Country postal services improved considerably after the introduction of the penny post in 1840, and a receiving office was set up in every village except in some of the very small ones. The Post Office contract for receiving and delivering local mail could be awarded to any small business or even private resident, and the county directory for 1847 shows how varied they were. At Arborfield, Thomas Chandler, publican at The Swan, was the Post Office receiver; at Barkham, George Collyer at The Bull; at Binfield, John Critcher, wheelwright; at Mortimer, William Ellis, farmer and land surveyor; at Theale, Walter Wise, ironmonger and blacksmith; at Bray, Charles Jones, baker and parish clerk; at Beedon, W Goodman, painter and glazier. Shopkeepers, such as Stephen Smith

Village shops, such as this one at Burghfield, began to stock a wider variety of goods as better transport broke down rural isolation. George Cooper was shopkeeper and sub-postmaster here from c1880 until the First World War.

at Bradfield, and James Sainsbury, grocer and beer retailer at Basildon, rarely served in this capacity. Some small villages, such as Boxford or Avington, still had their mail delivered by foot post or mail cart from the nearest town.

Vital links between villages and towns were maintained by carriers. The numbers of these providing regular services increased as the century advanced, and the lumbering hooded wagons familiar in earlier times were replaced by lighter and more solidly enclosed wooden vans. The number of journeys undertaken increased from Market Days only to two or three times a week, or even daily where the demand was sufficient. Carriers departed from their home villages early in the morning for the journey along a fixed route into town, where they delivered and collected parcels and supplies, executed commissions on behalf of villagers and tradesmen, and made ready to depart for home at the advertised time from whichever inn they regularly used. In Reading, inns commonly used by carriers included the Black Horse in London Street and the Lower Ship in Duke Street for those travelling south; and the Sun in Castle Street, or the Peacock, or the Duke's Head in Broad Street for those travelling west. For many years, certainly until the advent of the bicycle, carriers provided the cheapest alternative to walking for people who were prepared to put up with a slow, bumpy journey, crammed in with sundry goods and parcels, or even livestock. Carriers became well known characters in the places they served, for many of them travelled the same routes for 20 or 30 years before handing over to their successors. William Dodd's van, calling at the Sun in Reading, served Theale, Englefield, Bradfield and Stanford Dingley every Tuesday, Thursday and Saturday from the 1840s to the 1870s; while Ferribee's van, stopping at the Peacock in Reading, served Hampstead Norreys and Compton every Saturday during the same period. There were dozens of other carriers' routes, ensuring that even small villages had a service, however infrequent.

Reading was the busiest centre for the carriers' trade and its streets and inns grew more crowded as services increased. From Burghfield, for example, only three carriers ran in 1842, one daily and two on Saturdays only. By the 1890s there were seven carriers from Burghfield performing 21 journeys a week between them. Newbury was almost as busy as Reading, with carriers coming in from all over west Berkshire and parts of Hampshire and Wiltshire. Well used carriers' inns included the Black Bear, the Waggon and Horses, the Dolphin, the Jack, and the Catherine Wheel. By the 1890s twelve carriers travelled regularly between Newbury and Reading.

In contrast to the proliferation of carriers in west Berkshire, there were very few in east Berkshire. Better rail services, a higher proportion of residents owning private transport, and perhaps shorter distances to the nearest town, must have reduced the demand for their services. In Wokingham there were only two: Goodwin & Son, of Peach Street, who provided a daily service to and from Reading for over 60 years, and Brown's of Bracknell, running three days a week into Reading via Wokingham, and twice to Binfield. In Windsor, only a few short carriers' routes were advertised in directories, from Winkfield, Sunninghill and Maidenhead, apart from one service to London. In Maidenhead, William Emmett appears to have been the only carrier, travelling to Reading every Tuesday, Thursday and Saturday, and to Windsor every Friday. From Datchet, before the opening of the railway line into Windsor, a more sophisticated passenger vehicle described as Sharpe's (Datchet) Omnibus travelled to the City via Horton every morning, stopping at the Spotted Dog in the Strand.

An old industry which expanded hugely in the 19th century was brickmaking. This was carried on in most parts of the county but most intensively in east and central Berkshire, where the demand was greatest; and everywhere farmers and landowners were keen to profit from this largely untapped resource. A contemporary doggerel ran:

'The richest crop for any field
Is a crop of bricks for it to yield,
And the richest crop that it can grow
Is a crop of houses in a row.'

In the second half of the century technical improvements such as the Hoffman kiln, which made continuous firing possible and saved fuel, enabled the industry to supply the building boom, when every kind of structure, from labourers' cottages to lordly mansions, from workhouses to town halls, was built in brick, and there was an accompanying demand for tiles, drainage pipes and other clay products. The rash of brick buildings contributed in no small way to the changing face of the countryside, and it was fortunate that the variety of local clays and methods of production resulted in so many variations of colour and texture, avoiding an overwhelming effect of harsh or monotonous red.

The abundance of good clays around Reading made this the oldest and principal centre of the industry, but by the 1820s brickmaking had begun at Slough, in an area famously well-endowed with clay, and by the 1860s it had spread to Langley. By that time brickworks were beginning to open up around Bracknell, Binfield and Wokingham, and the industry expanded rapidly in that area. In all these places manufacturers made use of the railways to supply orders from other parts of the country, and some firms were linked by their own sidings. After 1882, in an unusual reversal of history, Slough brickmakers transferred their trade to the cheaper transport provided by the newly opened Slough branch of the Grand Union Canal, which helped the industry to develop further in that area. There were other brickworks in east Berkshire at Knowl Hill and Pinkneys Green, near Maidenhead. By the 1890s the largest Bracknell firm, Thomas Lawrence & Sons, had additional works at Easthampstead, Swinley, Warfield and Crowthorne, and was capable of producing twelve million bricks a year.

In west Berkshire brickmaking was carried on in a smaller way at works scattered around Frilsham, Basildon, Hermitage, Cold Ash, Donnington, Shaw and Beedon, where it was often the secondary occupation of a farmer or builder. Many new labourers' cottages were built in brick, replacing the old thatched and dormered type of cottage which Hardy lamented. The exchange of farming for brickmaking, however profitable, did the countryside no favours. Brickyards, with their kilns and chimneys, worksheds and long rows of drying bricks and tiles, were unsightly and occupied a great deal of space, while the pits from which the clay was dug pockmarked and laid waste to the land for miles around. At larger works there could be other attendant paraphernalia, such as the overhead cables at Tilehurst, which carried buckets of wet clay from pits (known locally as 'the treacle mines') on Norcot Hill for over a mile to Colliers' brickworks in Water Road.

Brickworks were often established on private estates for special purposes or buildings of exceptional size. Wellington College had its own brickworks, and so did the huge country mansion at Bearwood, built between 1865 and 1874 for John Walter III. The Bearwood works at California produced some 4,250,000 bricks for the house and also made bricks for *The Times* offices in London.

Bearwood was by far the largest of the new country houses added to Berkshire in the 19th century and, typically for the period, was built for one of the newly rich landowners – usually successful business magnates – who could still afford to realise ideals of country house life and hospitality on a grand scale. House and grounds were designed to demonstrate worldly success and new social standing; and there was no difficulty in obtaining the liberal supply of indoor and outdoor servants needed for the upkeep of the establishment. John Walter's father had bought the Bearwood estate in the 1830s, about the same time as another newcomer to local society, William Crawshay, bought the Caversham Park estate. Crawshay had made his fortune from the huge Cyfarthfa ironworks in South Wales, and in 1850, after a disastrous fire, rebuilt Caversham Park house in lavish style. Other large new houses were

169

The Harvest Home procession at Swallowfield was recorded in the *Illustrated London News* in 1863. Such traditional celebrations were already disappearing from the countryside.

Easthampstead Park, built for the Marquess of Downshire in 1860, and Marlston House, built in 1895–9 for W G Palmer, of the biscuit-making dynasty. Like Bearwood, these houses were built in brick with ample stone dressings, for brick, although inevitable on grounds of expense, was still considered plain and undistinguished on its own. It was not until the turn of the century that leading architects, such as Edwin Lutyens, began to work purely in brick. His Deanery Gardens at Sonning, built for Edward Hudson, the owner of *Country Life* magazine, was constructed in the finest red bricks made by Colliers' of Reading. By that time the decline in land values and other economic factors had virtually put an end to building over-large houses on extensive estates, and new houses were designed on a more manageable scale.

Among the casualties of this century of change were the seasonal customs traditionally associated with May Day, Harvest-time and Christmas, and in the later decades older people were beginning to mourn their passing. A few landowners and squires tried to keep them going. The Russells of Swallowfield Park held Harvest Home festivities until the end of the century, although even in 1863 the event was rare enough to merit an item in the *Illustrated London News*. The parishioners marched in procession to the church to give thanks for the abundant harvest, and listened to a sermon given by the Rev Charles Kingsley, at that time rector of nearby Eversley and already a famous author. After the service the congregation returned in procession to the park, walking behind a great wagon load of wheat drawn by four gaily decorated horses. The National anthem was sung and about 350 people, farmers, labourers and their wives, sat down to dinner, after which there were sports and games. In 1888 the *Reading Mercury* reported a less happy occasion when Sir George Russell, 'the genial and popular Member for East Berkshire', held his annual Harvest Home celebrations. Sadly the weather was very unfavourable, being wet and misty, and the harvest was poor, the wheat having been flattened by wind and rain. However, some 150 tenant farmers and men working on the estate were treated to a hot dinner served in marquees by the landlord of the George and Dragon inn, with Sir George presiding.

At Swallowfield, well into the 1890s, mummers continued to perform their medieval play at Christmas. The characters, believed to have originated in the time of the Crusades, included a Turkish Knight as well as Father Christmas, St George and the Dragon. This is an extract from the Swallowfield version:

'*Enter St George*
Here come I, St George, from England did I spring.
I'll fight the Dragon bold, my wonders to begin.
·I'll clip his wings, he shall not fly,
I'll cut him down, or else I die.

Enter the Dragon
Who's he that seeks the Dragon's blood,
And calls so angry and so loud?
That English dog, will he before me stand?
I'll cut him down with my courageous hand.

They fight and the Dragon is killed.'

17

VICTORIAN TOWNS

Up to the reign of Queen Victoria the great majority of the people of England lived in the country. Towns were mostly small to medium-sized market towns, where the products of local farms and local craftsmen were bought and sold, so that town and country were dependent on each other. Towns also provided banking, legal and other professional services, although most of their clients lived in the country; they tended to be very busy and crowded on market days but rather quiet for the rest of the week. By the middle of the reign this situation was reversed. The Census of England and Wales in 1871 reported that two-thirds of the population now lived in towns; that a new phenomenon, the large manufacturing town, formed a major category among towns; and that former villages and small places were rising up to the importance of towns.

In Berkshire, Reading still functioned as a busy market town but it owed its growth to a variety of industries and had developed into one of the most important manufacturing towns in the south of England. Its population increased from 18,937 in 1841 to 32,324 in 1871, and by 1901 to 59,018. The villages of Slough and Bracknell were 'rising up to the importance of towns', and both doubled their populations from around 2,000 to 4,000 between 1841 and 1871. Even towns such as Newbury and Wokingham, which remained essentially country market towns, showed some rate of growth, while favoured residential and commuter towns such as Windsor and Maidenhead showed very substantial increases in size and population. Windsor with Clewer rose from 9,488 to 15,662, and Maidenhead from 3,315 to 6,173.

Most of the new population moving into towns came from rural areas where its labour was no longer needed. A large manufacturing town such as Reading could offer a wide range of employment for skilled and unskilled workers; while in all towns where there was a growing number of well-to-do families, there was also a growing demand for service in homes and gardens, in shops, offices and transport. Census returns show that people were moving into Reading not only from the rural parts of Berkshire but from Wiltshire, Oxfordshire and Buckinghamshire. Others came from much further afield.

Because of its greater attraction as a place of employment Reading suffered the worst problem of overcrowding. A report of the Municipal Boundaries Commission in 1832 remarked on the large number of tenements let to poor people. It described Reading as 'a place of considerable size, population and apparent prosperity. A new high road into the heart of the town is in progress and will be an important improvement. The main streets are spacious, and contain very good shops and are well lighted with gas ... 1,700 or 1,800 houses are let to mechanics, labourers and other persons at very low rents.' The new road, i.e. Kings Road, served a pleasant residential area, developed in the 1830s and 1840s, of large and small houses for the middle classes. Similar developments were taking place on the other side of the town along Oxford Road. The new housing was in stark contrast to the older parts of the town centre, around Broad Street, Friar Street and St Mary's Butts, where ancient timber-framed houses survived, which may once have been occupied by merchants and tradesmen, but were now divided into tenements and rented room by room to much poorer families, usually the most recent arrivals. These areas soon degenerated into slums, where hundreds of people lived in overcrowded conditions without an adequate water supply or sanitation. Diseases flourished, and the prevalence of cholera, smallpox, scarlatina and typhoid fever made the death rate in Reading higher than anywhere else in Berkshire. Not only slum dwellings made the town centre offensive. There were numerous pigsties, and slaughter houses operated in full view of passers by. Street cleaning made little impression on the heaps of refuse lying in the gutters. Public complaints had been increasing over many years, mostly from better-off residents whose town was being rendered so unwholesome. A typical complaint in the *Reading Mercury* in August 1846 remarked that no-one could pass down a by-street without being offended 'by some stagnant pool of putridity, the insufferable stench of a slaughter-house, or the foul air of a half-choked drain'. Even the main streets were barely endurable in warm weather.

Such evils were common to all rapidly growing towns at the time, for the idea that public health should be a concern of central and local government was a new one. In the 1840s various official enquiries produced such masses of horrifying evidence that, in 1848, a Public Health Act was passed empowering towns to establish Local Boards of Health to deal with the problem. The Reading Board was set up in 1850 and carried out essential remedial measures, abolishing cesspools, demolishing slums, laying down a proper drainage system and water supply, removing slaughter houses from the centre to a new abattoir near the cattle market. Over-full burial grounds in the ancient parish churchyards were closed and burial in the new cemetery on the eastern outskirts was made compulsory. The town council made other improvements. Thoroughfares were widened by the removal of old buildings blocking their centres, street cleaning became more efficient. The untidy, rubbish-strewn open space of the Forbury was laid out as formal public gardens for the healthful recreation of the townspeople.

Although no other Berkshire town had such serious public health problems, Windsor, the next in size, had troubles with a new housing estate. The old town, strung around the foot of the castle walls, had begun to expand after the enclosure of common lands on the western side in 1817, and the Municipal Boundaries Commission in 1832 recommended the extension of the borough boundary to take in part of Clewer parish. Between 1841 and 1871 the population of Clewer increased from 3,975 to 8,078, while that of Windsor remained between seven and eight thousand. It was in Clewer that poorly built working-class housing, run up to cope with the rapid growth of population, produced problems similar to those in Reading's slums. Overcrowding and lack of adequate sanitation caused outbreaks of epidemic diseases, particularly cholera, and in 1850 the Windsor Board of Health was set up to carry out the necessary works, beginning with an underground system of sewers. Progress was slow, and at the end of the decade typhoid was still endemic in the town. At the castle, a new drainage system had been started in 1846 but left unfinished, and the ancient drains and cesspools which were allowed to remain were believed to have been the cause of the death of Prince Albert from typhoid in 1861. In the working class areas of the town a major difficulty was that so much of the cheap housing had been built below the flood level of the river, the receptacle of the town's sewage until 1875, and many homes were under water during the winter floods. A special report on the matter by two Government inspectors in the 1880s caused the town council considerable embarrassment, and a new byelaw directed that the foundations of all future buildings must be safely above flood level. In the 1890s the council began to clean up the river frontage and transform it into pleasant public gardens. The problems of Clewer had little effect on the attractions of the historic town of Windsor as a tourist centre, and tourism developed as a major industry after the dual railway links with the capital made it more easily accessible.

Newbury remained true to its role as a country market town, and was proud of the fact that its corn market was larger and more valuable than

174

The canal at Newbury in the 1860s. Newbury managed to retain its prosperity as a market town despite the agricultural slump.

Reading's. Records taken in the 1840s of business at the two markets showed very satisfactory results.

'Value of corn sold at Newbury,
July 1842–June 1843 .... £181,518 8s. 6d.
Ditto at Reading .... £153,652 18s. 11d.
On the market day previous to Christmas Day
1846 the value of corn sold at Newbury was .... £9,793 15s. 6d.
Ditto at Reading .... £5,301 17s. 3d.

The manufacture of wheat into flour and barley into malt were the principal trades of the town, and in 1847 it was said that, within seven miles of it, there were 26 corn mills and 70 malt houses, whose existence accounted for the magnitude of the market. The corn market continued to flourish throughout the 1860s, and a handsome Corn Exchange was opened in the Market Place in 1862. In the same year a wool market was started, some 2,300 tons of wool being deposited in the first year, and this market was held annually until the end of the century. After the collapse of corn prices in the 1870s Newbury's agriculture-based industries, together with its shopping and business centre serving a wide area in three counties, were sufficient to sustain a moderate level of prosperity. The opening of a new cattle market in 1873 followed on

S & E Collier's brickworks in Water Road, Reading, established about 1870, were the longest-lasting of the Victorian brickworks. They closed in 1967 and a housing estate now occupies this site.

the increased importance of livestock farming.

The Newbury Weekly News was launched in 1868, a significant year for the provincial press. The development of the electric telegraph had made news available all over the country within a few hours. In 1868 the Press Association was formed to provide a joint news service for provincial newspapers at low rates of telegraphic transmission, enormously widening their range of possible news coverage. Although only a weekly, the Newbury paper provided a valuable channel of news, information and advertisements, creating stronger links between the town and the rural communities it served.

The built-up area of Newbury expanded slowly, mainly to the south, where the ecclesiastical parish of St John was formed in 1859. Its Gothic church was designed in brick by William Butterfield. In 1878 the borough boundaries were extended into Speen and Greenham, and between 1876 and 1878 new municipal buildings were added to the 18th century town hall, providing a new council chamber and magistrates' court. A clock tower was completed in 1881. Newbury's slower rate of growth helped it to avoid such drastic changes as those taking place in Reading.

The firms which made Reading famous as a manufacturing town occupied large and prominent sites in and around the town centre. Sutton's Royal Seed Establishment on the east side of the Market Place extended over much of the former abbey precincts. Simonds' Brewery in Bridge Street had expanded along the canal, while Huntley & Palmers' stretched from King's Road to the railway, and was linked by sidings to the Great Western and South Eastern networks. The seeds, bulbs, beer and biscuits produced by these firms had won a high reputation all over Britain and across the world-wide market of the Empire.

Large employers of labour though they were, Reading contained many other industrial and commercial concerns which attracted people to the town in search of employment. There were several other large breweries, such as Blandy, Hawkins & Co in Castle Street, and Dymore Brown in Queens Road. Iron founding and agricultural engineering, and the Great Western Railway engineering works in Caversham Road, employed many hundreds of men. Brickmaking was the fourth industry for which Reading was famous. S & E Collier's works in Tilehurst were the largest and longest-lasting, surviving into the 1960s, and in addition to producing bricks and tiles for a great many important local buildings, also supplied thousands of tiles for London housing estates. Among other brickmakers were Poulton's in Elgar Road and Wheeler's in Katesgrove and Tilehurst. Building trades and the printing trade flourished; shops, offices and domestic service absorbed thousands of men and women; while country men experienced in horse management found work as grooms, ostlers, carters or cab drivers.

Far from declining, the number of horses in use for short journeys and delivery work in town and countryside increased in the second half of the century. The stimulus given by railways to travel, industry and commerce made station approaches and goods yards perpetually busy with horse-drawn traffic. Town streets were crowded with private vehicles, delivery vans, carts and hire-cabs; and noisy with rumbling wheels, clopping hooves and jingling harness. The smell and dirt of horse manure invaded even the smartest streets, and crossing sweepers plied a lowly trade clearing passages through the dirt for pedestrians, especially ladies, whose long skirts trailed along the ground.

The town centre was re-orientated towards the railways, and away from the Kennet wharves which had served it well for so many centuries. Simonds' Brewery, started in the 18th century, Sutton's Seeds, founded in 1806, and Huntley & Palmers' in 1823, had grown up with the canal but quickly transferred their business to the larger and faster distributive network provided by the railways. In 1865–7 the original Great Western station was replaced by a larger building, and Station Road, leading to it from Friar Street, began to be developed south of the Great Western Hotel, built opposite the station in 1844. However, it was not until the turn of the century that Queen Victoria Street was cut through into Broad Street, creating a direct access from the station to the heart of the shopping centre.

The improvements carried out by the Board of Health in the 1850s and 1860s were followed by a period of energetic civic and commercial building. As in other towns, the increased powers and responsibilities of local government called for more public buildings; not only council offices, but public baths, public libraries, police and fire stations, and most numerous of all after 1870, board schools. A new town hall was built in 1872–5, incorporating the 18th century hall. It was designed by the distinguished architect, Alfred Waterhouse, and Colliers' red and grey bricks and terracotta ornaments were used to great effect. In the 1880s this building was extended by a range containing a concert hall, public library, museum and art gallery. Reading School, which had declined to the point of extinction, was re-established in 1867 under the council's control, to provide a more efficient education for boys. The foundation stone of a new school building, also designed by Waterhouse, was laid by the Prince of Wales in 1870, and Reading school re-opened in 1871.

Reading School was built on part of the Redlands estate, which became available for development in the 1860s, and became one of several new residential areas to the east and south of Reading, extending towards Earley. On the western side of the town, more development was taking place along Oxford Road. Two important new buildings in this area were the Union Workhouse (later Battle Hospital), opened in 1867 in what was then described as 'a salubrious position about a mile from the town centre'; and in 1877, Brock Barracks, providing a headquarters for the Berkshire Regiment. In 1887–9 the borough boundaries were extended to take in parts of Tilehurst, Earley, Southcote and Whitley, thus doubling the area of the borough.

In 1832 Maidenhead was still making a living from traffic along the Bath Road, and was only just beginning to expand beyond its one main street. It had no manufacturing industries apart from a little brewing and flour milling, but it was said to be 'the centre of an opulent

178

neighbourhood'. A short distance away, North Town contained about 150 houses whose inhabitants worked in Maidenhead, and several new houses had been built between Maidenhead and North Town, indicating that future growth would be in that direction. A mile to the west, Boyn Hill was still a straggling village to the south of the Bath Road, and near a spring known as Reading pond, which was in great demand as a watering place for coach and wagon horses. Boyn Hill remained rural throughout the 1840s, when William Child, the publican at the Old Dog and Ferrets, eked out a living as a 'bird stuffer and herb distiller'.

Everyone who had derived trade from the Bath Road fell on hard times after the opening of the Great Western Railway, not least Maidenhead town council, which was forced to reduce its tolls on the bridge in an attempt to attract custom from its too powerful competitor. But within a year or two, trade in the town began to pick up as new residents moved into the area, delighted to find so pleasant and healthy a neighbourhood, with a railway station, within 23 miles of London. The population increased rapidly. New shops and businesses replaced trades which had been forced to close, and a large new brewery was started in 1840 by William Nicholson in place of the stables and coach houses of the old White Hart Inn. Houses and villas were built on the high ground in the Castle Hill area, and after the Maidenhead Improvement Company was formed in the 1860s the town began to grow in all directions. More shopping streets were added, and housing for the working classes as well as for the middle and professional classes. Boyn Hill, where a church designed by Street was built in 1854–7, became a smart residential area. As the Thames became more and more popular for pleasure boating, fashionable villas were built along the river bank, and large hotels, such as the Thames and the Riviera, opened up to accommodate weekend visitors. The old coaching inn beside the bridge, formerly known as the Orkney Arms, took on a new lease of life as Skindle's Hotel. In 1869, when the population had passed 5,000, the *Maidenhead Advertiser* began publication.

'Slough', said Kelly's Directory of 1883, 'which but a few years since consisted of a few inns and other accommodation for traffic on the High road from London to Bath, is now a well-built and rapidly increasing town, a polling place for the county and an important station on the Great Western Railway, being the junction of the Windsor branch . . . . The Grand Junction Canal Company, by Act of Parliament, 1879, have constructed a branch from Cowley to Slough. A new station is now (1882) being built, and the line widened between Paddington and Maidenhead.'

The railway gave a tremendous boost to the two industries which developed from Slough's rich and fertile soils. Brickworks had been opened up for special purposes in the past, notably for the building of Eton College, but these had been short-lived, and it was not until the 1820s that brickmaking started as a local industry and gathered momentum in mid-century as the demand grew for bricks for houses and many other kinds of buildings in London and other parts of the country. By the 1860s brickworks were opening up in Langley and, by the end of the century, brickfields covered large areas of that parish. The second industry, market gardening, had been carried on in a small way since the 18th century, but after 1838 the possibility of sending large quantities of fresh vegetables, fruit and flowers by rail to London, as well as selling to the prosperous populations of Windsor and other local towns, attracted more nurserymen to Slough. Considerable effort and expertise were put into the cultivation of new and finer varieties of fruit, such as the Cox's Orange Pippin, and of scented flowers such as lilies, roses and pinks, which were so popular in wealthy Victorian homes.

Meanwhile Slough village was expanding with new streets, shops and useful trades, professional firms, schools and chapels. It was not just a working-class town, for there were neighbourhoods within easy reach of the station containing high-class developments, such as the Upton Park estate of villas and terrace houses in a parkland setting. Since 1812, the *Windsor and Eton Express* had circulated in this area, but in 1883 Charles Luff, the son of the town's first postmistress, started the *Slough Observer*. By the end of the century Slough was the largest town in South Buckinghamshire, with a population of around 11,000.

Bracknell had begun to develop as a trading place on the Windsor Forest turnpike road, and a short distance to the north of the settlement of Old Bracknell, in the 18th century, when the Forest was becoming increasingly popular as a residential area for the nobility and gentry. In 1847 Kelly's Directory described it as 'a small village 28 miles west of London, in the parish of Warfield;. . . being in a woodland country, the scenery is rendered very beautiful; the roads are also remarkably good. The village itself consists of a long, narrow street, inhabited principally by small shopkeepers, who supply the surrounding neighbourhood, there being several large mansions inhabited by persons of distinction.' In addition to the many shopkeepers the locality also supported a solicitor, a fire insurance agent, a surgeon and a vet, and by the 1860s a land surveyor and house agent as well.

In 1851 Bracknell, which had hitherto contained parts of Warfield and Winkfield parishes, was formed into a separate ecclesiastical parish and a new church, of the Holy Trinity, was built. The arrival of the

Wokingham's red brick Town Hall was built between 1858 and 1860, replacing the 17th century timber-framed, many-gabled building which had epitomised this ancient town, originally within the bounds of Windsor Forest. East Berks is proud of its forest history. Bracknell has recently changed its name to Borough of Bracknell Forest.

railway in 1856 encouraged more rapid growth and brought a change in the character of the area through the introduction of industry. Bracknell had plenty of clay and brickmaking had been carried on formerly in a small way, using wood for firing kilns. The railway brought supplies of cheap coal, allowing brickmaking to develop as a major industry and to become the largest employer of labour in the area. Thomas Lawrence, who started his first brickworks in 1860, and by the 1890s had five works in and around Bracknell, producing millions of bricks a year, was only the best-known and most successful of many firms in the late 19th century. By 1900 Bracknell was a small town with modern amenities, such as gas lighting, mains water supply in place of the former wells and pumps, banks, schools, a hotel, churches of most denominations, and recreational facilities.

The market town of Wokingham served an area smaller and more compact than Newbury's, and in the 19th century, as the population of east Berkshire increased, it changed more rapidly as communications, housing and industry developed. Up to Victoria's reign the rustic character of the old Forest town was symbolised by the 17th century town hall, timber-framed and many gabled, which stood on a low mound where the three main streets converged upon the Market Place. In old prints it was shown picturesquely shaded by spreading oak trees. From the 16th to the 19th century the name of the town was commonly spelt Oakingham, from a mistaken but understandable belief that it was derived from the noble oaks of Windsor Forest. The character of the Forest began to change after the enclosure act of 1813. More development took place and some parts of the heath were planted with pine trees. Monarchs no longer hunted the deer, whose numbers were reported greatly diminished early in the century. The young Queen Victoria could be seen travelling sedately in her carriage through Wokingham, on her way to visit the Duke of Wellington at Stratfield Saye.

Wokingham's corn market had never been important. Although mixed farming was the principal occupation of the neighbourhood, poor and ill-drained soils had produced small rewards. The poultry market, which had been of prime importance in the 18th and early 19th centuries, had declined and by 1847 very small quantities were brought for sale. By 1877 Wokingham market was said to be unimportant and its decline continued to the end of the century. Wokingham flourished instead as a useful shopping and business centre for the gentry and farming communities living roundabout. The railways linking it with Reading in 1849 and Waterloo in 1856 greatly enlarged the range of goods and services available, and encouraged some new residents, although in 1877 the journey to London via Staines still took at least $1\frac{1}{4}$ hours, making Wokingham less attractive to commuters than Maidenhead, Slough, Twyford or Reading.

From the late 1850s the town began to change as old buildings disappeared and new ones were built. In 1858 the old town hall, which had served for innumerable social gatherings as well as official meetings, was judged at the end of its useful life, and a subscription list was opened towards the cost of replacing it. £1,500 was raised; the old building was demolished and work started on a new town hall, which would combine municipal offices, a police headquarters, and public rooms, including a reading room and parochial library of 1,000 volumes. In complete contrast to its predecessor, it was built in brick in the Victorian Gothic style. The new town hall was opened in 1860, and in the next 20 years many other buildings were added to the town, especially schools and churches to serve new parishes as the population grew steadily from 3,342 in 1841 to 5,043 in 1881, and 6,002 by 1901.

The number and variety of shops and businesses also increased, and some new industries, such as brickmaking and steam milling, were established. Three steam mills were working by the 1890s. Older crafts and industries which survived for many years were shoemaking and broom-making. A tannery on the Emmbrook supplied the shoemakers and leather workers who formed the largest body of craftsmen in the town. The heathlands, two or three miles to the south, supported a community of broom-makers, who cut birch and brushwood on the commons to make into brooms, many of which were sold in Reading. In 1862 the local clergy began to take an interest in these unlettered, almost heathen people, and a day school was opened for the children, followed in 1864 by their own church, St Sebastian's in Nine Mile Ride.

In 1885, in response to a petition to the Privy Council, Wokingham was granted a charter of incorporation, giving it a borough council with full municipal powers. Until then, government had been vested in an Alderman and a number of burgesses. Now the chief officer renounced his ancient Saxon title, and adopted the more usual one of Mayor.

Like Newbury, Hungerford faced a struggle for survival after the end of the coaching age. It had few other resources. Apart from milling, brewing and the fisheries it had no industries, and the rural area it served came within the sphere of its larger neighbour. However, it provided shopping facilities for an area with many small villages and hamlets with few shops of their own. The arrival of the railway in 1847 improved communications with Newbury and Reading, although Hungerford remained the terminus until the line was continued westwards in 1862. Trade along the canal continued although declining steadily. Shaw's barges still travelled between London and Bristol, calling daily at Hungerford wharf; while Parkes' barges plied between Reading and Bristol, calling three times a week. As the years passed, these journeys were shortened until, by the 1880s, barges ran only between Hungerford and Reading.

Barley was still extensively grown in the area. In 1847 Kelly's Directory recorded that a corn market by sample only was held but a pitched market was about to be established. A cattle fair was held each year in April and was well attended, and two hiring fairs took place at Michaelmas. It was thought that 'A sheep fair would be a great accommodation to Hungerford, the situation being well adapted for such a purpose, and a large stock being always in the immediate neighbourhood.' By 1887 the town had made remarkable progress. The decayed 18th century town hall had been demolished and a new town hall and corn exchange built at a cost of £4,000, and opened in 1871. In addition to the cattle fair, a yearly wool fair in June and sheep fair in August were held. A Literary and Scientific Institution established in 1865 provided

The sheep market at East Ilsley was said in 1844 to be the largest in England outside Smithfield. Sheep and lamb fairs took place annually at Easter and in November.

a public reading room which was supplied daily with London and provincial newspapers and periodicals. Social life was enlivened by the Royal Berkshire Yeomanry Cavalry, whose headquarters was in the town. Printing and bookselling were among new trades represented, and the range of employment had been widened by small engineering firms, such as Cottrell & Co., engineers and agricultural machinists at Eddington ironworks. In 1894 the boundaries of Hungerford were extended to bring Charnham Street into the town.

In 1847 Lambourn's huge parish of nearly 15,000 acres was said to contain 'the decayed market town of Chipping Lambourn', the market having been discontinued in the previous century. A fine large church and medieval market cross survived as reminders of past ambitions. The town was now no more than a large village, whose tradesmen and craftsmen drew their custom from the villages and farms of the upper Lambourn Valley and the Downs. The greater part of the parish consisted of Downland turf, which from the 1840s brought a new industry and new trade to the area. Race-horse training had originally taken place privately on owners' estates, but an increasing number of public training stables were set up and the fine turf of the Downs naturally attracted trainers. By the 1870s there were several training stables in Lambourn, and others in East Ilsley and villages roundabout.

Although smaller than Lambourn, East Ilsley had remained livelier because of the main Oxford to Newbury road passing through it. Its ancient corn market had died out at the end of the 18th century, but its sheep market still flourished. William Hewett, in 1844, wrote that 'East Ilsley has been celebrated from time immemorial as a large market for sheep, a reputation it still maintains; being, with the exception of Smithfield, the greatest sheep mart in England.' He also noted that a wool fair had been started at East Ilsley some years previously, and was increasing in importance. 'Its flourishing state must be ascribed to the liberality of the Marquis of Downshire, and other landed proprietors in this county, who have annually presented two silver cups to be competed for by the wool staplers and farmers.' Sheep markets were held in Broad

Street, which was formerly the Market Place, and Hewett recorded that as many as 80,000 sheep had been penned there in one day, of which 55,000 had been sold. Sheep and lamb fairs took place regularly between Easter and November, bringing dealers and graziers from all parts of the country.

Such fairs as East Ilsley's continued to fulfil their original purpose, but many smaller country fairs had ceased altogether, and in large manufacturing towns fairs were no longer of any importance as trading events. Even Reading's once-famous Cheese Fair, at which in the 18th century over 1,000 tons of cheese had been brought for sale from all the dairying counties of the west, had declined by the 1830s and became chiefly notable as a pleasure fair. As such it quickly fell into disrepute. The vulgar peep-shows, travelling menageries, rustic sports and other crude or sensational entertainments appealed to the labouring classes but respectable townspeople grew increasingly appalled and disgusted by them, and clergymen preached rousing sermons attacking the evils resulting from pleasure fairs. Public pressure over many years reduced them in size, and in 1871 the Fairs Act gave local authorities the power to abolish fairs which no longer served a useful purpose. Among the still useful fairs held at the end of the century were the hiring fairs, to which farm workers and domestic servants came to seek employment for the coming year. Traditionally, those with special skills carried distinctive symbols, such as a shepherd's crook, carter's whip or housemaid's broom, to advertise them to potential employers. Hiring fairs continued to be held in Newbury, Hungerford and Reading, but began to die out after labour exchanges were introduced early in the 20th century. Hiring fairs of a sort were held by large manufacturing firms such as Huntley and Palmers, and on these dismal occasions, a crowd of the unemployed would stand outside the factory gates, waiting for them to open, when a few lucky ones would be picked, almost at random, and given work.

Market days continued to be the most important day of the week for market towns, but shops were now the main attraction of town centres, making them busy throughout the week. For middle-class women with money to spend, shopping had become a leisure activity, and shopkeepers were encouraged to extend the range of their goods beyond what was necessary and serviceable. Shops grew larger and their displays more elaborate. Next to food trades, clothing and furnishing trades expanded rapidly. Drapers and dressmakers were among the most successful high street traders, and it was not unusual for their shops to expand into department stores. John and William Heelas of Wokingham both went into the drapery business, one remaining in that town and the other moving to Reading, where he started a shop in Minster Street, in

1854, which had grown by the 1890s into the largest and most palatial store in the town. Other department stores competing with Heelas' were Wellsteed's, Bull's and after 1903, the huge and architecturally fantastic McIlroy's store.

Shop assistants formed one of the largest classes of employees, attracting men and women, although the hours were long, the wages low, and prospects minimal. At some stores it was usual for the younger, unmarried assistants to 'live in', and the miserable conditions they endured were experienced by H G Wells, and used as material for his novel, *Kipps*, published in 1905. In 1880 Wells was apprenticed at the age of 14 to Messrs Rodgers and Denyer, a firm of drapers in Windsor High Street. His working day began at 7.30 in the morning and ended at 8.30 in the evening. He lived in, and shared a room with three other junior assistants. Meals were eaten in a canteen in the basement, into which daylight never penetrated, and out of the 24 hours, only two were theirs to call their own – between 8.30 and 10.30 in the evening. It was then that they had their only chance of getting a breath of fresh air or taking any exercise. They had to be back at the shop promptly by 10.30 pm, for then the lights were turned out and the doors locked, and latecomers were unable to get in. Wells found the business of selling materials by the yard over the counter tedious and depressing; and, perhaps fortunately for him, Messrs Rodgers and Denyer found Wells so unsuited to the job that, in under three months, they cancelled his apprenticeship articles. His brother Fred, however, had a similar post at Heelas' store in Wokingham, and was apparently better suited to that kind of work. Rodgers & Denyer were at 25 High Street, Windsor, when Wells worked there, and the firm remained at that address until c 1905. During that period, Caley & Son, at 19 High Street, grew into Windsor's leading store, and were 'court dress makers, mantle makers, milliners, ladies' tailors, etc., and linen drapers'. By 1911 Caley's had expanded into Rodgers & Denyer's former premises at number 25.

The range of specialist shops also increased: numerous commercial and home dressmakers created a demand for sewing machines; sports equipment warehouses opened up in response to the spread of organised games; piano and music shops flourished in an age of home entertainment. Some new trades were introduced, notably that of the commercial photographer. Frances Dann's business in Reading was established in 1856 and grew into the well-known firm of Dann & Lewis, surviving well into the 20th century. S Victor White and William Salmon were among many others whose work was to leave a permanent record of Victorian Reading. By the 1870s photographers were in business in other Berkshire towns – four in Windsor, three in Maidenhead, and one in each of Bracknell, Newbury, Hungerford and Pangbourne. There was a world of opportunity for photographers. The Victorians sat enthusiastically, in groups or individually, to have their portraits taken, and outdoor scenes in town and country featured in new illustrated guidebooks. Picture postcards gave the trade an additional boost after 1894, when the Post Office agreed to accept them. It is not easy to imagine nowadays the novelty and interest of sending to friends or relatives a genuine likeness of a place being visited, whether it was a large town or a small village.

In the 1870s improved models of the bicycle were developed and, in the 1880s, cycling became enormously popular both for pleasure riding and for getting to work. At first there were few dealers, and these were also makers, such as William Goddard in Reading, and Timberlake & Co. in Maidenhead, who were both in business by 1877. Within a few years there were many more makers, and also dealers and agents for famous named models – the Monarch, the Rover, the Zephyr, and others. The most famous firm was that of John Warrick in Reading, founded in 1877, which specialised in bicycles and box tricycles designed for town delivery work and became one of the leading manufacturers in the country. Continual improvements to bicycles stimulated demand and prices were soon within the reach of all but the poorest people. In 1900 the Humber Cycle Depot in Market Place, Reading, was advertising 'Machines built to order, fully guaranteed for 12 months. Free wheels, rim brakes, long cranks, high gears. All prices from £8 to £30'.

Shops and businesses started by local enterprise dominated town centres until the end of the century and it was not until the 1890s that the first small branches of multiple chain stores began to appear. Home and Colonial Stores, selling cheap and imported foods, were in Reading and Maidenhead by 1895; Freeman, Hardy and Willis, mass produced footwear, were in Reading, Newbury and Windsor in the same year. Lipton's, tea and provision merchants, appeared in Reading in 1899, and Boots' Cash Chemists in Reading and Windsor in 1903. W H Smith's, originally only station newsagents, had bookshops in Newbury and Reading by 1907. Marks and Spencer opened a penny bazaar in West Street, Reading, in 1904 and another in Broad Street in 1912.

18

COUNTY PROGRESS:
1889–1939

Berkshire began to be called the Royal County in the 1880s. The style was unofficial – it did not receive royal approval until 1957 – but it had popular appeal as the Golden Jubilee of Victoria's reign approached, and it was adopted with enthusiasm by the recently formed Berkshire Archaeological and Architectural Society. 'The Royal County possesses vast fields for archaeological discovery which have never been explored,' stated the Society's journal in 1889, while its Secretary, the Rev P H Ditchfield, pressed Berkshire's claim far back into the past: 'For 800 years it has enjoyed the proud distinction of being the Royal County; Windsor Castle, the ancient home of the kings and queens of England, is within its borders.' In 1877 Wantage, the birthplace of King Alfred, had been honoured by the erection of an imposing statue in the Market Place, put up at the expense of Lord Wantage and unveiled by the Prince of Wales. Other royal associations abounded: Royal Ascot, the Royal Military College, the Royal River; and in 1885 the Berkshire Regiment was awarded the prefix 'Royal' in recognition of its gallant conduct in the recent action at Tofrek. National and local history were becoming popular subjects of study, stimulated partly by the great achievements of the Victorian Age, partly by the disappearance of ancient landmarks as the process of change accelerated in town and country, and partly by the spread of education and the growing thirst for knowledge.

Looking back at the past, to the beginnings of the royal castle and to the Saxons who created the shire, seemed particularly appropriate at a time when the county faced a new administrative future. Since Tudor times counties had been administered by justices deriving their authority from the Crown, whose principal qualification for office was ownership of substantial property in the county. These men belonged to the upper layer of county society, by long tradition bound up with the land, the Church and Parliament. For the most part, they had performed their duties conscientiously in the civil government of the county as well as in

Berkshire County Council's first Shire Hall, opened in 1911, stood alongside the entrance to the stables (later the garage) of Sutton's Seeds establishment in Reading.

the administration of justice. At Quarter Sessions they met together in Reading, Abingdon, Newbury or Wokingham to attend to the business of the court and to discuss local affairs and politics, while their wives and families patronised the local shops and, in the evening, they might all attend a ball in the town's assembly rooms. Their control over local affairs had remained unchallenged for generations, but by the end of the 19th century it was no longer so willingly accepted by the growing numbers of the rural population who were educated and enfranchised.

In towns, middle-class ratepayers had been able to vote in local elections since 1835, and in 1867 the vote had been extended to the working classes. As the responsibilities of local government widened, the principle of election was applied to new bodies charged with areas of special concern, such as Boards of Guardians of the Poor, Local Boards of Health, Highways Boards and School Boards. Each of these added to the burden of the rates, so that country ratepayers were driven to protest against further taxation without representation. The Local Government

Act of 1888, and the County Electors Act of the same year, were designed to put county government on the same democratic footing as that of towns by setting up elected county councils. These would take over the administrative, but not the judicial, duties of the justices in Quarter Sessions and would control the whole of the county except towns with populations exceeding 50,000. These were designated county boroughs, and would continue to manage their own affairs. Reading amply fulfilled the requirements for this status.

Berkshire County Council began to hold its quarterly meetings in 1889, the venue then, and for over 20 years until a Shire Hall was built, being the Assize Courts in Reading. The 68 elected members were all men experienced in public office, and many had previously served as magistrates. Mr W G Mount, of Wasing Place, was elected Chairman. He was already Chairman of Quarter Sessions and Member of Parliament for South Berkshire. Membership was very largely Conservative, with a few Liberals; there was no Radical element to disrupt the smooth transfer of responsibility from one body to another. To begin with, only a few committees were found necessary to deal with the business in hand: Finance and General Purposes, Highways and Bridges, Technical Education, and Diseases among Farm Animals. If the workload was small, so was the budget. The county rate in the first year yielded only £11,944, a sum which the Council took care to manage with the strictest economy, so that none of its newly powerful electorate could accuse it of waste. A Government grant of £6,478 was received for technical education, a forerunner of higher education, which aimed to train young people for useful occupations in farming, dairying, farriery and building trades.

The management of police forces had presented a problem to the Government, which was unwilling to transfer full control to county councils. Arson and other violent crimes, many resulting from the continuing war between landowners and poachers, were still common in rural areas, causing the Prime Minister (Lord Salisbury) to remark that 'the civilization of many English counties is sufficiently backward to make it hazardous for the Crown to part with power over the police'. A compromise had, therefore, been decided on, whereby control of each county constabulary was vested in a Standing Joint Committee, half of whose members were magistrates and half county councillors.

At their early meetings Berkshire County Council's most pressing concern was the matter of roads and bridges. Barely 20 years had passed since the last of the turnpike trusts had been wound up, bankrupted by the loss of traffic to the railways and heartily detested by the remaining road users. Since then, main roads had been much quieter than in the days of long-distance coaching, and their condition had deteriorated. Responsibility for their upkeep had passed to local Highways Boards, each covering a large part of the county; but several important bridges, including those across the Thames at Windsor, Maidenhead, Cookham, Whitchurch and Streatley, remained in private or corporate ownership, and tolls for their upkeep were still demanded from travellers. Freeing these bridges by purchase would require far greater expenditure than the council could then contemplate, and the process of freeing them was to take many years and some hard-fought campaigns by local people. Windsor's bridge was freed in 1898, Maidenhead's in 1904, Streatley's in 1923, and Cookham's in 1946. Whitchurch's remains a toll bridge to this day, and provides a bone of contention between that village and Pangbourne.

Roads which were formerly managed by turnpike trusts were now designated main roads, and became the responsibility of the County Council, while other roads remained with the Highways Boards. A statistical survey revealed that a considerable disparity existed between the mileage of main roads in east Berkshire and that in the west, the former having only 43 miles and the latter 71 miles. This situation was not acceptable to east Berkshire, which was busier, more populous, and whose ratepayers paid higher rates than those of west Berkshire. Moreover, the use made of many minor roads had increased, especially where they approached towns, bridges or railway stations, and it was necessary to upgrade these to main road standard. Eventually, the Council decided that, in order to even up expenditure, east Berkshire should have 116 miles of road maintained up to main road standard, and west Berkshire 115 miles. The difference in rates was unchanged. Another much-debated question concerned the advisability of purchasing a steam roller. Even the best road surfaces consisted only of small stones compacted by rolling, and in dry weather these produced clouds of choking dust. In 1893 a decision was reached not to purchase a roller as it was cheaper to hire one when needed.

The roads began to get busier in the 1880s, and by the 1890s traffic was already causing problems. Cyclists at first, and a few years later, motorists, agitated for better road surfaces. Bicycles, to begin with, had been few in number and ridden only by daring enthusiasts. An early trial of their capabilities took place in 1869, when H J Timberlake of Maidenhead, riding a velocipede, challenged the winner of the Chertsey Steeplechase to a race over one mile of the Bath Road through Maidenhead Thicket, the cyclist being the loser. Further trials took place in 1870, when two pioneers undertook to cycle from London to Bath and back, and took five days for the round trip. Rapid advances in

Edwin Lipscomb's cycle shop in Broadway, Newbury, in the early years of the 20th century. Bicycles brought freedom of movement to all but the very poor and focussed new attention on the state of Berkshire's roads.

engineering enabled another cyclist, in 1880, to complete the same journey in 23 hours, riding a penny-farthing. The development of the low-built, chain-driven safety bicycle and the pneumatic tyre introduced in the 1880s made cycling a popular pastime, as well as a means of conveyance for women as well as men. The growth of bicycle manufacture soon brought prices down, so that, for the first time, a cheap and independent form of transport was available to the masses. Thousands of people cycled to work, and at the weekends town-dwellers were able to get out into the countryside for fresh air and exercise, while country-dwellers were less isolated than before. Numerous cycling clubs were formed, and guidebooks recommended routes and tours for cyclists. Such books were keenly interested in road surfaces, and critical of roads such as those in the Lambourn valley, which were 'covered with quantities of loose stones and rubble, perilous and risky indeed to tyres, promising a goodly crop of punctures'. Cyclists discovered a pleasure in hills never before experienced by travellers. The mile-long run downhill into East Ilsley was recommended as marvellously exhilarating, 'poetry in motion on wheels' – provided that no strings of horses or flocks of sheep got in the way. The Cyclists' Touring Club put up warning notices at danger spots, such as steep hills, but many cyclists ignored the signs and the County Council received many complaints about dangerous speeding on various hills in the county. Cyclists were also accused of frightening horses, sheep and pedestrians, cutting up road surfaces, and raising excessive clouds of dust. But whatever trouble they caused, complaints about cyclists were nothing like so hostile as those directed at early motorists.

In 1895, people living in the neighbourhood of Windsor were able to watch the Hon Evelyn Ellis, a pioneer motorist who lived in Datchet, driving his four horsepower Panhard-Levassor around the country lanes. His average speed was between nine and ten miles an hour, well above the legal limit of four mph, fixed many years earlier with steam ploughs and threshing machines in mind. Another enthusiast was Alfred Harmsworth, owner of the *Daily Mail*, who leased Calcot Park, near Reading, in 1899, and entertained his motoring friends there at weekend house parties. Influential motoring interest got the speed limit raised to 14 mph in 1896, although local councils were empowered to reduce it to 12, which Berkshire did. In 1900 Harmsworth sponsored a 1,000 mile trial run round Britain, which attracted 83 entrants. Calcot Park was a scheduled stop on the route, where drivers were entertained to a champagne breakfast.

Not surprisingly, motor cars were regarded as playthings of the rich and idle, so that complaints about dangerous driving, noise, dust, road damage and frightened animals tended to be soured by class hostility. Motorists were accused of driving at double the speed limit and refusing to stop for anyone, so that it was impossible to identify them in order to lodge a complaint. At a meeting of the County Council in 1900, Alderman Major Thoyts, of Sulhamstead, reported that even if the driver of a horse turned round and galloped after an offending car, it was impossible to catch it. Only those who used the roads on which motor cars travelled knew what a nuisance and inconvenience they were. His was only one of many complaints at the meeting, and it was resolved that the Clerk should write to other County Councils asking for their co-operation in seeking legislation from the Home Secretary to control motorists. In the meantime, the county police were under orders to stop and caution motorists exceeding the speed limit and to report second offenders. In 1903 speed checks were carried out in Bracknell High Street, where policemen were stationed with stop watches, and several drivers exceeding 12 mph were fined £10 by Wokingham magistrates. Later that year, the Motor Car Act raised the speed limit to 20 mph, but required all vehicles to be registered and to carry lights and number plates front and rear. The first year's statistics, in 1904, showed that there were 8,465 cars in Britain, and this number was almost quadrupled by 1907. Road accidents and traffic offences increased and motorists remained widely unpopular. In Kenneth Grahame's *Wind in the Willows*, published in 1908, the character of Mr Toad represented the type of wealthy, arrogant motorist whose reckless driving involved him in frequent accidents and troubles with the police. No doubt there were some, among Grahame's older readers, who felt profoundly satisfied when Toad was sentenced to 20 years' imprisonment!

The pressing need to improve road surfaces led to the appointment, in 1904, of a County Surveyor of Highways, who organised a more efficient system of maintenance. Gangs of six or seven men were employed in each district to spread a water-bound macadam in front of a roller, and 89 lengthmen were each responsible for about four miles of road. In 1909 tar spraying equipment was purchased for use only on main roads, and it was soon remarked that its use lessened the need for excessive watering, which had formerly been so detrimental to surfaces. The busiest road was still the Bath Road, which absorbed an inordinate amount of surfacing materials because of heavy traffic. In 1912, a Government grant of £30,000 was received towards the reconstruction of this road from Maidenhead to Hungerford, and also of the London road via Ascot.

The work of the County Council increased steadily from the early years of the 20th century. In 1902 School Boards were abolished and the Council became the Local Education Authority, responsible for secondary as well as elementary education. The power to levy a penny rate enabled it to build more schools, and by 1910 the Education Committee had established four new secondary schools: Newbury County Girls' School, Maidenhead Boys' Grammar School, Maidenhead County Girls' School, and Windsor County Boys' School. Ranelagh School at Bracknell, a grammar school for boys and girls, had been rebuilt with the aid of Council funds. Also in 1902, the Council appointed its first Medical Officer of Health, only part-time to begin with, but full-time with two assistants from 1908, when his department took on responsibility for regular medical inspections in schools. Home health visiting by district nurses and midwives began in 1918, and a school dental service in 1927.

The increase of staff resulting from these new duties had obliged the Council to take over additional accommodation, including a row of houses next to the Assize Courts for use as offices. Between 1904 and 1911 these were demolished and Berkshire's first Shire Hall was built

Vincent's motor works at Reading. In 1900 Berkshire County Council ordered the local police to stop and caution any motorist exceeding the speed limit of 12 mph and to report second offenders.

on the site. Externally, this was a handsome and dignified building, but internally it was too small and the office space provided was so inadequate that not many years had passed before staff were again moving into 'temporary' accommodation elsewhere.

The women's suffrage movement was much in the news in the early years of the century. From 1907 women were entitled to serve on county councils, although the first woman councillor was not elected in Berkshire until 1921. Women could already vote in local elections but, after several years of campaigning, were still denied the right to vote in parliamentary elections. After 1912 the militant suffragette movement became more violent, smashing windows and carrying out arson attacks on churches, hotels and other public buildings. Three other churches in England had been destroyed by fire, and 18 others attacked and damaged, before Wargrave church was burned down on Whit Monday 1914. The fire was discovered at 3 am, but by the time local fire brigades reached the scene, only the outer walls and the tower remained standing. Parts of three bombs were found in the wreckage, and postcards left lying about bore messages protesting against the forcible feeding of suffragettes in prison. Typical ones were: 'A reply to brutality and torture'; 'Let the Church follow its own precepts before it is too late

Wargrave church was burned down by suffragettes in 1914. Threats were received that St Mary's, Reading, would be next but no further outrages occurred in Berkshire.

– no surrender'; 'Blessed are those that suffer persecution for justice's sake'. On the same day, a house near Windsor was set on fire and similar postcards left lying about.

Although suffragettes had been holding meetings in the neighbourhood, the presence of militants had not been suspected and it was believed that those guilty came from outside the county. The committee of the Wokingham Women's Suffrage Society wrote to the Vicar of Wargrave expressing sympathy for the loss of his church, and condemning such violent actions, but the vicar's post also contained a great many anonymous letters threatening further violence to local churches, one of them stating that St Mary's, Reading, would be the next one destroyed. In the general state of alarm, many churches were kept locked for several weeks, and were only opened during service hours. Notices were displayed similar to this one outside Mortimer church. 'Owing to dastardly outrages by frenzied criminals who have no regard for God or man, this church will for the present (though with the greatest regret) be kept closed except at the hours of divine worship.'

On the Sunday following the fire at Wargrave, a service for a huge congregation was held among the ruins. At a service in Windsor, when the vicar condemned violent suffragette activities, a woman stood up and shouted 'God bless Mrs Pankhurst', and was escorted to the door. The police took special precautions at Ascot races that month, but there were no more serious incidents in Berkshire. When war broke out a few weeks later, the suffragettes abandoned their campaign for the duration, and joined in the war effort.

The early months of the war saw long queues of men at recruitment centres, inspection parades, crowd scenes at railway stations as people bade goodbye to units of regular and territorial forces, and numerous fund-raising events and street processions. Regiments from elsewhere arrived and were encamped or billeted. Newbury racecourse was occupied for a while by the South Midlands Mounted Brigade but later became a tank repair park and a prisoner of war camp. In east Berkshire a prisoner of war camp for German officers was set up at Holyport. Hospitals allocated wards to the wounded, and additional hospital accommodation was prepared in large country houses, such as Heatherside at Crowthorne, Bisham Abbey, which was a hospital for Belgian soldiers, Bearwood, used as a convalescent home for Canadians, and Basildon Park, made available by its owner, Capt J Morrison, as a convalescent home for the Brigade of Guards. The Long Gallery of Englefield House was converted into a hospital and received its first batch of wounded in October 1914. The owners, the Lord Lieutenant Mr J H Benyon and Mrs Benyon, were responsible for the high standard of efficiency maintained by the Berkshire branch of the Red Cross throughout the war.

Women replaced men in offices, factories, workshops and on the land. They worked as postwomen, tram conductresses, and on delivery rounds. For the first time, women teachers were not made to resign their posts on marriage, but were allowed to continue teaching until the end of the war. Their contribution to the war effort encouraged the Government to extend the vote to women over 30 in 1918. Shortages of men in the police forces were made up by special constables drawn from many trades and professions. By 1917 the shortage of horses for farm work brought motor tractors into use for ploughing. Messrs Vincents, motor car builders in peace time and agricultural machinery organisers for the county during the war, trained men to drive a 16 horsepower tractor capable of pulling a three-furrow plough. Two horses were normally needed to plough a single furrow.

In 1916, a recently built jam factory in Coley, Reading, was taken over for use as a technical training school for the Royal Flying Corps. Headquarters was at Coley Park House. Flying training went on from a field near the Kennet, and lessons in aerial reconnaissance and radio were held at Wantage Hall. By 1917 hundreds of members of the Corps were billeted in south Reading homes during the winter months, but were under canvas in Coley Park during the summer. In April 1918 the Royal Flying Corps was amalgamated with the Royal Naval Air Service to form the Royal Air Force, and the technical training school was moved to Halton. Undoubtedly, the most famous pilot to learn to fly at Reading was Captain W E Johns, creator of 'Biggles'.

Berkshire families suffered their share of the appalling losses inflicted by the war, and in 1919 and 1920 the County Council received a stream of applications for permission to erect war memorials on roadside verges. These were usually granted, but a request from Pangbourne for permission to place a torpedo, which had been presented to the parish, on the parapet of the bridge over the river Pang, was firmly refused.

During the war years at least one new enterprise was successfully established, in spite of many difficulties and shortages, such as petrol rationing. In 1915 the Reading Branch of the British Automobile Traction Company started a motor bus service, operating two buses between Reading and Maidenhead and Reading and Streatley. Until then, only limited road passenger transport had been provided by carriers, but more frequent services, capable of carrying more passengers, were badly needed. The company was encouraged to increase its fleet and its services to cover the whole of the middle Thames

A patriotic May Day ceremony at Sulham village school in 1916.

region, so that, by 1920, when it became the independent Thames Valley Traction Company, it controlled a route network of 147 miles, with services reaching out to Oxford, Newbury, Mortimer, Crowthorne, Windsor, Maidenhead, High Wycombe, Henley and Stoke Row.

From 1920 other services were provided by the Aldershot and District Traction Company, operating in east Berkshire and the Reading area; while from 1932 Newbury and District Motor Services increased those in west Berkshire. Country buses played a vital part in economic and social life, giving villagers much better access to towns for work, schooling, shopping and visits to the cinemas and theatres. Buses provided some of the comfort and convenience of the motor car to the vast majority of the population who would never own private cars, and offered a welcome alternative to rail travel. Private hire and excursion coaches soon became very popular, one of the earliest firms being Smith's Luxury Coaches, started by A E Smith in Reading in 1922. His first advertised excursions ran to Bracknell, Bagshot and Camberley; and within a year or so he was running day trips to Southsea

Osiers (a species of willow) for basket-making were still grown in Berkshire in the 1930s, though the ancient craft was dying out. In this scene near Ruscombe the osiers are being stripped of bark.

and to exhibitions at Wembley. Private hire by local organisations greatly increased his business. The public enjoyed the novelty of exploring the countryside and places which were still largely unfamiliar and unspoiled.

The sights and sounds of the countryside had not changed very much since Edwardian times. The land was divided among many small, mixed farms, and in rural parishes most of the inhabitants were employed in agriculture. The tractor had arrived, but horses were still widely used for ploughing and draughtwork. A great deal of haymaking and harvesting was still done in traditional ways, employing large numbers of extra hands. Corn was still carted to rickyards to be stacked and threshed during the winter, usually by a travelling threshing machine driven by steam. But many associated rural industries were dying out. The beds of osiers, grown for basket-making, and once a familiar sight along the Kennet and Loddon valleys with their glowing masses of scarlet and gold tints in autumn, were no longer so extensively cultivated. Before the war they had been a profitable crop, growing on land too wet and heavy for ploughing or pasture, and providing employment for farm hands in the winter months. Women and children, too, had earned a little money helping to sort the rods and strip the bark. The regenerative power of the osier willow was so great that, according to an old saying, a willow would buy a horse before an oak would find him a saddle. A proportion of those grown in Berkshire was sent to local towns, where there was a large demand for baskets of all sizes from fruit and vegetable growers, bakers, laundrymen, shopkeepers and housewives, but the bulk of the crop was sent by barge to wholesalers in London.

Woodland crafts had also been carried on for generations in the Kennet valley, where deep, wooded gulleys running down to the river were too steep for other forms of cultivation, and the underwood had been used for making hurdles, barrel hoops, rakes, brooms, mopsticks and bowls. Thatcham was at one time an important centre for under-wood products, and large numbers of turners could be seen working in the Broadway there until the use of machinery in Thatcham turneries put them out of business. By the 1920s all these woodland industries were dying out with the older woodmen, for few young men were interested in learning trades which required considerable skills and experience, and were poorly rewarded.

In the period of financial stringency following the war, development in the county could only be slow, and it was only when substantial assistance had been promised by the Carnegie Trust that the Council agreed, in 1924, to adopt the Public Libraries Act of 1919. The Trust granted about £1,600 for the purchase of books, shelving and other equipment, so that it was estimated that, if the scheme was started in a modest way, the cost to the Council for the first full year would be no more than £400. A book circulating system was adopted whereby each village centre received a fresh supply of books three or four times a year. A full-time librarian was appointed at a salary of £300 per annum, and the County Library headquarters was set up in the former St Lawrence's School in Abbey Street, Reading. All the village centres were in makeshift buildings.

In 1929 a much heavier burden had to be shouldered when the responsibilities of Poor Law Guardians were transferred to county councils. The Boards of Guardians were abolished and their Union workhouses renamed Public Assistance Institutions. These were now hospitals for aged and sick paupers, although most retained casual wards for tramps and unemployed people on the road in search of work. Poor and disadvantaged children were cared for in cottage homes. The Public Assistance Committee was also responsible for financial assistance to the poor at home, after a means test, and for administering the payment of unemployment benefit.

Even in Reading the rate of growth had slowed down, although the 1920s saw some notable achievements. The size of the borough had been greatly increased by a boundary extension in 1911, taking in most of Tilehurst and Caversham. The latter addition made better road communications with the town a matter of the first importance, as the only existing link was a narrow iron bridge across the Thames, erected in 1868, on the site of the dilapidated medieval bridge. Before the war started, plans had been under discussion for two new bridges, one to replace the iron bridge and a second entirely new bridge linking east Reading with Lower Caversham. These plans had to be postponed for the duration, but they were revived in the 1920s, by which time it was obvious that much wider bridges were needed to cope with the increased volume of traffic. The new Reading bridge was opened in 1923, and the replacement for Caversham bridge in 1926. Reading's status was further enhanced in 1926 when Reading College, founded as a University Extension College in 1892, was granted its charter of independence and became the University of Reading.

The most spectacular growth in the 1920s and 1930s took place at Slough. Towards the end of the war, the War Office had established a Motor Repair Depot on farmland just outside the town. When the war ended the 600 acre site was left strewn with vehicles, many damaged or derelict, and a number of unfinished buildings. It quickly became known as The Dump. However, in 1920, a group of enterprising businessmen agreed to relieve the Government of this embarrassing white elephant for the sum of £7 million, the price to include the land, the buildings, plant, and all the vehicles, plus the thousands of British and American war vehicles still overseas. The Slough Trading Company was formed, the buildings were completed, the damaged vehicles repaired, and by 1924 all the vehicles had been sold. In 1925 Parliament authorised the Company to build roads and to install electricity, water and drainage. Manufacturing firms had already begun to move in; Gillette, Johnson and Johnson, Hygenic Ice and Citroen Cars Ltd, being among the first. The Slough Trading Company changed its name to Slough Estates Ltd and set to work building a large number of new factories, of varying sizes but all equipped with basic services. By 1930 over 100 firms from all over the country were established there. The estate was ideally situated, with its main gates opening onto the A4, and had its own railway station, banks, post office and restaurant. In 1932 Forrester Mars from America started his first sweet factory in England on the Slough estate. The employment opportunities drew thousands of workers to the area, creating a huge demand for houses. In 1930 the boundaries of Slough Urban District were extended east and west to Langley and Cippenham, more than trebling its size; but within a few years housing estates, built by the Council and by private developers, had almost covered it. By 1937 the population had grown to more than 50,000. In that year an important public building – the town hall – was completed, and in 1938 Slough was granted the status of a borough.

19

THE SECOND WORLD WAR

These, and many more instructions, printed by the Home Office well in advance, were distributed to all householders in September 1939:

'If you have not already done so, get fitted for your gas mask . . . . Arrange to have your windows and skylights completely covered at night, so that no ray of light can be seen from outside. Blinds and curtains should be of thick dark material . . . . If you have a garden, prepare a small trench as protection from blast and splinter . . . . See that you have a bucket of dry sand or earth, with a long-handled shovel, ready to deal with small incendiary bombs . . . . See that your wireless set is working, or arrange to receive wireless messages from a neighbour should an emergency arise . . . . Keep calm. The services for your protection are well organised and efficient.'

Preparations for war had begun in 1937, when local councils had appointed Air Raid Precautions Committees and asked them to prepare comprehensive plans for the organisation of ambulance and first-aid services, anti-gas training and other necessary measures. In the expectation of heavy air attacks on London and other large cities as soon as war started, the Government had prepared and rehearsed plans for the mass evacuation of children into the country. Berkshire was considered safe enough to be a reception area, and by the end of August it was known that Reading was to get 25,000 evacuees, about half of them children under five with their parents, and half schoolchildren with their teachers. Other parts of the county were to receive smaller numbers; Wokingham Rural District, for instance, 6,500 and Wokingham borough 1,800. In the event the numbers fluctuated considerably as evacuees drifted back to London, and returned to the country again when the bombing started. By 2nd September the first trainloads of evacuees had arrived and billeting was in progress. Official propaganda claimed that the operation went well, but people working behind the scenes had to cope with a great many complaints from dissatisfied householders and evacuees, while confusion was caused by schoolchildren arriving with the wrong teachers, or no teachers at all. There was a serious lack of rapport between 'townees' and country dwellers.

In the unsettled, often chaotic, early months of the war, officialdom was everywhere. Reading was one of twelve regional centres set up to co-ordinate Civil Defence throughout the country. The town had 2,500 air raid wardens, and these, in their dark blue boiler suits and tin helmets, were soon familiar figures, distributing and fitting gas masks, checking blackout curtains, and advising on air raid shelters. Town halls and other public buildings were heavily protected by sandbags, and Reading's historical archives were removed for safety to chalk caves at Emmer Green. In the caves were also stored a large supply of cardboard coffins for use in the event of a gas attack. Thousands of people enrolled for first-aid and ambulance services, and the Women's Voluntary Service, founded in 1938 by Stella, Lady Reading, assisted local authorities with billeting evacuees and with the organisation of emergency food and clothing supplies. By January 1940, food rationing and the Dig for Victory campaign had started, and people were beginning to grow accustomed to a new way of life under wartime restrictions. By June, Reading was playing host to about 700 men evacuated from Dunkirk.

During the war the Women's Voluntary Service and Women's Institutes operated a meat pie scheme, delivering pies and other snacks made by village bakers to farmworkers in the fields.

Under the threat of invasion, the Local Defence Volunteers, later the Home Guard, was formed, for which there were 6,000 volunteers in Berkshire.

Factories were converted to war-work, taking on thousands of extra employees. Women were called up and began to replace men on the production lines. Reading became a centre for the production of photo-reconnaissance Spitfires, which up to September 1940 had been made at Southampton. But after heavy bombing of the works there, Lord Beaverbrook, Minister of Aircraft Production, ordered production to be dispersed among a number of smaller units in southern England. Vincent's Garage in Station Square, Reading, was requisitioned for the manufacture of Spitfire fuselages; Great Western Motors in Vastern Road assembled wings, and a small factory in Star Road installed engines, fuel tanks, wiring and plumbing, and checked all systems. Spitfire tanks and a variety of small parts were made at Markham's the coach-builders in Caversham Road. At the beginning of the war, aircraft were taken by road to a small airfield at Cockpole Green, near Wargrave, for test flying before delivery to units, but later RAF Benson, the headquarters of the Photographic Reconnaissance Unit, was used for this purpose. Factory employees worked long hours. Women worked alternate months of day or night shifts, 8 am–7.30 pm or 8 pm–7.30 am, slightly shorter hours than men.

At Woodley aerodrome, Phillips and Powis' factory had begun to build aircraft for the RAF before the war. The aerodrome, started in 1929, had been used in peacetime by Reading Aero Club, and by many leading aviators for light plane racing and aerobatic displays. The work of the designer, F G Miles, had attracted the attention of the Air Ministry in 1935, when the Miles Hawk was approved for training Air Force personnel. In 1938, when the Air Force was being expanded, Phillips and Powis were awarded a large contract to build the Miles Magister, a military version of the Hawk. In 1939 Sir Kingsley Wood, the Air Minister, came to Woodley to open a new factory to build the Miles Master, a high-speed training aircraft for pilots who were to fly the new Spitfires and Hurricanes. Between 1938 and 1945 the factory, known from 1943 as Miles Aircraft Ltd, built more than 5,000 planes, as well as repairing or rebuilding 3,000 other planes damaged in action. At its peak the factory employed over 7,000 workers. The basic flying training unit of pre-war days became No. 10 Flying Instructors' School, and remained at Woodley throughout the war.

White Waltham aerodrome was built just before the war by De Havilland's as a base for a flying school, but in 1940 it became the home of the Air Transport Auxiliary, a newly formed unit consisting of civil pilots whose job was to fly communications aircraft and deliver fighter and bomber planes from factories to fighting units. During the war the ATA flew 308,567 ferrying trips. Among the famous pilots who flew for the unit was Amy Johnson, who joined in 1939 and who was presumed killed when her plane, carrying material for the Air Ministry, was lost over the Thames estuary in January 1941.

When the war started there were emergency plans, in the event of invasion, to move all the aircraft at Woodley to an airfield at Great Shefford, but such a move was never necessary and Great Shefford was used only occasionally by training aircraft. At Sheffield Farm, near Theale, another airfield was built originally as additional landing space for Woodley aircraft, but in 1941 an Elementary Flying Training School was established there, with 24 Tiger Moths and 60 pupils. Their accommodation in Nissen huts, on fields notorious for flooding in winter, was so poor that Sulhamstead House was requisitioned for their use.

In 1942 the BBC moved into Caversham Park, and the Monitoring Service was working there by 1943. This service had been set up in 1939 by the Ministry of Information as a listening unit to record and translate broadcasts from enemy and neutral countries, and throughout the war it performed the vital role of collecting and translating information for the Government and for the BBC news bulletins. Many of the people employed there were refugees, often listening to news from their own countries. By the end of the war Caversham Park had grown into the largest and most efficient listening post in the world, monitoring over a million words a day in 30 languages.

The fall of France was followed by the period of most frequent bomb attacks on this part of the country. Air raid warnings sounded and hundreds of bombs and incendiaries were dropped on various parts of Berkshire, but the haphazard nature of the damage suggested that they were dropped by lone raiders getting rid of their bombs before returning home. Scores of houses and other buildings were damaged, roofs were torn off, windows blown out, and craters left in roads, gardens and farm fields. Local newspaper reports for security reasons named no places, but were perfectly comprehensible to their readers. 'A terrace of eight cottages was badly damaged, the fronts of the dwellings being smashed in, when a lone Nazi raider dropped bombs in a village in the south-east of England early on Sunday morning,' ran a typical report in a Reading newspaper in October 1940. 'Housed in the cottages were 45 men, women and children, and the only casualty was a man, James Saunders, who is now in hospital suffering from facial injuries, including a serious eye wound. One old lady, Mrs Dearden, who has lived in one of the cottages for many years, told the village constable a few minutes after the raider had passed: "I'm going back to bed. I shall be jolly unlucky if they come this way again".'

Air raid wardens, auxiliary firemen and other helpers were always quick to reach the scene of an explosion to prevent fire spreading and to find accommodation for people rendered homeless, but sometimes there was a trickier problem to be dealt with. At Basildon, in September 1940, a German parachute mine floated down on the village and lodged in a tree between two houses almost opposite the Crown Inn. These mines were then a new and frightening form of aerial attack, and were a kind of airborne torpedo which bomb disposal men had to deal with. They succeeded in detaching it from the tree and moving it a little way up the hill behind the village to an old chalk pit. Every house in the neighbourhood was evacuated and all doors and windows were left open before the mine was exploded, leaving a huge crater and causing damage to buildings over a large area. Many houses had windows broken, ceilings brought down and doors wrenched out. St Bartholomew's church, standing by the river some distance away, suffered damage to its stonework and stained glass windows. A 14th century stone canopy, re-used to frame a memorial to Sir Francis Sykes who died in 1804, was broken and bears the scars of the explosion to this day.

After 1941 raids were less frequent but included the two most serious attacks on Berkshire towns. 'Hit-and-Run Raid on Town', ran a headline in a local paper after the attack on Reading on Wednesday, 10th February 1943. 'Up to Thursday mid-day it had been ascertained that of the people killed and injured in the "hit-and-run" raid which took place on a Home Counties town on Wednesday, three are children. It is not yet known whether this is the complete casualty list, as ARP workers were still searching the debris on Thursday. The raider at first machine-gunned the streets, then dropped bombs, and finished up by another burst of machine-gunning. The bombs fell in a shopping district of the town, and the premises in three streets and the streets connecting them practically all received damage, some being completely demolished. The first bomb dropped near a furniture repository, a second struck the rear part of a departmental stores, a third scored a direct hit on a British Restaurant. Great havoc was caused by the bomb which fell on the departmental store. It was to some extent fortunate that the raid took place on early closing day, otherwise this store would have been crowded with shoppers. As it was there was a number of girls living on the premises, and some of these were among the casualties .... By far the greater number of casualties occurred at the British Restaurant. It was tea rush hour, and at the time the restaurant was fairly crowded. Most of the kitchen staff and some of the customers were buried when

During an air raid on Newbury, on 10th February 1943, St. Bartholomew's almshouses were reduced to rubble. These stood at right angles to Lower Raymond's almshouses, which have survived, and overlooked the site of the 18th century Cheese Fair. They have been replaced by the Fair Close day centre.

the building collapsed. Throughout the night ARP workers were digging in the debris of this building, searching for bodies, several of which they succeeded in extricating, using the light of torches and flares to carry out their work.'

Four bombs had fallen in a line across the town centre from Minster Street to Friar Street, wrecking the back of Wellsteed's (now Debenham's) and damaging the covered Market Arcade which contained the British Restaurant, known locally as the People's Pantry. The fourth bomb caused severe damage to St Lawrence's church, the offices of Blandy and Blandy, solicitors, and one end of the Town Hall. The toll of dead was 41. The seriously injured numbered 49 and the slightly injured 104.

On the same afternoon a single Dornier plane carried out a similar raid on Newbury, demolishing Newbury Senior Council School opposite the station, St John's church, St Bartholomew's almshouses and ten other houses. Fifteen people were killed and several injured. Over 300 buildings were damaged, 16 of them so seriously that they had to be demolished. Among other Berkshire towns, Windsor and Maidenhead also suffered damage in various minor raids. These places were just within range of the flying bombs which, from 1944, caused 202 alerts and many nerve-wracked hours as people waited for the bombs to fall. There were many casualties and over 1,000 houses were damaged in the area. One flying bomb alone, which fell in Cookham Road, Maidenhead, injured 62 people. Slough escaped lightly from the war, and perhaps one of the most unpleasant aspects was the pall of black oily smoke put up to camouflage the trading estate, where many of the factories were engaged on war work. Slough, too, was involved in the production of Spitfires, while Hurricanes were built at the Hawker airfield at Langley.

From 1943 airfields in west Berkshire were taken over by American Army Airborne Divisions. Greenham Common airfield had been built in 1941–2 and intended for an RAF bomber training unit, but it served that purpose for only a short time. In October 1943 the Americans arrived with Mustang and Thunderbolt fighter planes, but soon the airfield was expanded to make room for over 50 troop-carrying Dakotas. An intensive training programme, involving parachuting and glider-towing was carried out in preparation for the D-Day invasion, and during the night of 5th June 1944 the airfield was heavily guarded for a visit of General Eisenhower to discuss with General Brereton the airborne element of Operation Overlord. Eisenhower addressed the paratroopers and air crews assembled and ready for departure: 'The eyes of the world are on you tonight,' he told them. In the morning the two generals watched the first Dakotas take off for Normandy.

Welford airfield was used for similar training. Americans began to arrive there in September 1943, followed by the Dakotas of the 315th Tactical Carrier Wing, and troop training commenced. Early in 1944 the unit was chosen to demonstrate before a distinguished audience including Winston Churchill and Eisenhower. The demonstration involved 97 gliders being towed off, flying a cross-country route, and returning to land at ten second intervals. On D-Day this training was used to good effect in dropping the 101st Airborne Division, the 'Screaming Eagles', near Cherbourg. On the following nights, more gliders were towed across the Channel to deliver troops to the front line, and as landing strips in France became available, the planes returned with wounded who were taken to Berkshire hospitals.

Aldermaston airfield was established in 1942 on requisitioned land on the Aldermaston Court estate. It was used partly by American training units with Dakotas, partly by No 3 Glider Training School flying Miles Masters and Hotspur gliders, and, from July 1943, partly by Vickers who used the facilities for the assembly of Spitfires, using parts made at factories in Newbury and Reading. On D-Day Aldermaston's role was to fly 52 troop-carrying gliders to a landing ground behind the Omaha beach-head, and after that to send supply flights to the battle front for the rest of the war.

Membury airfield, lying between an Iron Age camp and the future site of the M4 service station, was originally planned as an RAF bomber training station but was re-allocated to the Americans in August 1942. The first unit to be based there was a photo-reconnaissance group using Flying Fortresses, but later the 53rd Tactical Carrier Wing moved in and took part in the D-Day drop of the 101st Airborne Division and many subsequent supply missions.

Two units of the 101st Airborne Division were among the many soldiers, British and American, who occupied Basildon House during the war. The Screaming Eagles completed their training there before D-Day, and after the invasion of France, returned there to prepare for the invasion of Holland.

Associated with Greenham airfield was General Depot 45 in Station Road, Thatcham. Originally a British Government depot, this was allocated to the American Army in November 1942 and became the largest G Depot in Britain. Dozens of storage sheds and several miles of railway sidings were installed, extending across Thatcham Moors. The depot dealt with supplies and stores of all kinds and was hectically busy around D-Day, when nearly 7,000 people were working there. Greenham airfield was serviced from G 45, which remained in use until 1946, when over 800 American soldiers, 600 civilians, and 2,000 prisoners of war were still employed there. It was handed back to the British in May that year.

20

POST WAR EXPANSION AND MODERN BERKSHIRE

In the years of austerity which followed the war, everything was in short supply and, apart from war-damaged areas, everywhere looked much the same as it had done in the 1930s, only a good deal shabbier and dingier. No-one had any idea of the immense changes which would take place in the next decades, altering familiar places beyond recognition. The floods which devastated the Thames Valley in the spring of 1947, following a bitterly cold, snowy winter, seemed like a return to a wartime state of emergency. Low-lying streets in towns and villages from Goring to Maidenhead were under water, and the Thames Valley was declared a disaster area. All the resources of the WVS, the police and rescue services were called upon to assist hundreds of families in need of temporary accommodation, and to deliver food and fuel to thousands of people marooned in their homes.

By the end of the war a huge housing problem had been created, due partly to overcrowding by evacuees, many of whom decided to stay on, and partly to the fact that no new houses had been built for six years, whereas many had been destroyed by bombing. In 1945 cheap, prefabricated bungalows were provided to house some of the needier families, and geometrically neat rows of these appeared in many towns and villages, but they were meant to be only a short-term measure while supplies of building materials were restricted. Town and country planning, a concept which had scarcely been considered before the war, was now seen as an essential preliminary and form of control. No more ribbon development was to be allowed to increase urban sprawl. In 1946 the County Council set up a Planning Committee and, over the next few years, the county's future development plan was prepared, identifying the use to be made of each area of land. However, the first major new development in Berkshire was not entrusted to the Council but to a Government agency, and resulted from Sir Patrick Abercrombie's scheme for the reconstruction of Greater London, and his far-reaching plan to re-house some of its population in new towns.

It had long been recognised that London had been allowed to grow too large and congested, and that it provided poor living standards for many of its inhabitants. Post-war rebuilding presented the opportunity to found new towns, which would offer a better way of life in smaller, self-contained communities, where work, education, social and leisure amenities would be within reach of everyone, as well as easy access to the countryside. White Waltham was at first considered for the site of Berkshire's new town, but was rejected on the grounds that it would use too much high quality agricultural land and would conflict with the interests of the aerodrome. The choice fell on Bracknell, then a small town with a population below 6,000, situated on a main road and railway line between Reading and London. The area of the new town was to be 2,623 acres, most of it poor quality land. The forested area to the south was to be retained as it was well-managed and produced a valuable crop of timber.

Bracknell New Town was originally planned for a population of 25,000. The town centre was developed around the existing High Street and was planned to include a variety of shops, offices and businesses, central and local government administrative buildings, police and fire stations. Around the town centre four residential neighbourhoods would each have their own shopping facilities, primary school, church, meeting hall, public house and play area. Bracknell Development Corporation was set up in 1949 and began the lengthy process of acquiring all the necessary land and carrying out detailed surveys. One survey was concerned with trees in the western half of the town, and the planners determined that as many of these as possible would be preserved. Large old houses standing in their own grounds were also considered to have a high amenity value and were retained in the plans. The first new neighbourhood to be built was Priestwood, where the houses began to be occupied in August 1951. Easthampstead, Bullbrook and Harman's Water neighbourhoods followed. By 1960, 4,026 dwellings had been completed, providing homes for over 14,000 people. Twenty-three new factories gave employment to 3,574 men and 1,165 women, and more factories were under construction. Among firms already established were Racal Engineering, Ferranti, Sperry Gyroscope Company, Wayne Tank and Pump Company, and the Heating and Ventilating Research Association. Fifty-six new shops and eight new schools had also been completed.

In order to balance factory employment the Development Corporation decided in 1958 to increase the possibilities for office employment. This new policy began to bear fruit when the Meteorological Office moved to Bracknell, occupying the first block of its huge building in 1960 and the

One of the county's new shopping centres. Princess Square was the last part of Bracknell's new town centre to be built, and was opened by Princess Anne in 1984.

whole of it by 1962. The population of Bracknell had reached 20,000 by 1961, but the decision was then made to extend the area of the new town. Wildridings was the first of the new neighbourhoods to be built following this decision, and its first residents moved in in 1967. By 1981 Bracknell's population had grown to 49,000, nearly double the number originally intended. South Hill Park, the house built by William Watts in 1760 and enlarged by Lord Haversham in the late 19th century, was opened as an Arts Centre in 1973, and the Wilde Theatre was subsequently established there.

Far-reaching social and economic changes in the 20th century have caused the break-up of many large private estates and the sale of country houses as families of the old landed gentry have died out or have been crippled by estate duties. Thousands of acres have been sold off in lots, very often for building developments, and many large country houses have been demolished. But some historic houses have been preserved and adapted for institutional or commercial purposes. Bearwood, the latest to be built, was among the first to be put on the market. Financial troubles hit *The Times* in 1889, and in 1908 the newspaper passed from the control of the Walters to that of Lord Northcliffe. After the First World War, when it was a convalescent home for Canadian soldiers, Bearwood was sold to Sir Thomas Devitt, who converted it into an orphanage and training college for the sons of merchant seamen. Since the Second World War it has become an independent school for boys.

Aldermaston Court, a Victorian mansion built to replace the 17th century house badly damaged by fire in 1843, was put up for sale in September 1939, together with the estate containing Aldermaston village, farms and a magnificent park five miles in circumference. The mansion and its immediate grounds were purchased for £17,000 by Associated Electrical Industries for possible use as an evacuation centre for London office staff, but before long it was requisitioned by the Government and used to accommodate various women's services during the war. The park was laid waste, the woods burned and the deer shot, to make way for the runways and Nissen huts of Aldermaston airfield. The house and grounds were handed back to Associated Electrical Industries in 1947, but in 1950 it was announced that the Atomic Weapons Research Establishment had taken over the airfield site. All roads through the area were closed and high security fencing went up all round it. From here, in the 1950s and 60s, 'Ban the Bomb' marchers set out on Good Fridays for their Easter rally in Trafalgar Square.

Among other country houses too big and expensive for continuing private occupation were Easthampstead Park, sold by the Downshire family in 1949 to the County Council for use as a teacher training college; Bisham Abbey, conveyed in 1946 by Miss Vansittart-Neale to the Central Council for Physical Recreation, as a memorial to her two nephews who had been killed in the war; Sulhamstead House, acquired by the County Council for the Berkshire Police headquarters and later a police training college; and Swallowfield Park, sold by the Russell family in 1965 to the Mutual Households Association, Ltd, for conversion into flats. The happiest rescue took place at Basildon Park, derelict after use by British and American troops during the war, but purchased in 1952 and restored over a period of 25 years by Lord and Lady Iliffe, who presented it to the National Trust in 1978. Two other superannuated buildings enjoying an entirely new lifestyle are the mills at Bagnor and Sonning, both converted into theatres with restaurants.

Some of Berkshire's older lines of communication had also reached the end of their working lives. Both the Newbury-Didcot railway and the Lambourn Valley railway had been well used during the war but passenger services on the Newbury-Didcot line ceased in 1962 and goods traffic in 1964. On the Lambourn Valley line, passenger services ended and the line between Welford and Lambourn was closed in 1960. The United States Air Force based at Welford, and some goods traffic, continued to use the remaining part of the line into Newbury until 1972, but in the following year this too was closed, and the end of the line was marked by a farewell journey enjoyed by nearly 3,000 railway enthusiasts.

For a time it looked as though the Kennet and Avon Canal, too, was doomed to closure. By the end of the war it was used only by a few traders and pleasure craft, and maintenance had suffered badly from shortages of labour and materials, so that most locks were in a bad state. In 1948 canals were nationalised and came under the control of the Railway Executive, who wanted to close the Kennet and Avon. They might have succeeded had it not been for the determination of John Gould of Newbury and John Knill, a fellow trader, who started to operate small carrying businesses along the canal. In 1951 the Kennet and Avon Canal Association was formed with the object of preventing any further deterioration of the canal and, ultimately, of seeing it restored to full working order. John Gould fought a long legal battle and petitioned

In November 1992 the world was shocked by news pictures of Windsor Castle on fire. Smoke and flames engulfed the north-eastern corner of the magnificent building and severely damaged the Chester Tower, St. George's banqueting hall and the Queen's apartments. At the height of the inferno, 200 firemen were fighting the blaze, while staff strove to rescue priceless paintings, furniture and works of art. The tragedy was followed by controversy over the cost of restoration.

The Kennet and Avon Canal was reopened in 1990. This view is near Tyle Mill lock.

Parliament to save the canal from closure; and, as a result of official enquiries and reports on the inland waterways, responsibility for the canal passed, in 1963, to the newly created British Waterways Board. The Board was interested in the canal as a leisure amenity as well as a means of transport, and was sympathetic and constructive. In 1962 the Kennet and Avon Canal Association had re-formed itself into a registered charity, the Kennet and Avon Canal Trust, and through the combined efforts of Board and Trust over a period of 28 years, the canal, with its 104 locks, was gradually restored throughout its course from Reading to Bath. In the summer of 1990 there were celebrations along the canal, and on 8th August, the Queen performed the opening ceremony at Devizes wharf, and travelled a short distance along the canal in the narrowboat *Rose of Hungerford*.

Soon after the war, road traffic began to build up, and the County Council battled with the task of repairing and improving badly neglected roads and considered schemes for by-passing towns and villages which were causing traffic bottlenecks. Since 1936 the Ministry of Transport had taken overall responsibility for the two trunk roads, the A4 and the A34, but the County still carried out maintenance work on an agency basis. On the A4 a bypass to relieve Maidenhead of through traffic had been proposed as far back as 1927, and a route had been surveyed, but in 1930 the Government withdrew its consent under the National Economy Act. However, in 1935 the Ministry of Transport concluded that a Maidenhead bypass was 'an urgent national need', and two years later work began on a new bridge near Bray to carry the bypass across the Thames. In 1939 bulldozers, then new and unfamiliar machines, arrived to start work on the road, but on the outbreak of war the project was halted, and the 1,680 tons of steel ordered for the superstructure of the bridge were diverted to more urgent uses. The bypass plan was revived in 1959, when the roadwork begun 20 years earlier and now overgrown was cleared for further progress. By that time there were plans to build a motorway from London to South Wales, into which the bypass would be incorporated, and accordingly the partly built river bridge had to be re-designed and its approach roads altered.

By the time the Maidenhead bypass was opened in June 1961 a number of proposed routes for the M4 motorway across Berkshire were under discussion. This major new east-west route was to have a profound effect on the future development of the county, but in spite of traffic chaos it was not generally welcomed, and every proposed route met with strong and vociferous opposition. The Downs Preservation Society, the Ramblers' Association, the National Farmers' Union, private landowners, racehorse trainers, archaeologists and naturalists were all involved, and each section of the route was the subject of enquiries and revisions. By 1967 the motorway to the east and west of the county was built, but across Berkshire the now hopelessly inadequate A4 carried an increasing volume of modern traffic, so that long queues of impatient drivers crawled through one bottleneck after another. By 1971 it was estimated that the busiest stretch between Maidenhead and Reading was carrying 70,000 vehicles a day. Eventually construction of the M4 across Berkshire commenced early in 1970 and the motorway was opened on 22 December 1971.

No sooner had Berkshire begun to adjust to the motorway and the new pattern of transport than it was faced with a far greater upheaval in the reorganisation of local government and the alteration of county boundaries. Under the Local Government Act of 1972, which came into force on 1 April 1974, the old sub-divisions of the county – Urban and Rural Districts and the County Borough of Reading, created in the previous century – were abolished and replaced by six new Districts with equal powers and status, subject to the overall control of the County Council. At the same time the revision of county boundaries resulted in the loss of old north Berks and the addition of parts of south Buckinghamshire, including Slough. The new Berkshire Districts are centred on the largest towns: Newbury, Reading, Wokingham, Bracknell, Slough and the Royal Borough of Windsor and Maidenhead. The last-named contains Eton, Datchet, Horton and Wraysbury as well as rural parishes extending from Sunninghill to Waltham St Lawrence, Hurley and Cookham. When the new Royal Borough came into being it was recognised that the one common factor to all its parts was the river Thames; and in order to promote a sense of unity the Queen was invited to make a river journey through the borough from Hurley to Magna Carta Island, coming ashore at towns and villages along the way. The journey took place in October 1974, unfortunately in pouring rain, but thousands of people turned out to watch the royal progress.

Racing at Ascot began in the 18th century and is still one of the highlights of the summer calendar, combining the attraction of royalty, horse racing and fashion.

Maidenhead had built a new town hall in 1962, and in 1974 this became the administrative headquarters of the new borough. The previous Maidenhead town hall, dating from 1777, was demolished. In Reading, the borough council had felt the need for larger accommodation since the boundary extension of 1911, and the situation grew worse as the population and the council's services increased. By the 1950s council departments were dispersed around the town in a number of makeshift buildings. Post-war slum clearance to the west of St Mary's Butts eventually made space for new and much larger council offices, and an impressive modern Civic Centre was completed in time for all departments to move in during the summer of 1976. On one side the building is flanked by a new Thames Valley Police divisional headquarters, and on the other by The Hexagon, an all-purpose entertainment centre. In the 1970s Berkshire County Council, still based in its 1911 Shire Hall, was in an even worse plight with some 14,000 employees scattered in 16 separate office locations around Reading. After considering various sites, the new Shire Hall was built just outside the borough boundary at Shinfield Park, formerly occupied by RAF Training Command HQ. The huge complex consisting of six pavilions around a central core, and situated on rising ground overlooking the M4, was ready for occupation by 1980.

The Arlington Business Park at Theale, one of several huge new enterprises taking advantage of the M4 motorway.

The M4 brought economic growth and prosperity to the whole county. The motorway's links with London, Heathrow and the M25, and with the Midlands and Southampton docks via the A34, made Berkshire a prime site for business and industrial expansion. In the 1980s the rapid growth of high-technology and service industries, such as finance and distribution companies, caused land and property values to rocket as developers competed for huge sites to build prestigious office accommodation and business parks. The demand for premises was so great that more than two million square feet of new industrial and commercial floorspace was being built in the county each year. Around Reading, in addition to new developments such as the Worton Grange industrial estate near junction 11 of the M4, and the Thames Valley Business Park at Lower Earley (near junction 10), several older industrial sites have been redeveloped, such as the Forbury Industrial Park on the former site of Huntley and Palmer's biscuit factory. Such homely names as theirs have disappeared from the town and giant multinational concerns such as the Digital Equipment Company have taken their place. To the west of Reading, the Arlington Business Park at Theale occupies a 48-acre site next to junction 12 of the motorway, and can provide 720,000 square feet of office space and jobs for up to 3,000 people.

Hi-tech industries along the M4 corridor have given it the name 'Silicon Valley'. It brought wealth and growth to every town across county, and in rural areas of west Berkshire the demand for property rescued many decaying houses and cottages in villages which were suddenly within easy reach of London and Heathrow. Perhaps the most spectacular change took place at Newbury, in the 1980s no longer just a country market town but 'Thatcher-town', a boom town transformed by new industry and free market economics into one of the busiest and most prosperous in the south of England.

Sadly Newbury, like the rest of the county, has been badly hit by the recession of the early 1990s, but Berkshire has all the necessary potential for economic recovery, and there can be no doubt that it will prosper again. Its vital position in the centre of England cannot be altered, and throughout the ages, its links with the nation's capital have been strengthened and increased.

BIBLIOGRAPHY

Material for this book has been drawn from many sources. I would like to acknowledge my debt particularly to the following.

Ashmole, E *Elias Ashmole: his autobiographical and historical notes* edited by C H Josten, 1966

Astill, G G *Historic towns in Berkshire: an archaeological appraisal* 1978

Berkshire Archaeological Society Journals, vols. 37, 39, 44, 54–5, 57, 59–63, 65–72. 1933–85

Bond, M *The story of Windsor* 1984

Briggs, A *The age of improvement, 1783–1867* 1979

Bracknell Development Corporation. Annual reports, 1952–60

Calamy, E *The Nonconformist's memorial* edited by S Palmer 1775

Clew, K R *The Kennet and Avon Canal* 1985

Davies, D *The case of the labourers in husbandry* 1795

Davies, E R *A history of the First Berkshire County Council 1889–1974* 1981

Defoe, D *A tour through the whole island of Great Britain, 1724–6*; edited by P Rogers 1971

Dils, J, ed. *An account of early Victorian Wokingham* 1984

Dils, J *100 years of public service: a history of Berkshire County Council* 1990

Disbury, D *Berkshire in the Civil War* 1978

Domesday Book: Berkshire; edited by P Morgan 1979

Evening Post Berkshire at war 1988

Footman J *History of the parish church of St Michael and All Angels, Chipping Lambourn* 1894

Fulford, M *Calleva Atrebatum: a guide to the Roman town at Silchester* 1987

Gelling M *The place-names of Berkshire* 3 vols 1973–76

Hadcock, R N and Millson, C *The story of Newbury* 1990

Hewett, W *The history and antiquities of the hundred of Compton* 1844

Hill, C *The century of revolution, 1603–1714* 1980

Hobsbawm, E J and Rudé, G *Captain Swing* 1969

Holzman, J M *Nabobs in England* 1926

Hunter J *The story of Slough* 1983

Indge, W *A Short History of the Berkshire Constabulary, 1856–1956* 1956

Karau, P, Parsons, M and Robertson, K *The Didcot Newbury and Southampton Railway* 1981

Kelly's Directories of Berkshire 1847–1939

Kerry, C *A history of the municipal church of St Lawrence, Reading* 1883

Lacey, P *Thames Valley: the British years, 1915–1920* 1990

Margary, I D *Roman roads in Britain* 1973

Mavor, W F *General view of the agriculture of Berkshire* 1809

Mingay, G E *The Victorian countryside* 1981

Over, L *The story of Maidenhead* 1984

Pevsner, N *Berkshire* 1966

Phillips, G *Thames Crossings* 1981

Pihlens, H *The story of Hungerford* 1983

Read, D *England 1868–1914* 1979

Richards, J C *Archaeology of the Berkshire Downs* 1978

Robertson, K and Simmonds, R *The Lambourn branch* 1984

Royal Commission on Local Government *Local government in South East England* 1968

Russell, C *Swallowfield and its owners* 1901

Sansom, O *An account of many remarkable passages in the life of Oliver Sansom* 1710

Sharp, A M *The history of Ufton Court* 1892

Shorland, E *The pish (parish) of Warfield and Easthampstead which includes Old Bracknell* 1980

Thacker, F S *The Thames highway: general history* 1914

Victoria History of the County of Berkshire 4 vols. 1906–27

Victoria History of the County of Buckinghamshire vol. 3, 1925

Walker, J W *A History of Maidenhead* 1931

Wokingham Society *Wokingham: a chronology* 1977

Wolffe, B *Henry VI* 1981

Wymer, J *Lower Paleolithic archaeology in Britain, as represented by the Thames Valley* 1968

Acknowledgements

I have pleasure in recording my thanks to the following for their help and kind permission to reproduce photographs and prints.

The University of Reading, Rural History Centre, for illustrations on pages 114, 117, 126, 141, 154, 157, 158, 166, 170, 176, 181, 184, 189, 196, 198, 199, 203. Those on pages 158 and 198 are from the collection of Mrs Iris Moon, deposited at the Centre.

Newbury District Museum for those on pages 33, 62, 85, 91, 95, 101, 113, 125, 129, 149, 152, 175, 192.

The Trust for Wessex Archaeology Ltd. for the illustration on page 45.

Arlington Property Developments Ltd. for the photograph on page 218.

Ascot Services for the photograph on page 217.

Jack Hole for the cover photograph (repeated on page 4) and the photograph on page 207.

Len Murchison for the photograph on page 214.

Margaret Morgan for her help with the map on pages 6 and 7.

Photographs on pages 13, 14, 18, 21, 28, 31, 37, 40, 44, 48, 66, 70, 82, 98, 102, 146, 212, 215 were taken by the author.

Daphne Phillips

Index